NOT FROM HERE,
NOT FROM THERE/
NO SOY DE AQUÍ
NI DE ALLÁ

NOT FROM HERE,
NOT FROM THERE/
NO SOY DE AQUÍ
NI DE ALLÁ

The Autobiography of NELSON A. DÍAZ

With a Foreword by HENRY CISNEROS

TEMPLE UNIVERSITY PRESS
Philadelphia | *Rome* | *Tokyo*

TEMPLE UNIVERSITY PRESS
Philadelphia, Pennsylvania 19122
tupress.temple.edu

Copyright © 2018 by Temple University—Of The Commonwealth System
of Higher Education
All rights reserved
Published 2018

Frontispiece by Joe V. Labolito/Temple University

Library of Congress Cataloging-in-Publication Data

Names: Díaz, Nelson A., 1947– author. | Cisneros, Henry, writer of foreword.
Title: Not from here, not from there / No soy de aquí ni de allá : The
   autobiography of Nelson A. Díaz / Nelson A. Díaz ; with a foreword by
   Henry Cisneros.
Other titles: No soy de aquí ni de allá
Description: Philadelphia, Pennsylvania : Temple University Press, 2018. |
   Includes bibliographical references and index. |
Identifiers: LCCN 2018008772 (print) | LCCN 2018031392 (ebook) |
   ISBN 9781439913628 (E-book) | ISBN 9781439913604 (cloth : alk. paper)
Subjects: LCSH: Díaz, Nelson A., 1947– | Hispanic American Judges—Biography.
   | Judges—United States—Biography. | Civil rights workers—United States—
   Biography. | Lawyers—Pennsylvania—Biography
Classification: LCC KF373.D479 (ebook) | LCC KF373.D479 A3 2018 (print) |
   DDC 347.748/0234 [B]—dc23
LC record available at https://lccn.loc.gov/2018008772

♾ The paper used in this publication meets the requirements of the American
National Standard for Information Sciences—Permanence of Paper for Printed
Library Materials, ANSI Z39.48-1992

Printed in the United States of America

9 8 7 6 5 4 3 2

CONTENTS

FOREWORD

I HAVE LONG BELIEVED that the most compelling narrative in the American story is our tradition of strivers, the people who struggle from humble beginnings and fight relentlessly throughout life to make something of themselves. The strivers are those who start with little, sometimes nothing, and push themselves to achieve extraordinary successes. They work hard and sacrifice in the present to create something worthwhile for the future. The strivers are driven, determined, and dogged, and much of America's legacy of greatness can be attributed to their spirit.

Nelson Díaz is a lifelong striver. He learned from his beloved mother, Maria, the importance of determination in working for a better future. One might say that he learned this lesson before he was born, when his mother journeyed to New York from Puerto Rico, young, alone, and pregnant. From the time she arrived in New York with nothing, soon to deliver her son into its vibrant and rambunctious community of Puerto Ricans, she imbued in Nelson a capacity for hard work, impatience with the status quo, and a sense of justice. Maria manifested her love for her son through her passion for his education, her prayers for his spiritual formation, and her sacrifices in matters small and large to support his physical needs and build his emotional strength.

As a young boy Nelson perceived the injustice around him and noted that people with authority and standing could promote the path to pos-

itive change. As an adolescent he first recognized the connection between applying himself to his studies and creating patterns of cumulative
achievement. He also saw the heartbreak and loss associated with those
who took routes of lesser resistance, those who became gang members
and ended up in prison or dead.

Nelson hungrily sought out mentors among his teachers at Rice High
School and among community leaders who spurred his ideas of a better
life for working people. He valued the encouragement of family members: his mother, his stepfather in New York, his aunts and uncles, and
his biological father in Puerto Rico. The adults in his life introduced him
to St. John's University, to community service, to productive jobs, to
Temple University Law School, and to political involvement. Nelson's
awakening as a young man drew sound guidance, opportunities, and
sparks of idealism from myriad sources of loving support. It was inevi-
table that the presence of his energetic, driven talent would make those
around him sit up and take notice.

Each phase of Nelson's education and community involvement
added a dimension to his public awareness and leadership skills. During
his years at Temple University Law School, he gained a respect for the
law and for its applicability to addressing the contentious urban issues
of the early 1970s. Joining groups of Latino activists, he found his voice
as a spokesperson for their grievances. After law school he served as a
public defender, contending with difficult cases, and became executive
director of Philadelphia's Spanish Merchants Association. His immersion in local politics with an eye toward resolving community concerns
earned him the respect of Mayor Frank Rizzo.

A stint as a White House Fellow in the office of Vice President Walter
Mondale gave Nelson insight into national politics, with a front-row seat
to the deliberations of the nation's highest and most skillful public servants. This young man from the mean streets of the Bronx and Philadelphia, who was able to observe, participate in, and contribute insights to
high-level national discussions, thus affirmed an interest in public policy
that would shape the rest of his life.

This is when I first heard of Nelson Díaz. Having been a White
House Fellow myself some six years earlier, I was attentive to subsequent
classes of Fellows and particularly to the Latinos who were selected. By
this time I was a city council member in San Antonio, Texas, and I took
pleasure in following the trajectory of Latinos who were rising in public
service. So I took note of Nelson's return to Philadelphia and watched

with pride as he became a state judge and Philadelphia's city solicitor. He earned citywide respect for his judicial decisions and his leadership, particularly with respect to exposing corruption in the Philadelphia court system. He also earned the enmity of criminal networks, which threatened his life. His reputation for courage and unshakable honesty grew in Philadelphia and in the Latino community nationwide. Through the 1980s I met with Nelson at Latino meetings and municipal conferences across the nation and was always impressed by the intensity and consistency of his commitment to the public interest.

When President Bill Clinton nominated me as secretary of the U.S. Department of Housing and Urban Development (HUD) in late 1992, it fell to me to recommend people for fourteen assistant secretary–level positions. One of the positions was general counsel of HUD, chief lawyer for the department. It was a job that would entail interpreting congressional laws, drafting departmental regulations, handling litigation, and setting the legal parameters for almost every aspect of HUD's daily operations. This was a key position in a department that had complex operations in every one of the 50 states and every U.S. territory—operations that, in keeping with HUD's mandate to address the needs of the least advantaged Americans and the most resource-deprived communities, were located in some of the most troubled places in the nation. I needed someone who would remain undaunted by the toughest, most challenging regions and who would work tirelessly to break legal logjams and find pro-active ways to get help to those who needed it most. Nelson came immediately to mind.

Fortunately, Nelson agreed to serve as HUD's general counsel. He resolved legal impasses that had hamstrung the department for years. He found creative ways to expedite funding, launch new programs, settle disputes, and carry out congressional mandates. He devised emergency measures to, quite literally, rescue residents from dysfunctional public housing in major cities across the nation. His work was crucial in such places as Vidor, Texas, where HUD addressed serious discrimination in public housing, and earthquake-stricken Southern California. He crisscrossed the country, visiting nearly 200 cities, hearing out and working for the least advantaged. Perhaps his most lasting legacy is his "disparate impact" decision, which the Supreme Court upheld a few years ago and which Justice Anthony Kennedy referred to as addressing "consequences of actions and not just the mindset of actors." In everything Nelson did, I saw the passion of a legal professional who recalled his own days in run-down, hazardous tenements and who wanted to save another generation of children from living even one day longer in the same conditions.

In the years since HUD, Nelson and I have been in close touch. He is more than a friend; he is my brother. It is impossible not to love as family someone who cares so deeply about values that too many public officials consider mere words and abstractions: values such as justice, fairness, due process, equity, inclusion, integration, and social mobility. To Nelson these ideals are reasons to engage his love of the law, to eke out another jolt of life's energy, to sustain the lifelong fight. Whether the intervening years have found Nelson working in a law practice, serving on a corporate board, advising a community organization, running for mayor, campaigning for others, sharing the quest for a better society with his beloved wife, Sara, or passing on his values to his own family and to other young people in classrooms and organizations, he has always been the striver who never stops trying to make life better.

So I come full circle to the preeminence of the strivers, the people who more than anyone else make America the unique place that it is. When Americans with burning aspirations, with physical determination, and with raw talent are unleashed in a nation where limits are meant to be surmounted, the result can only be individual achievement and community progress. Of course, our country, like any other, has its shortcomings, including too many generations lost to rigid class barriers and too much talent lost to discriminatory inequity, but slowly and surely the barriers are lifting. Nelson Díaz's life is a twofold testament to these advances in that he has hurdled impediments in his own life and he has worked to dismantle age-old obstacles for future generations.

This book, which movingly describes the passage of a striver, holds important lessons for Americans from many backgrounds. It is a primer for those who start life with few advantages, a lesson—from Nelson's story—of the possibilities that life holds for them. It is a revelation for those who have enjoyed advantages, a message of respect for the unlimited potential of every person to enjoy the blessings that our great country holds. For those who study the mindsets of the underestimated, the underappreciated, the marginalized, the invisible, and the newcomer, it is a clinical diagnostic, an exploration of those who blossom into examples of the leaders we most need. This book is sure to inspire young readers who aspire to a life of contribution and to instill pride in my contemporaries for taking part in remarkable social progress.

I consider myself fortunate to have witnessed the making of an extraordinary man. Nelson's story is one of dynamic continuation: he first dreamed, and then he prepared; he listened, and then he acted; he learned, and then he taught; he followed, and then he led; he engaged in spiritual reflection, and then he fought for justice and fairness. This book continues the sequence: Nelson has lived a contributing life, and now he shares his motivations, dreams, and aspirations in the honest and straightforward language that kindles our admiration for the man and rekindles our love for the country that makes this life possible. In a time of anxiety and division, of uncertainty and doubt, Nelson Díaz has bestowed on us this priceless gift of hope and confidence, of faith and belief.

—*Henry Cisneros*

PREFACE

ONE NEED LOOK NO FURTHER than the recent coverage of Puerto Rico and Hurricane Maria to understand my reasons for writing this book. A lovely island sitting in the Caribbean and under U.S. rule since 1898, it has somehow evaded Americans' awareness as one of the last standing vestiges of New World colonialism. And now it is barely standing.

No soy de aquí ni de allá, we Puerto Ricans say, meaning "I am accepted neither here nor there." We were handed over as a trophy after the Spanish-American War, and we have been Almost-Americans ever since. Cuba immediately, the Philippines later, and other U.S. territories have gone on to full statehood, but Puerto Rico stays in limbo as it slowly collapses, like an old house no one can be bothered to look after.

And then the hurricane came and wiped out an electrical grid that was fragile and badly outdated. The system, which has changed little since it was created some 70 years ago, costs four times as much as electrical grids on the mainland when it functions at all.

When President Donald Trump finally visited the island, almost two weeks after the hurricane made landfall, he had already lashed out at the mayor of San Juan and insisted that nothing more could have been done. He took it personally that the mayor had warned that people were in real trouble, even dying, as a result of the flooding, the lack of power, and the overwhelmed and underfunded emergency services. Then he showed up, chided Puerto Ricans for being a drag on the national budget, and tossed out paper towels, as if they were party favors, to a passive crowd. And after either growing bored or seeing no further point in staying, he left an hour earlier than scheduled.

Watching the whole sad, inadequate response on television, I could not even focus on the president's actions. I was watching my fellow Puerto Ricans. When it took Trump weeks to show up, we said little. When he arrived and opened with a complaint about how much we were costing the United States, we said nothing. Everywhere he went, we stood and watched, waiting for something good to happen. When he tossed out paper towels as if they might mop up the flooding, we clapped, we smiled, we caught them, and were grateful.

When he said that the debt would probably have to be wiped out, we knew he was only saying so to get out of the room, and then he left and took his promise back. Of course, he did. And what will we do about it? Probably nothing. The island is saddled with a municipal debt of more than $70 billion—not to mention an additional $22 billion in bonds owed by the government-owned electric company—and almost half of its citizens live in poverty. But we are unwilling to take any steps to change our predicament. We wait for better days. This has forever been the way. But now Puerto Ricans, not from here and not from there, face the possibility that there will no longer be any "there."

Growing up in New York City, Puerto Ricans had little standing and no identity. We seemed to be more timid than other groups. Perhaps because we always had somewhere to flee to, we chose not to stand and fight. As citizens of the United States, we are free to move between the island and the mainland, and with cheap travel, we could always go somewhere else when things got bad. I count myself lucky that I grew up in the time of the civil rights movement, among people who helped me take my sense of justice and aim it at something. I learned how to take my frustration at a system that abused its power over people and turn it into action. I was fortunate to grow up during a time when, as a teen and as a law school student, I could join African Americans in their fight for civil rights.

The Latino population in the mainland United States was tiny in the 1950s, but it has rapidly grown, and with our increasing numbers can come greater political power. This book aims to show what one determined Latino can do, and I hope it provides a path for others to follow. Moreover, I hope that the coming generations push further, do more, and can change the world. This will take not just hard work but also community- and online-initiated common cause with like-minded people.

I believe that education is paramount to success and that it must be more equitably provided to all. Better-educated children become more civic-minded adults, more effective citizens, and more willing advocates for the needs of their communities. This book tells my story. I spoke no English when I entered a school where no one spoke a word of Spanish to me. I was behind when I began, and I had to fight to catch up. I didn't do it alone—I had help and inspiration from my mother, from my church community, and from many other mentors.

I believe in Philadelphia. This city, my home for almost 50 years, has much to offer and much work to do. It's the ideal place for people who want to make a difference. It has taught me a great deal, and it has been good to me. I hope this book helps pay it back and pay it forward.

I was born into poverty and squalor, and bad things happened in my life. But I was also fortunate, even blessed. I made many mistakes, and I often had doubts, but I kept moving forward. I strove to improve life for everyone, and while I did not always triumph, I believe that I made a difference. This book is not intended as an instruction manual for community activism or for any other endeavor. It is simply my story, and I hope it will speak to those who read it, remind them of what's possible, and inspire them to keep working toward what they know to be right.

ACKNOWLEDGMENTS

A
FEW YEARS AGO, I told the president of Temple University that I was thinking about writing my life story. He introduced me to Micah Kleit, Temple University Press's editor in chief at the time. Micah helped take that general idea and craft it into a proposal. He also put me in touch with Justin Coffin, who helped take the proposal and craft it into this book.

Casey Swiski did dogged and valuable research on housing, the courts, and Philadelphia history for this story.

A few special others provided support along the way, including Terri Capece, Lindsey Leonard, and all my friends and partners at Dilworth-Paxson. Bill von Hoene at Exelon Corporation provided valuable resources as well. All helped bring this narrative from a few stories that I would tell over dinner and eventually forget to the book that readers now hold in their hands.

NOT FROM HERE,

NOT FROM THERE/

NO SOY DE AQUÍ

NI DE ALLÁ

1

PUERTO RICO AND
FAMILY HISTORY

TWENTY YEARS OLD, pregnant, and alone, my mother, Maria Cancel, stood before the SS *Marine Tiger,* docked in its berth in the Port of San Juan on September 5, 1946. It was the day she would sail from Puerto Rico, bound for New York City. I think of her feeling small and alone before the gangplank that would take her away from everything she knew onto the deck of what must have been the largest thing she'd ever seen—a ship a tenth of a mile long. She was one of 800 passengers boarding that day, and one of thousands headed to the mainland United States during the Great Migration of the 1940s and 1950s. The *Marine Tiger* had been used as a troop transport during World War II but was converted back after the war to a passenger ship that shuttled from San Juan to New York City and back. With nothing but a suitcase in her hand and a child in her belly, she was leaving home behind and boarding the 12,000-ton steamship that would swallow her up like Jonah's whale, take her away, and spit her out on the shores of a land she'd heard of only in stories and her sister's letters. How many on that voyage were just like her? How many had gone before? How many more would come after?

Life wasn't easy in Puerto Rico in 1946. Opportunities were few, but industry jobs, growth, and hope awaited in the mainland United States. Maria was one of more than 150,000 Puerto Ricans who migrated during the 1940s, more than had done so in the previous five decades combined. Many came to the mainland in search of better lives, to earn some money that they could send back home. Some came for seasonal work, and some to start a life. Most at the time came to make some money and to return, a little wealthier, to Puerto Rico. They wanted something more, and they flocked to the land of opportunity to find it. But what they encountered was often hardship, poverty, discrimination, and exploitation.

Maria's oldest brother had gone first. Paulino volunteered for the army and sent part of every paycheck back to the family in Puerto Rico. After his stint in the service, he landed in New York. Maria's sister Pepita had followed Paulino. Maria and Pepita looked alike and were inseparable growing up; everyone said that Pepita and Maria were like twins. Pepita had flown to New York and was working in a factory. She too sent money back, and it was she who wired the $100 to pay for Maria's ticket and a little extra so Maria could join her in the Bronx.

Food on the voyage was scarce, and the ship was loud: the deep persistent roar of the engine, the incessant high chatter of voices in the hall, shouting strangers, people coming in and out of the shared cabin. Maria knew no one on board, and every time she returned to her berth she felt that things had been moved around or that something was missing. She kept to herself below decks, sitting with her belongings for as much of the journey as she could, eating very little, and feeling the air grow colder the farther north she sailed. Each turn of the huge turbine counted out the growing distance between her and home, each wave beating against the hull brought her closer to an irreversible future in an alien land. She was battling severe seasickness and was ill prepared for September in New York. She'd packed what little she had, which included nothing that would keep her warm outside of the tropics. Still, she was overcome with a sense of hope and relief when she first caught sight of the Statue of Liberty on September 9. Perhaps only because it meant the journey was over, but maybe she sensed the significance of her arrival. She had made it to the mainland. With the end of her voyage she had graduated into a new life.

It was cold when she disembarked, but Maria was flushed with excitement. A friend of Pepita's met her at the pier and took her to Pepita's house on Jackson Avenue in the Bronx. Maria couldn't know it then that only six months earlier the man who would become her husband had arrived from Puerto Rico and was living on that same block of Jackson Avenue.

The trip to New York took her away from her home, from her mother and her brothers and sisters, and from the man who had put that new life in her belly. She had been with a man in Puerto Rico, a man named Luis Díaz. She was in love with him, but he was much older and had no interest in starting a new family with her.

Maria had lived outside Vega Alta, which in the 1940s was one of the most prosperous towns in Puerto Rico, and Luis Díaz, the only son of a man from the Canary Islands, was the big man in town. A Levi-Strauss factory sat just outside of Vega Alta on the military road that is the main thoroughfare in and out of the town. A long, low sugar factory with tall smokestacks that still stand today was a big employer not far from the town's central plaza. Luis owned an appliance store, a movie theater, and a two-story department store that sold clothes and sundries, called Comercial Luis Díaz.

As a young child, Maria lived with her family in the neighborhood of Candelaria. When she was nine years old, to spare her from the wrath of her father—who would beat the children with little provocation—Maria's mother put a quarter in her pocket and sent her to live, first in San Juan with her sister Modesta and then in Vega Alta with Tomasa, an older woman who was a friend of the family. Maria never returned to live in Candelaria again. She stayed with Modesta and then with Tomasa. At 13 she began working as a maid to support herself.

Maria had been to Luis's department store and his movie theater many times as a child, and she would have known who Luis was. He was a fixture there, every day running his businesses, keeping an eye on things. He didn't drive—he hired a car to take him into town every day. His son Fernando used to say that the sun wouldn't dare rise on Vega Alta unless it knew Luis Díaz would be there to greet it.

I'm not sure how they came to be together. Perhaps he met her through Tomasa, whom he knew. Or he could have noticed Maria when she came into the store. In my family's stories, she would sometimes take shoes, shoes she may have bought but might have stolen, and they first met when he caught her. Or perhaps they met when she started working for him. He needed someone to clean and there she was. But now she was 19, and maybe she just caught his eye. My uncle Willie didn't like Luis and didn't trust him; he said Luis took advantage of Maria and it's hard to imagine he didn't. She would have been a teenager and he 25 years older. She was hardly out of childhood, barely a woman, and he was in his middle age, with children older than she, and grandchildren.

By today's standards their relationship would be considered inappropriate. But that was a different time and a different place. All that is certain is that they began to see each other, sharing an act that meant something different to each of them. She was in love with him, but Luis had enough love in his life already. He had businesses and a wife and a family of his own, and he was carrying on another affair with a woman whom he'd set up in Dorado. (A few months after Maria left for the mainland, the other woman too would become pregnant.) When Maria got pregnant, she found out that she and her unborn child did not figure into Luis's very full life in the way she wanted.

And so Maria set sail for the mainland United States at a time when New York City was undergoing a huge influx of Puerto Ricans. The Census Bureau counted 61,000 Puerto Ricans living in New York City by 1940. By 1950, that number had tripled to almost 190,000. The city was immediately confronted with the problem of how to deal with this spike in population. Where would all these newcomers live, and how would they be treated? The immediate answers were not always satisfactory, and, ever since, our nation has wrestled with these questions. For my entire life, they have informed my sense of right and wrong.

I arrive in my own story on May 23, 1947, eight months after Maria Cancel landed in New York. She delivered me, a healthy baby boy, at Bellevue Hospital, a place that is shorthand for "loony bin." I joke that I am the way I am because I caught a little of the crazy when I was born, but Bellevue has always been more than just an insane asylum. It was founded as the Almshouse Hospital well before America declared its independence and, as that name suggests, it cared for the poor. It has always served the public, and in 1799 it opened a maternity ward. To this day Bellevue ministers to the indigent and the uninsured and counts the immigrant community among the major groups it serves. But I have wondered whether Maria faked some kind of psychiatric disorder to be admitted, or whether she didn't have to try very hard to manufacture symptoms of exhaustion or to convince a doctor that she was having a nervous breakdown. She was resourceful, for certain. She was a survivor. There were closer hospitals in the Bronx, but she did what was best for her baby.

My mother says I was born with a pale face, and when she passed she still had a lock of my blonde hair among her things. Where my coloring came from is a mystery when you consider my heritage. My father's father sailed to Puerto Rico from the Canary Islands, off the coast of Morocco. Prevailing winds make Puerto Rico a natural sailing destination from Gibraltar and thereabouts; these are the winds that brought Columbus and the slave trade that followed. Consider, for instance, the Calima, a wind that lifts sand from the Sahara and carries it all the way to the Caribbean. I have seen Sahara sand drop like rain in Puerto Rico.

My father's maternal grandfather came from Africa in chains, a slave in the Spanish slave trade. In 1835 the queen of Spain abolished the slave trade in Spanish colonies, including Puerto Rico, but slavery itself was not abolished until 1873.

My mother's grandparents immigrated to Puerto Rico from Murcia in southeastern coastal Spain, taking the town's name with them. My mother's mother's name, as traditionally rendered in Puerto Rico, is Iluminada Gonzalez Murcia. She was known to everyone as Mina.

My family is a mixture of Taíno and Spanish, with bloodlines tracing back to Europe and Africa. I carry in me the blood of the native people of Puerto Rico, the colonialists who claimed it for their own, and the immigrants who came from almost every continent that touches the Atlantic.

So there I was, newly arrived to New York City. My mother and I were still in Bellevue when she received Amparo Canales and her daughter, Diana Díaz. Amparo was Luis Díaz's wife, and she happened to be in the Bronx visiting Diana, a ballet dancer. They came to the hospital and offered to take me back to Puerto Rico, where I would be raised as Luis's son. I could learn the family business and one day have a stake in it myself. It wouldn't be a terrible life. I would have a kind of security that Maria, raising me on her own in New York City, could not provide. I would be well taken care of. My mother thanked them for the offer and sent them away.

That was my arrival. But does my story begin there? In New York City, at Bellevue? Surely my story reaches back to Puerto Rico, where my parents were born and where they lived and where they met. It moves forward to Philadelphia, where I went to law school and made my career. It bounced me back and forth between Philadelphia and Washington, D.C., to the White House as a Fellow, to the Philadelphia courts as a judge, back to D.C. for a post in the Clinton administration, and then back again to Philadelphia as a lawyer and city solicitor. It took me all over the world and put me squarely in the middle of vital communities that pulse with life even while they struggle. But where do I begin? How

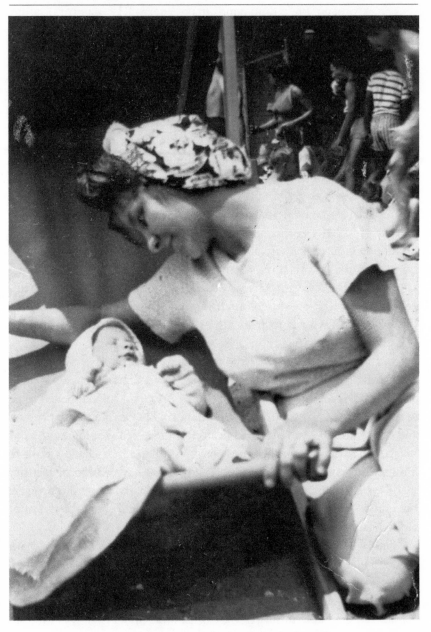

As a newborn in the Bronx, with my mother looking down at me.
She came to the mainland to make a life for me.

do I tell you who I am and how I got to be where I am? Let's go farther back.

My mother was one of 13 children, and she survived a childhood with 11 siblings and the memory of another who died. The family moved from house to house in the Candelaria area, around Vega Alta. My mother's mother, Mina, was very poor, and she and her children never had much of anything. They relied on help from others. Mina would sometimes resort to taking fruit growing in the yard of one of my grandfather's other lovers to feed her family. She was so poor, so destitute that she lost a child to starvation. I cannot imagine how helpless she must have felt watching her own child starve. I don't know how she bore it.

My story runs back through a maternal line of struggle and strife, as men appear and disappear. My father wasn't there to raise me; I didn't meet him until I was 10 years old on my first trip to Puerto Rico. My mother's father, however, was a man out of a song. Grandpa was a rolling stone. Perhaps my story can begin with him.

Pedro Cancel Pantoja had four children with his wife. With Mina he had 13 more, and with other women other children, the number of which I will never know. He rode a fine horse from one side of the island to the other, following the seasonal work in the sugar cane business. The cane grew around Vega Alta on the Atlantic side of Puerto Rico and Humacao on the Caribbean side. Tall and handsome, strong and well dressed, he cut an impressive figure riding along the road. But he was not a kind or generous man, and he could be violent and cruel. He would come around to see my grandmother when the cane was being harvested and he'd give her another child, but he took little interest in the children he'd already sired unless they bothered him. And then his discipline could be vicious. He provided no support and Mina was left to care for her children alone, sleeping with a gun under her pillow for protection, in a house that was always short on money and never long on love.

Mina has her story and Maria hers. My family's story is our own, but it is a song sung all across the island. Times were tough in Puerto Rico and my mother grew up poor, as did her mother, as did I. This is the history of Puerto Rico and the history of Latinos in the mainland United States. It is the history of the New World.

As a Latino, I am several things at once. Being not any one thing makes identity a difficult thing to hold onto. It feels provisional and unsteady, as though there is no solid ground beneath my feet. I am an American and a colonized person at the same time. And if I am not any one thing, am I anything at all? I am a stranger in my own country and a citizen of an island where I have never lived. I have never been truly at home or accepted in either place.

2

TURNING POINTS

ALONE, WITH A THIRD-GRADE EDUCATION and no English, my mother arrived in New York to start a life with the child she was carrying and to help her family back in Puerto Rico. She moved in with Pepita in the Bronx at 156th Street and Jackson Avenue, and Pepita helped her find work. When I was just one or two years old, she met Miserain Rodriguez at a storefront church on that same block. He lived across the street from the church and, before they met, had admired Maria from his window as she came and went with her baby.

Maria had come to the mainland a Roman Catholic, but the church in New York did not cater to Spanish speakers. Catholics in New York, the priests, the nuns, and many of the parishioners, were Irish and spoke English. For the Irish, it had been important to assimilate to the American way as quickly as possible. Friction arose between them and the incoming Puerto Ricans, who did not speak English and kept to themselves in the very neighborhoods the Irish had worked so hard to carve out for themselves. Many Puerto Ricans therefore turned to storefront Pentecostal churches, which catered to the new immigrant population in a way that the Catholic Church did not. My mother could understand the language that was spoken from the pulpit and by the other parishioners at that little church on Jackson Avenue. There, the music, unlike the stoic chanting of the Catholic mass, was celebratory. My mother felt supported at the little church on Jackson Avenue with its ad hoc social services, its welcoming community, and its minister who would listen and counsel.

Soon after Miserain Rodriguez met my mother, he courted her, and, when I was three years old, they married. They had a little girl, whom they named Noemi, but she's always been Cookie to me.

Before Cookie was born, my mother carried another child to term and gave birth to him. But he was stillborn. My mother agonized over him most of her life. When she told the story, what seemed most to afflict her was the callous way the hospital treated her. In her telling, the nurses brought the body to her and accused her of killing her baby. They said she'd had an abortion and this was the result. She had, of course, done no such thing. She had gone to the hospital expecting to bear a healthy baby, only to endure first the heartbreak of his stillbirth and then the humiliation of being blamed for it. It must have been devastating.

Such an exchange is hard to imagine, but I have to allow that it's possible. It could be that the hospital staff saw a poor Spanish-speaking woman and made assumptions based on their prejudices. When it became clear that something had gone terribly wrong, I can imagine that it was easy for the staff, harboring suspicions spawned by bigotry, to blame her rather than to attribute the stillbirth to the fragility of human life or any other of several possible factors. I can imagine, too, how easy it would have been for a misunderstanding to occur when a grief-stricken woman sits on one side of a language divide and a roomful of non-Spanish-speaking medical personnel sits on the other. A fraught environment with no course for clear communication created a vacuum in which an accusation bloomed. Whatever the cause, the incident stayed with my mother for the rest of her life and added suffering to the grief of losing a child. Maria's plight was the plight of other Puerto Rican migrants at the time—to have to fight to be understood and to understand because of our language and, despite our citizenship, our essential foreignness. In the decades since, many things have improved because we have fought for improvement, but we still have a long way to go before we can say that we are, all of us, treated equally.

Back in 1950, on Jackson Avenue, my aunt Pepita's apartment was going to be too small for our growing family. There was no room for Miserain, and then my mother got pregnant with my sister. It was time to move out. My mother's good friend Gineta, who had been her matron of honor, her *madrina,* a woman who always looked out for us, helped us find a single-room occupancy (or SRO) on 133rd Street in West Harlem. As the name suggests, an SRO was a one-room apartment with a shared bathroom in the common hallway. Like many poor families with few options, we took what we could afford at the time and packed into close quarters. SRO buildings, like tenements, had been built for single families or split into larger apartments and were later divided up and segmented and rented room by room to the poor people arriving in New York on the wave of postwar migration. The apartments were often squalid, owned by landlords who didn't want to invest in upkeep because they didn't have to. Housing in New York at the time was a free-for-all with very little regulation or oversight, and the typical SRO was overcrowded, rundown, and substandard.[1] For the time, our SRO was not bad. One could certainly find worse places to live, and soon enough we did. A year after moving to 133rd Street, our little family moved down the block, around the corner, and into a first-floor tenement apartment on 134th and Broadway.

My mother had left Puerto Rico holding tight to the migrant's dream of a better life in the mainland United States, but soon she was confronted with the reality many like her faced when they arrived in New York City: life wasn't much better stateside, and in some ways, it was far worse. A tenement in the 1950s was not a good place to live, especially if you're raising children, and I can tell you it's terrible if you're a child yourself. My first memories are from that little overcrowded, rat-infested building. My mother and stepfather shared one bedroom, Cookie had the other, and I slept on a sofa in the living room. There never seemed to be enough room or enough light or enough air, and I don't remember a time when there wasn't at least one relative living with us. The five-story tenement building was close to where the elevated Broadway train line began, and right in the middle of a changing neighborhood. West Harlem had been Irish, but with the arrival of so many Latinos, it was now in transition. And the transition was tense. The Broadway musical *West Side Story,* in which a Romeo-and-Juliet lovers' tragedy is played out between rival ethnic street gangs, the Puerto Rican Sharks and the white Jets, was based on my West Harlem neighborhood.

---

1. Suzanne Daley, "Court Ruling Brings Fear to S.R.O. Hotel Rooms," *New York Times,* July 10, 1989.

Celebrating my fifth birthday, with my mother, at the Reverend Ramon Gutierrez's church at 135th and Amsterdam.

Our first-floor apartment faced the building's backyard, and we could look out on the kids playing stickball, Chinese handball, and other games. Staring out those windows at night I saw things a little boy is not equipped to see. I would see muggings and shakedowns, violence and strife, and people having sex in the very yard where I played during the day. Around the neighborhood and in the building itself, I regularly saw people accosted, searched, and roughed up by police for no discernible reason other than that they were poor and Latino. I remember when the police raided an apartment and arrested an entire family for playing lotto, a game of chance that is now advertised as a wholesome game and a civic support for the state of New York. And yet, in all the time I've spent throughout my life on golf courses, I have never seen a single golfer arrested for wagering on a game.

Our apartment's windows, set in a quiet spot away from the street, were perfect for break-ins, and we were burglarized more than once. But that was not the worst of it. Rats had the run of the lower floors; roaches were everywhere. We stayed in that awful place for seven years, in close proximity to drugs, crime, health risks, and the police. It was dim, dirty, close, and unsafe, like permanent midnight in a jungle full of predators, and you could avoid them for only so long.

It's painful to recall those years. Teenagers would expose themselves to the younger kids, and we'd all act out sexual behaviors in the yard behind the building, behaviors we might have seen but were incapable of either performing or understanding. It was unwholesome and de-structive, and it would be many years before I felt I could move past my idea of sex as something that was only for self-satisfaction rather than a way for two people to express their love for each other.

My mother's relationship with my stepfather did little to offer a healthy example, either. Their marriage was contentious, and in most of my memories of them at the time, they are fighting. My mother would shout at my stepfather, berating him for having no ambition, for not being like my biological father (a shadowy figure whose face I had never seen, a mysterious nonpresence who haunted my childish imagination from his tropical island hideout), who was important and successful. Sometimes their fights would get physical. Neither Cookie nor I brought many friends to our home for fear of being embarrassed. And yet my mother and stepfather managed to stay together, locked in a strange affiliation full of strife and recrimination but also love and support, for 67 years.

The worst thing that happened in that godforsaken place on 134th Street took only a moment, and I kept it secret for years. My mother had gone shopping and had taken Cookie with her. I was five years old, an age at which, in that neighborhood and at that time, children were often left alone. The memory is murky, but I remember playing in the first-floor hallway when another tenant in the building grabbed me. He was naked under his robe and he nearly penetrated me with his penis. Some-how in the struggle that followed, I got away from him. Did he hear someone coming in the door or down the stairs? Did he feel a pang of conscience? I'll never know. I never told anyone and have lived with a memory that has not faded over the years. It has become distorted like a nightmarish painting that has been stored out of sight and made weirder by warping over the years. Maybe if I had said something about it at the time, I would remember who he was. But I kept it to myself, even though sometimes I felt it would grow too large for me to contain, and all the trauma and the shame and fear that went along with it would crush me or blow me apart. But to whom could I have turned? That little boy I was back then just wanted to leave it behind, to act as though it hadn't happened. He didn't see how telling someone would have helped. Now, more than six decades later, as I think about that boy's situation and the few people he had around him, I see little hope of comfort or support among the adults to whom he could have turned at the time.

I was a vulnerable child, left alone in a building overstuffed with people who were living in squalor. That is no way for anyone to live. No one deserves to live in conditions that make them sick, that expose them to so many threats to their health, to their development, to their very spirit. And yet this is what the most powerless among us often suffer at the hands of those who seek only to squeeze as much money out of them as possible. How, then, did that traumatized five-year-old manage to navigate his childhood? How did he survive his own upbringing? It wasn't will or strength or any aspect of character that spared him. No, I survived, I managed to grow from that poor, harmed child to who I am today because of grace. I thank God that we were able to move out of the tenement and into public housing, out of a place where I felt alone to a place where I found mentors. It was as though I had been confined to hell and then set free.

As I see it, my survival is evidence of grace. Others reading this story may attribute it to luck or hard work or the stewardship of good men. The only distinction I can make between, on one side, luck or work or guidance, and on the other side, grace has to do with whether or not you attribute the results to the work of God. That brief moment could have crippled me, and yet it did not. Was it grace? I believe it was, and I further believe that the way grace played out in my life had everything to do with housing.

I further believe that God has a sense of humor. The kid who lived in the SRO, who lived through hell in the tenement, and who then moved into public housing would grow up to be a public servant instrumental in the implementation of a change in U.S. public housing policy. My dedication to public housing and my belief in everyone's right to a clean, safe place to live was born in those buildings and grew to maturity there, just as I did. Housing is a basic human right, and the foundation on which so much else rests. I lived through the culmination of a housing crisis in New York City. For decades, the city had wrestled with the fundamental question of how to reach beyond the concept of mere storage and find ways to house the poor people who were migrating to the city in waves. In short, the question was "How can a large, crowded metropolitan area provide shelter for its most vulnerable without destroying them?"

Moving to public housing affected me profoundly and helped me survive. But my situation would have to grow worse in order to get better. In addition to the traumas and the everyday meannesses of my life in the tenement, and because of them, I developed asthma. My mother always insisted it was the result of the pneumonia I came down with after my stepfather's aunt bathed me in cold water, but I attribute it to our living conditions. Asthma was a common affliction in the tenements, and it reached far beyond Harlem, far beyond the range of one old woman and her cold baths. Between the roaches and the filth and the coal heat and the poor ventilation that caught the lingering smoke and dust, the air we breathed was unhealthy. My parents addressed the issue as best they could. I had my tonsils removed at Knickerbocker Hospital, right across the street from my grammar school. That operation kept me out of school for three weeks. Often I was confined to my makeshift bed for long stretches of time.

Asthma attacks are terrifying, and I suffered them fairly regularly as a child. I felt as though I was suffocating, which I was, and that I was going to die. Asthma is a serious health issue that can disrupt your life, but my asthma saved us. My poor health was our ticket out of hell. The attacks qualified us for the new public housing that was going up around Manhattan at that time, so I am grateful for every last gasping breath I had to take.

My mother applied and we were accepted at the brand new Grant Houses, a high-rise housing project at 125th Street and Amsterdam Avenue in West Harlem. Grant Houses was the tallest public housing development in New York when it opened in the summer of 1956. We moved in the following year, on August 1, 1957, and it felt as though we had made it to the middle class. We had three bedrooms in our 16th-floor apartment, one for Mom and Pop, one for Cookie, and at long last one just for me. And in my room, I had a radio. At night I would listen to Cousin Brucie on WABC, to the Good Guys on WMCA, and to Murray the K's *Swingin' Soiree* on 1010-AM WINS. Sunday nights I fell asleep listening to Howard Cosell or Billy Graham.

We were the first tenants to move into our apartment at Grant Houses. It smelled like fresh paint, and fresh paint smelled like hope. In my own room, from my own window, I could look down on P.S. 125 and see the park. That view was so different from the view of the courtyard I had been exposed to in the tenement. Here I could look down on a basketball court and a baseball diamond. I could look out and see whether any of my friends was there. We did not have the luxury of air conditioning, and so when it was hot, the windows were thrown wide open. Voices drifted up from the courtyard below, and I would listen to the groups singing doo-wop by the community center. It was wonderful to hear.

People with real talent lived in that building. Little Ronnie of the Ronnettes, who would become Ronnie Spector, came from my building. I remember seeing a long black Cadillac pull up to the front of the building and watching her climb inside. I didn't know what it meant, whether it was a good thing or a bad thing. A black Cadillac could take you to a wedding or a funeral. I guess for Little Ronnie it might have been a mixture of good and bad, marrying a mercurial and powerful record producer like Phil Spector.

Relationships with powerful men can often be both good and bad. And whether New York City liked it or not, when I was growing up, it was in a relationship with Robert Moses, who brought sweeping changes to housing. His almost singlehanded and massive rearrangement of the demographics, of the transportation systems, of the city itself was ruthless and comprehensive. His solution to rundown tenements and nearly unlivable conditions was to evict the tenants without giving them a place to move to and then offer them the right of first refusal months or years later when the buildings were brought up to code. It's a fine promise, to hear that things will be better when the place is updated, but it is no consolation when you no longer have a roof over your head, even if that roof leaked. And he did it all without having to consult with Mayor Fiorello La Guardia or anyone else. This was not a federally overseen public housing plan. Eventually it would become part of a federal program, but at the time, Robert Moses was, essentially, the sole governing body for housing policy. For years the city slumlords had used the lack of oversight to their advantage, packing their buildings with as many people as they could, doing as little maintenance and upkeep as possible, and collecting as much as they could in rents. Moses's solution was to condemn the slumlords' buildings and throw out their tenants. And while the slumlords' practice of stuffing six families into the six rooms of what had formerly been a single-family apartment was unhealthy, and the sharing was difficult, Moses's solution upset everyone: the property owners who had been making money off the arrangements, the now-evicted tenants who had to scramble for any available living space they could find, and the municipal government watching its city being torn up and having no control over what was happening.

There had never been anyone like Robert Moses before, and there hasn't been anyone like him since. No one can duplicate what he did up and down Manhattan. When I was living at 134th Street, the city condemned everything from 133rd Street down to 129th or maybe even farther south. What replaced those places was much better. But Moses did it all without mercy.

I wish I had the power Robert Moses had. I imagine every urban planner and city commissioner, everyone who has ever pushed for reform in public housing does, too. After his success in New York City, other cities put up high-rises. In Chicago, they became shooting galleries. In Baltimore, they were failures—the elevators never worked. In Philadelphia, they became hotbeds of criminal activity. Those cities took one of Moses's most problematic ideas and copied it, even though they did not face the issue of population density that made Moses's approach necessary in New York. In New York Moses had nowhere to go but up; Chicago, Baltimore, and Philadelphia had plenty of land to spread out. They didn't have to put up high-rises, but urban planning in that era was marked by a profound lack of imagination. Those other cities took a cookie-cutter approach to the most prominent feature of public housing and thought it a substitute for actual planning. But that approach led to many of the problems that have plagued public housing. In the 1990s, however, during the Clinton administration, when I served as general counsel at Housing and Urban Development under Secretary Henry Cisneros, we were able to change the copycat mentality that in solving some problems had created many more.

Moses found a way to function as an autocrat without a thought to the tens of thousands of people he was displacing. If I had his resources, his control, his carte-blanche manifest, I'd take practically every block of North Philadelphia, condemn them and rebuild them. And then I'd do the same in Camden. But no one can do what Moses did with any amount of money. People cannot be evicted now without being provided with a place to live in the interim, just tossed out and wished good luck finding shelter. By law, they must be relocated while the rebuilding process goes on. And, of course, that's only right. Moses's way worked because of his guts and his complete lack of compassion. He threw people out on the street, but he changed New York for the better. And not everything he did was done for the sake of creating better housing for the poor. He shunted many of the poor and minorities to high-rise public housing along the shores of Manhattan, and in the vacated neighborhoods they left behind he built places designed for the wealthy.

All of these changes in New York housing, in essence, saved me. Nineteen fifty-seven was a great year for me. I turned 10, we moved into public housing, and my family took me to Puerto Rico for the first time. We went in January for the Puerto Rican celebration of Christmas, January 6. That flight was my first time on an airplane, and we took off from a cold and gray New York and touched down in lush greenery on the island. As we drove over the dirt roads to my grandmother's house, I was overwhelmed by the abundance of strange nature. Here I was, a kid from a place of asphalt and concrete, accustomed to cold New York City winters, where most of the greenery was walled up between Central Park West and 5th Avenue, limited to the leaves of an occasional street tree, and where pigeons flew through the little bits of sky that peeked between the buildings. In the tropical island of Puerto Rico, where it stays verdant year-round, I felt as though I was exploring the jungle. The weather was beautiful, with low humidity, and the skies were mostly clear. There were no streets, and what roads we traveled barely qualified as roads at all. They were dirt, and sometimes nothing more than two ruts running through the vegetation. The houses, made of wood with zinc roofs, looked like sheds with rickety fences around them.

We were going to stay with my grandmother, whom I would meet for the first time. I was dressed in a new white suit, hoping to make a good impression on her. Her house was small, just another two-room shack with a zinc roof. Vegetable plants and fruit trees surrounded the house; chickens ran around the yard. But most astonishing to me was the sight of a pig. To this day, Pop gets a big laugh out of my exclamation when I saw it: "Look! A pig in person!" I had seen pigs on television and I'd seen them in pictures, but I'd never been in the presence of one. I walked over for a good look at this fascinating creature standing by the latrine, in a muddy area that could be called a pigpen, though it was not enclosed. As I approached, my feet came out from under me, and I fell into the mud and slop. My brand new white suit was ruined.

My poor mother had bought that suit for me in Greenwich Village, bartering with the shop owner because it was December and no one was buying a white suit in New York City. She would barter for almost everything or work out a trade, always looking for deals and making offers at opportune times. And here was the result of all that planning and expert scheming, lying in a pigpen, covered in mud before I'd even set foot in my grandmother's house. I had to take it off so they could wash it in a big bucket.

My grandmother lived like many others on the island at the time. She had no bathroom, only an outdoor latrine. No shower, no sink, no washing machine—in place of all of these machines was a bucket of water and a washboard. My trip was like a visit to a totally new world. There weren't a lot of pigpens you had to avoid in West Harlem. The weather and the land figured much more prominently in daily life than they did in West Harlem. You couldn't drive on the roads in Puerto Rico after a hard or sustained rain in a two-wheel-drive car or you'd find yourself stuck in the sandy mud. And when the rains came, they beat so loudly on the metal roofs of the huts there that even if you were out of the rain, you could hear it. Inside, it seemed as though the rain was trying to get at you by beating its way through the thin roof. Once I saw high winds pull the roof off a house. I had never seen anything like that in New York City. Also, in New York, you bought all your food at a store or from a vendor. My grandmother bought only milk and bread at a store. Everything else she fed us she grew in her yard. And that pig that I'd thought of as a person became a meal later in that same trip.

I had an asthma attack when I was there. It might have been an allergic reaction to the plants, I'm not sure, but I remember it was serious enough that my uncle Diego picked me up and carried me to his house in Vega Alta. He was in the middle of his honeymoon, and every year that I came back I'd stay in the nursery with a new baby. He and his wife would have 10 children in all, one every year.

I met my father for the first time during that trip to Puerto Rico. My mother took me over to his store and introduced us. It was another pivotal moment full of significance, too much for a young boy, so what I felt at the time was mostly awkwardness and confusion. Everything felt out of place when I stood before him. Here was my father, finally, but in the flesh the thing that was most clear about him was that he was a stranger. When I could bring myself to look into his face, I searched it for features that matched my own. Did I look like him? Would I one day? Before meeting him, I had wondered in some inexpressible way whether I would be able to trace a path from the boy I was to the man I might become, to make sense, somehow, of myself.

He invited me into the store and told me I could have anything I wanted. What I wanted, though, was not to feel like a scruffy, poor kid from New York who wasn't as good as his other, already grown children. People walked in and out and spoke to each other about me, referring to me as *americanito*. No one seemed to speak out of spite or to use the term as a pejorative, especially not in front of my father, but it made me feel even more uncomfortable. Everything felt like its own opposite. I was meeting a man who was both my father and a stranger, and I was doing it while visiting my family's homeland for the first time. The moment may have looked like a homecoming, but it simply added to a rising suspicion that was emerging in my young mind: that I did not belong anywhere. In New York I was just another Puerto Rican kid, another brown body filling up a public housing high-rise; in Puerto Rico I was as out of place as a lit candle under the noonday sun, a pale kid from New York, wilting in the tropical heat. In each place I felt as though people saw me as someone away from home, an unwelcome visitor somehow both invisible and conspicuous, bumbling around on someone else's native soil. But something else stirred inside me, too. In that first meeting with my father, it was as if something were tapping on its shell, beaked and clawed, preparing to emerge. It was new. I was discovering something I had unknowingly been carrying around within me, because now it had awakened. This new creature was ambition.

I wanted to become somebody, to be like my father's other children, to get an education and become someone people respected, to find a place that I could claim as my home. My father's oldest son was an optometrist, his second son was an engineer who helped bring electricity to many towns in Puerto Rico, his third son—the son with whom I would become the closest—was a dentist, and Eddie, the youngest of my father's sons born of his wife, managed the store. My father's daughter, Diana, the ballet dancer who came with her mother to Bellevue to ask whether they could take me back to Puerto Rico, had married a football player, and they ran a school that taught sports and dance. They had taught the children of the elite of Puerto Rico, including future governor Ricardo Rosselló, who had gone on to be a champion tennis player. Who was I? Just a poor kid from New York who lived in a high-rise apartment in West Harlem and struggled to make it through school.

My father knew that we were poor, that my mother struggled. But he knew she was tough. He told me so. I wanted some of that toughness, to use it to become somebody that he could be proud of, not just the little American boy. The day I met my father was the day I first felt the ache and impatience to be more than I was. Every year thereafter, until I graduated from law school, I would travel to Puerto Rico and meet him at his store. Those visits were a measuring stick, to see how I'd grown and what progress I'd made during the previous year.

Decades later, I discovered what may have led to my finally being able to meet my father. It was not until I was a White House Fellow during the Carter administration, when I needed a passport to accompany Vice President Walter Mondale on my first trip outside the United States. To get a passport, I needed to provide an official birth certificate. I ordered one from the New York City Vital Statistics Office, and when it arrived I noticed an amendment, dated 1954. When I was born, I was given the name Díaz, after my father, but the space for "Father's Name" had been left blank. Now, at the bottom of the form, the name Luis Díaz appeared in that space; it had been added when I would have been seven years old. When I asked my father about it, he got angry and wouldn't explain it. My mother said she didn't want to talk about it and never did, so all I can do is speculate.

I think my mother contacted him and demanded some support. My father probably didn't want to provide anything for a son for whom he was not recognized as the father. I suspect they struck a deal. Submitted as Exhibit A, I offer that it was about that time that he sent me a bike in a box as a gift, and from then on he sent money every month—$50, I think. That's the extent of my theory, but it is nothing but speculation, an attempt to trace the outlines of my parents' relationship, and to color it in as best I can.

What did my father see in that pale asthmatic boy from New York City, come to meet him for the first time? I don't know. But much later I was able to learn what he thought of me as a man. My father died in Puerto Rico in 1994. After his death, my niece Carmen, whose father was my half-brother Victor, the engineer, gave me a packet of letters and photos that my father had saved. I had written to my father every month and included pictures of my children and descriptions of the events of our lives. Carmen, who had been very close to him, said he would always show her the latest letter and photos and tell her about me. He'd brag about my accomplishments. I cannot know what he thought when he met his 10-year-old son, but I know in the end that he was proud of who I became.

Back in New York, the short trip from the tenement to Grant Houses 10 blocks away was every bit as formative as my first trip to Puerto Rico. I had never experienced the sense of civic responsibility I now encountered. The men in that neighborhood believed in the importance of a man's presence in a boy's life. They were mentors. Several men reached out to me and to other boys my age, including one who invited me to join the Boy Scouts.

I knew what the Boy Scouts were, but I had never thought about joining. I had never gone camping, and I had left the city only to fly to Puerto Rico. There was no way my family could afford the uniform anyway. The only place you could get one was at Macy's. But I had been invited to join, and my parents, in an uncharacteristic moment of weakness, said I could. Somehow I got a uniform, too. It never occurred to me to wonder where it came from or what it cost, but someone had procured it for me. I loved it. I could put it on and be enveloped in a sense of belonging. The shirt with the kerchief and the patches and all of it said that I had a troop. I had a tribe.

I was excited when our troop leader told us that a special day was coming when we would be allowed to wear our uniforms to school. When the day came I put on my uniform and thought about how much I would be admired as I walked the halls in it. I'd pass other scouts in their uniforms and we'd give each other the Boy Scout salute and share an identity borne of secret knowledge about camping and adventure, things the other boys didn't have. But when I got to school, I was surprised to discover that I was the only one there who had worn his uniform. I found no one in the halls to salute, no one to share the secrets of different knots and whittling techniques, just merciless classmates making endless fun of me that day. They were relentless, and I wound up feeling ashamed. I never wore my uniform to school again.

I didn't stay in the Boy Scouts for long, because, like many other Puerto Rican parents in the neighborhood, my mother and stepfather were not inclined to let me go anywhere overnight, particularly not outside of the city. But through the Boy Scouts I went to my first dance, at the community center. We were there in our Boy Scout uniforms, and the Girl Scouts came in theirs. That night I danced with a girl for the first time. I remember it all: her hair, her uniform, what she smelled like, everything about her but her name. That detail is not lost because I have forgotten but because we barely spoke. I never got her name or told her mine. I learned nothing at all about her. After mustering the courage to cross the room and ask her to dance, feeling the eyes of all my friends on me, I had little else to say. I was blazing a trail and making a life free of the old rules, such as the one that said 10-year-old boys don't dance. Here were all these girls, and I wanted to dance with one. I asked her, she consented, and that mystery Girl Scout and I danced together, each of us in our uniform. Nothing else needed to be said.

Despite my parents' reluctance to let me off Manhattan Island, I remember that they allowed me to take one trip, to Alpine, a Boy Scout camp in New Jersey. I helped to build a fire and we cooked hotdogs over it. I remember the cabins with the rows of bunks inside. I remember a hike we took and the leaders and older scouts who told us to stay on the trail. We would not listen, and as we blundered our way through the woods, we happened upon a bear. A real wild animal! In the woods! The "pig in person" paled in comparison. I didn't see it at first. Instead I saw my friends in their uniforms, who had been so brave just moments ago as they blazed their own trail through the underbrush, now running the other way, their faces frozen in masks of terror. When I first saw the bear, I, too, lost my adventurer's spirit. And though our time together was brief, and though I never asked its name, I will never forget that bear either.

I don't remember whether we slept overnight at that camp, but as far as my mother was concerned, that was more than enough time out in the wild for little Nelson. After about a year in the Boy Scouts, I lost steam. I couldn't really be a Boy Scout without going to the Jamborees and on camping trips. I could study the scout manual, but I couldn't earn the merit badges in outdoor skills if I wasn't allowed to venture outdoors. Even though I never made it past the rank of Tenderfoot, my year in the Boy Scouts was a positive and horizon-expanding episode. In so many ways, I and other boys like me were having our lives saved by the outreach of black, white, and Hispanic men in the community who took it upon themselves to help.

Without a doubt, a man who slept on a bench in the park and hustled quarters from us was the most influential mentor I ever had. Leroy

Otis was a homeless man who sold Converse Chuck Taylors for $10 a pair. Whenever he saw a group of boys in the park, he'd round us up and take us to the baseball diamond by P.S. 125. He'd arrange us in the infield and the outfield and hit grounders and fly balls. He taught us how to play and he made us a team. And then he went out and hustled jerseys for us. He'd put us in leagues and coach us all summer.

We played in a twilight league at the P.S. 125 field, finishing our games before it got dark. He'd take us to Morningside Park, part of Columbia Park and owned by Columbia University, at 110th Street and Morningside Avenue. We also played in Washington Heights, on the same field that the Columbia University baseball team played on. We could walk all the way from the park at 125th Street down to 110th Street, where we'd play fast-pitch softball, and we'd never have to walk in the street to get there. Columbia Park is still there, with two baseball fields on opposite corners. We won a lot of championships there.

Leroy had us in three leagues most summers, finding jerseys and sponsorships wherever he could. In one league we were St. Joe's, in another we were Freeland because we were sponsored by a liquor store of the same name. We won the league championship as Freeland, and because we won, we were invited to a picnic in upstate New York, outside of Yonkers.

We played with some remarkable talent in those days, and some real characters as well. Like the 12-year-old kid we played softball with. He'd sit in the park and smoke a marijuana joint and then pitch in the game, windmill-style the way they do in women's softball. His curveball was almost impossible to hit.

I played with Leroy almost all summer every summer from the time I was 10 until I was 17. I lost track of him after I went to college, and I always wondered what had happened to him. Not until decades later did I find out.

Around 1999, when I was the Hispanic chair of the Democratic National Committee, I sat next to a minister from Harlem during an Executive Committee meeting. I told him that I had grown up in his neighborhood, and we got to talking. I brought up Leroy and the great impact he had had on my life and said I had been looking for him, to thank him for all he had done for me. This minister told me that Leroy used to work for him at the Church of the Masters, which was across Morningside Avenue from P.S. 125, but that he had died just the previous year.

*Twilight league baseball team. Leroy Otis, in the white shirt, stands
in the back, and I stand smiling to his left. The team was sponsored by
Lucas Electrical Service, but anyone offering funds had a shot
at being displayed across the front of our jerseys.*

Leroy had done well. Almost right up to the end he had coached kids,
which was no surprise. He was a natural coach and leader. How else
could a homeless man, a bum we might have called him if we hadn't
known better, get a bunch of rowdy kids to listen? How else could he
have guided them, molded them into a team that won championships? He
had a gift, and I was glad to know that he never gave it up. And somewhere along the way, things had turned around for him. He'd been able
to buy a house in suburban New Jersey, where he'd lived until his passing.

When I met Leroy, he bit on the filters of his cigarettes, he bit his
nails, and he was always hustling. After he coached us, he would shake
us down for a little money for his trouble. He'd sell us sneakers if we
needed them and he'd go and buy fish and chips for a quarter. It was
worth what little we paid. He slept in the park then. But things had

turned out all right for Leroy. I will always be grateful for his guidance. I was crushed at the time to learn he had died before I could stand before him, show him what I had become, and shake his hand and thank him for the very important role he played in molding me. But I am glad to know he found a home.

Mentors like Leroy changed my life. And it all began with our move from the tenement on 134th Street to public housing on 125th, where we found a sense of community and possibility. Housing is much more than where people go to get out of the rain. Pack them together like cordwood in bad conditions so they can be forgotten and you will get a predictable result. Give them a little room and some opportunities and see what happens. Housing matters. Where you live says something fundamental, to you and to everyone else who sees you, about who you are. It is profoundly important.

The changes that happened in my 10th year turned my life around. But I still faced many struggles. The high-rise was neither free of problems nor devoid of bad options. Kids in my building were a rough bunch, and to survive without being picked on and beaten up, you had to join a gang.

Outside of Grant Houses, school was a continual struggle for me as well. My lack of English hindered my learning from the time I entered first grade, and I was often in trouble.

I didn't go to kindergarten when I was supposed to, which was fine with me. And when it came time to go to first grade, I was in no hurry to do that, either. On the first day of school, my mother walked me the few blocks from our tenement on 134th Street to P.S. 192 on 137th Street and Broadway. When she tried to leave me there, I started to cry and then got so worked up that I bit her. But she left me there, and so, over my most zealous protests, my scholastic career began.

The two things I remember from first grade were that my teacher was named Mrs. Brown and that I was terrified. Everything was taught in English, and I couldn't understand most of it. If I learned anything at all that year, I don't remember what it was.

In my home, in my building, and out on the street, I spoke only Spanish. I knew very little English and sat all day in classes taught in a language I couldn't understand. At the time there were no courses in English as a Second Language, so my school years were a struggle. I passed many years with a D average and was identified throughout as a discipline problem.

My mother didn't like P.S. 192 any more than I did, and when it came time for second grade, she took me to Annunciation Catholic School, down on 133rd Street. She hadn't enrolled me, and when we arrived at the school she was told that all the classes were full, that Annunciation was already overcrowded, and that the school couldn't possibly take any more students. My mother, however, was not going to give up. I wasn't going home, nor was I going back to the public school. I was going to Annunciation. My mother told me that when the other kids went into the school, I was to follow them, and when they went into a classroom and sat, I was to do the same. And then she left me there. I knew better than to get upset. I did as I was told.

The Dominican nuns didn't know what to do with me. They didn't know who this little boy was who spoke almost no English and couldn't be found anywhere on the rolls. With no answers coming from me and no one there to speak on my behalf, they made a guess and put me in first grade. Somehow I got across to the first grade teacher that I didn't belong there. When they put me in third grade, I managed to communicate that it was too advanced for me. Finally they put me in second grade, with a lay teacher. And there I stayed.

The next year, my second crack at third grade, was often disrupted by asthma attacks. That was the year I had my tonsils taken out and spent three weeks recovering. Once I fainted and my teacher carried me to the principal's office, where I stayed until my mother came to get me.

I remember little of fourth grade but getting in trouble. Throughout my time in Catholic school, however, I was a discipline problem. My fifth grade teacher, Sister Mary Martha, brought my mother in and advised her that she should slap me. My mother responded that perhaps she should slap Sister Mary Martha.

Mine was very much the clichéd oppressive Catholic school education. The nuns were authoritarian, and they would beat you—hitting you on the palms of your hands with a ruler—for what today would be considered very minor infractions. Catholic school was something you survived. Each class had 40 or 50 kids, who sat in rows, arranged in alphabetical order. I would try to behave, but often I would be lost, unable to understand the teacher's instructions or to follow the lesson, and I'd ask one of the students beside me what the teacher had said. That got me into trouble a lot. Frustration and boredom set in, and I chafed at the thought that my teachers considered me little more than a mischief-making nobody. I looked for things I could do that might keep me out of trouble or make a better impression on my teachers, so in fifth grade I joined the choir. In sixth grade I became an altar boy at the church associated with Annunciation. That responsibility sometimes allowed me to get out of class for weekday Mass and the occasional funeral.

Throwing myself into these additional activities was my way of demonstrating to the school that I wanted to be a good boy and a good Catholic. I think I was also out to prove something to myself, and if God happened to notice that this scruffy little discipline problem was now helping at Mass and singing in the choir, that couldn't hurt, could it? I would often pray about my behavior, asking God what I had to do to be a better student, a better son. Becoming an altar boy seemed like a good-faith effort. I knew that the school thought I was bad and my teachers thought I was bad, so I mounted a small public-relations campaign, hoping my good deeds and actions would counterbalance the problems that would continue to arise because I couldn't completely stop misbehaving.

Yet while being an altar boy might have helped my image at school, it was certainly not the best way to develop faith. We altar boys messed around a bit. We liked the priests who mumbled their way through the Latin in Mass, because we'd spend less time kneeling. The more devout priests were far less beloved, because everything took longer. After Mass, we were supposed to take the excess communion wine and pour it into a bowl from which it went down into the earth somewhere. Once, after a weekday service and before returning to class, feeling curious, I took a sip. When I returned to class, my teacher smelled something on my breath and surmised what had happened. The school called my parents to come take me home.

I remember the feeling of frustration I had. I knew I had done something wrong, but it seemed like a minor act of misbehavior. I had been trying earnestly and sincerely to behave—I was on a sustained campaign to be a more righteous person—but I was still a kid, still curious, still mischievous. I felt as though the nuns took notice only when I misbehaved and ignored my efforts to do better. I hadn't drunk a glass of the wine, I hadn't stolen a bottle; I'd taken a sip. Yes, that had been wrong, but I felt that no one at the school appreciated that I had committed that little misdeed while helping out in the church. No one seemed to notice my efforts to be better, my desire to serve the greater good. It was all blame and no credit.

In sixth grade, toward the middle of the school year, a new kid arrived who would take my teachers' attention away from me. His name was Robert Díaz. His background, like his last name, was the same as mine. Robert was the most disruptive kid I'd ever seen. He called out, he made noises, and he continually got out of his seat. If he were a student today, he'd probably be placed on the autism spectrum. But back then he was just a problem. No one in our class understood him, and no one liked him. We had no way of knowing what afflicted him. All we knew was that he was loud and obnoxious. My teacher had no idea how to handle him. Her techniques were limited, and when yelling and the usual punishments did not work, she turned to torture.

I will never forget the day she brought him to the front of the class and told him to bend over her desk, face down. Then she told all 40 of us to line up and one by one to hit him on the backside with a ruler. At first we were excited, and I remember feeling glad to have a chance to hit that infuriating, annoying kid. But the justified anger I felt when we began gradually turned to shame and horror as every kid in the class took a turn beating and humiliating Robert.

One of those kids was George Mercado, powerful even as a 12-year-old. I played baseball with George, and he would go on to play in the minor league system for the Los Angeles Dodgers. Another was James Wright. Everyone was scared of James. He was already running with gangs in the neighborhood. It was an awful thing as these two took out their anger on poor Robert. I took part in the beating like everyone else. It went on for a long time, and we didn't stop till every one of us had hit him. It was brutal, it was criminal, and if it had happened today, our teacher would have gone to jail. The following day neither Robert nor the teacher was in the classroom, and we never saw either one of them again. Robert was removed from the school, and we heard that the teacher was put in a mental institution.

Our replacement teacher was a young, beautiful recent graduate from City College of New York named Miss Graniela. She was the diametric opposite of the teacher she replaced. She was full of optimism and ideals, and she saw potential in each one of us. She lived not far from me and sometimes after school I would walk home with her. She didn't look like a nun to me, and she didn't behave like one. With her, for the first time, I developed a relationship with a teacher that was something other than hostile. She never saw me as a problem or a disappointment.

School was hard but somehow I passed all my subjects. Math was an exception. I excelled at math. Still, very few of my teachers expected anything from me. In seventh grade I had Sister Christopher, and I remember her as a very good teacher. My English by then was vernacular and incorrect, what might be called street English. And though I was beginning to understand more and was able to speak and write in a more acceptably academic way, I knew I still had problems and I wanted very sincerely to improve. I had never done much reading, and that year I realized that I had never learned the basics of grammar and that if I was going to get better at the subjects that required writing, I'd have to learn on my own and be my own teacher. And so I started to do that by playing to my own strengths. I would study mathematical word problems to better understand English.

When I think about all my discipline problems, and all the trouble I had in my humanities classes, I realize how lucky I was to make it out of grammar school, much less out of high school and into college and law school. My life was saved over and over again. And while I was mentored and watched over by men like Leroy Otis, it was my mother who led me to turn my life around when I was a teenager, just by asking me for a birthday present.

3

RELIGIOUS AWAKENING

I COUNT MYSELF LUCKY to have had a mother like Maria. The sometimes frightening power of her love guided and protected me when I was young. As an adult, I could do no wrong in her eyes, but when I was a kid, she ran the household like a correctional facility. She was tough. She would discipline me for my grades, for my behavior, for anything. And if I wasn't home by 6:00, by 6:01 she was heading out to the street to find me.

Our neighborhood was poor and violent, and rival ethnic groups were in a long-running war for control of it. Many people worked to make it better, but my mother had good reason to worry. Several times, while coming home from an evening shift at a restaurant or from his job as a doorman downtown, my stepfather was mugged by gangs of stickup kids who ran the streets. And so my mother started bringing a baseball bat with her when she went to wait on the stoop for Pop as he made the last treacherous leg of the journey from the subway to our building. She also took the bat with her when she walked the streets looking for me. She was small, but no one messed with Maria and her baseball bat, including me.

When I was a teenager, I could be a little reckless. I didn't often stay out late, but sometimes I was not as conscientious about the time as I should have been. I ran with a bad crowd in those days, and when I wasn't playing baseball or being an altar boy, I was one of those stupid kids running the streets and making trouble.

My associates were the kids in my building and the gangs around Harlem. In my neighborhood that's how a young man survived. You joined up with boys who would offer some safety and protection. And with few constructive outlets, we were often up to no good. We broke into buildings and stole things; we went into stores and shoplifted and robbed. Some of the kids I ran with had knives, some even had swords, but none of us had guns back in the early 1960s. Most often we'd play hooky and take girls over to someone's house for a party.

It was pretty clear I was going nowhere with this bunch of hoodlums headed for the very same place, many of whom were reaching their destination early. Most of the kids I knew back then have long since died. They overdosed, they got sick, they were murdered, or they died of AIDS. I joined with them to fit in and to have the protection and safety of numbers, but being with them was getting me in trouble, too.

One afternoon I was picked up by the police. I was walking with some friends down Amsterdam Avenue near 129th Street, a notorious area of West Harlem that was the site of frequent rumbles. There had been a big gang fight just that afternoon. I steered clear of the big battles—they were too violent and too dangerous. We just happened to be out on this day, and I'd picked up a broken car antenna that I'd found in the gutter. The police were sweeping the area looking for kids who'd been in the fight. When they saw me with something that could have been a weapon, they arrested me and took me in.

I had been chased by the cops before, for doing things like opening up a fire hydrant, but I had never been taken to the precinct. I was angry that the officer assumed that either I'd been in the rumble or I had been ripping the antennas off cars in the neighborhood, and I was scared that my parents would find out I was in trouble again. I had been in fights before, but in this instance I was innocent. As I sat there in the station, miserable and sullen, I saw a police officer whom I knew as a director of the Police Athletic League. He recognized me, too, from the summer baseball leagues I played in, and he came over and asked me what had happened. I told him the story: I was innocent, the cops were committing a great injustice, and could he please help to make sure my mother never found out? I think his name was Officer Harris, and he was the first black police officer I'd ever seen. Thank God for him. He listened, and then he went and talked to the officer who'd brought me in, telling him that he knew me and that I was a good kid. The officer did write me up, but then he let me go, and my parents never found out about it.

My mother may never have found out about that particular incident, but she knew enough. She knew the caliber of kid I was running around with. She knew that I was getting in trouble at school, when I was there. She would often complain that she had heard from someone that I'd been seen playing hooky, hanging on the corner, or, very often, that I'd been seen in the company of some no-good skinny girl. She was always most troubled by the skinny girls that she'd hear about.

On one particular and very memorable night when I was 13 or 14 years old, at just a few minutes past my 6:00 curfew, I was hanging out in the park and talking tough with my idiot friends from the corner. I don't remember whether I had lost track of time or had decided to defy my mother. Sometimes I'd find my way home while she was still out looking, but on this night she found me. She had brought the bat.

I may have been stupid in my youth, but I was no fool. The calculus was simple: the embarrassment would be nothing more than a twinge I would feel when I dropped the little-thug façade and ran from my tiny, terrifying mother, but the bat would leave a mark. So I ran home with my mother hot on my heels.

My mother did not care whether she embarrassed me or made me look foolish in front of friends. Inevitably she would find an opportunity to mortify me by talking to any friend I brought home or by yelling at me or by fighting with my stepfather. No one wanted to call me, because my mother would interrogate anyone who called and would do worse than that when a girl was on the other end of the line. And so I never brought any friends over to my home in the high-rise. I kept company in the streets.

This was how my mother raised me, time and again chasing me down, shoving and hectoring me into making good decisions against my own worst instincts. Some people were blessed to have a mother who inspired them, guiding them gently like a still, small voice inside them. As for me, my mother would chase me home yelling and swinging a baseball bat.

It wasn't always dignified, but it worked. It was much in this way that my mother chased me from my life of frustration and failure. Many of my stories begin with my mother and her determination. She did whatever she needed to do to make sure her children were safe and headed down the right path. Sometimes she used a bat, and once she even used her own birthday, but she kept at me until she knew I was safe.

Faith was important to my mother. And so as she watched me wandering further astray, floundering in school, repeating by rote the words I was told to learn while remaining uninspired by the Catholic faith, and spending more and more of my time as a little street hoodlum, she must have felt desperate. She knew I was an earnest kid and she knew that I was trying, but she saw me running myself to exhaustion between the two poles of my life. Sometimes I was the boy who fervently participated in the sacraments and went on Franciscan retreats and considered the priesthood as a way to make myself worth saving. And other times I ran around with a loutish group of little criminals in Harlem.

She saw what they thought of me at Rice High School, too. She didn't need any English to see me cast in the school play as a lazy, drunken Mexican with a big sombrero, lying in the shade of a tree slurring Spanish songs. She saw that, even with all the church, the Mass, the sacraments, and the study, I was in trouble. I had no living faith. I needed help and no one was helping, so Maria saved me. And to tell the story right, let's again, for the third time, go back to her arrival in New York City.

Most of the Puerto Ricans who migrated to New York City were Catholic, Maria included, but the Catholicism she had grown up with on the island differed greatly from the Catholicism she found on the mainland. On the island, the church services her grandmother had taken her to were filled with a spirit of celebration. The music was loud and joyous. In New York, the church services, like everything else in the city, made Maria feel like an outsider and intensified her sense of alienation and exile. None of the words was in her language. The priest spoke from the pulpit in Latin, and everywhere else—in confession and in any aspect of community or fellowship she might have had access to—she heard only English. The staid, archaic music seemed like another coded message she wasn't supposed to understand. She felt no spirit of celebration and found no support. Maria had arrived in New York at a time when the American Catholic Church was ill prepared to minister to a Spanish-speaking population. In the Bronx—and West Harlem as well—the church was run by and catered to Irish Americans, who were unwilling to yield their place to newcomers who did not seem to care about assimilating. Like most Puerto Ricans in New York, Maria felt no more welcomed by the church than she did by the neighborhood, by the city, or by the country itself.

Solace, comfort, and community were to be found much closer to home, in the storefront church on the block where she lived in the Bronx. There she heard a service in her language. She could sing songs in a style that was familiar, uplifting and joyful, songs that felt like home. She received counsel from a Spanish-speaking minister. And the parishioners were just like her. She made connections there. She found community.

Storefront churches were so named because they were often set up in an otherwise unoccupied building or in a rental space that had formerly housed a store. In contrast to Catholic priests, who needed years of higher education and a post-graduate degree, ministers in these storefront churches did not need a college degree. Anyone who wished to preach the gospel had only to attend a Bible institute, earn a degree in a few months or a year, and open a church as a 501(c)(3). Mom and Pop both earned diplomas from a Bible institute and proudly hung them on the wall of our home.

A ministry that emphasized community support and outreach was precisely what the growing Puerto Rican community was seeking. Many Protestant churches, Baptist and Pentecostal, popped up in New York in the 1950s and 1960s.

My mother knew better than to show up to places where she was not wanted. And so shortly after her arrival, she stopped going to the Catholic church and began attending the Pentecostal church on Jackson Avenue, unaware that Miserain Rodriguez would sometimes watch her from his window across the street as she came and went. He lived with his brother, who knew Pepita and who had brought him to New York from Puerto Rico when his job at Ramey Air Force Base ended. Miserain asked to be introduced.

After Mom and Pop were married and moved to West Harlem, they found another Pentecostal church, this one on 135th Street, a couple of blocks from the SRO where they lived. The pastor was Rev. Ramon Gutierrez. I have a picture of myself at the pulpit of that church, celebrating my fifth birthday. When we moved to Broadway, below 134th Street, we continued to go to that church until my parents had a fight over my stepfather's infidelity. He had cheated on my mother with a woman in the building. Somehow this incident led to a break with the church. (To be fair, my mother herself had some fidelity issues, and she and my stepfather would regularly accuse each other of cheating. But they were married for 67 years, until my mother's death in 2016, so who's to say what works?)

The year my mother stopped going to church was the year she pulled me out of public school and sent me to Annunciation. She would walk me to the door of the Catholic church—predominantly Irish American and English-speaking—but she did not go in.

Everything changed when I was 15. I knew that my mother was going to church again, to a Pentecostal Assembly of God church uptown, but I wasn't interested in going. I was a Catholic, after all. I'd been one since I was seven. But she kept asking. Then one fall day she mentioned that her birthday was coming up and all she wanted as a present from me was to go with her to her church one Sunday. Just one time. For her. What could I do? So on Halloween weekend, just after my mother's birthday, I gave her the birthday gift of attending her church.

John 3:16, as the church was then called, had started as a storefront at 126th Street and Old Broadway but had grown so much that the congregation had gone looking for a larger space to purchase. When I first visited, the church was in a big old house that had once belonged to a judge. Next door at 146th Street and Hamilton Place was a City College of New York fraternity house. Vicente Ortiz, who later became my father-in-law, had founded the church. By the time I came along, he had been named head of all the Assemblies Churches on the East Coast, and his wife was the pastor of John 3:16. But because women were not allowed to be pastors in Assembly of God churches, John 3:16 would, soon after I arrived, become an independent church and change its name to Tabernaculo de la Fé.

Cookie had been going to services with my mother, and when the three of us walked into the church on that first Sunday in late October, I thought it was a joke. I didn't recognize it as church at all. It was like watching a riot unfold. I knew that what I was seeing and hearing was the sort of religious experience my mother had had when she was a girl, what she had always thought of as "church." The music was upbeat and raucous; people were calling out and speaking in tongues. It was overwhelming and strange, and everyone was so young! The congregation was mostly teenagers and young adults barely into their 20s. Up on the altar I saw a kid named Agapito whom I'd known when we ran together in the same gang. Agapito had disappeared and I hadn't seen him in months. Now here he was, helping out the minister.

The experience was different in every way from what I thought of as church, right down to the part where, as uncomfortable as I was, I felt welcome. From the moment I walked in, the young people there reached out to me and kept reaching out when we saw each other during the week in the high-rise or on the street. These gestures meant a lot to me as a young man who'd been searching for a place to fit in. I kept going to church with my mother, and soon I was leading a different kind of double life. I gave up struggling with Catholicism by day and making trouble in the neighborhood at night and became a secret Pentecostal pretending to be a good Catholic. And ironically, I became a much better Catholic.

I had been brought up Catholic, I had studied Catholicism, and I had always considered myself a Catholic. But as much as I wanted to be a part of that church, I never felt that the church really wanted me in return. I had kept trying through far more failure than success, because even though the church had felt inaccessible, difficult to understand, and unconcerned with me, I wanted a part of God's mercy and I knew no other avenue to it. This new place embraced me, ministered to me, and accepted me as an important part of its congregation. God was here, too, wasn't he? Things began to make some sense. I jumped into church activities. I started bringing kids I knew with me to church. Some Sundays I'd round up as many as 30 kids in the projects, and we'd all go up Broadway to the church, walking, taking the bus, or packing as many in a car as we could fit and driving.

When I was 16, I was asked to teach Sunday school. I swelled up with pride at being asked, and I took the responsibility seriously. I knew that in order to step up to it, I had to know better what I was talking about, and I had to be confident speaking in front of people. In order to teach I had to learn. I had to read up on the teachings of the church and its foursquare gospel faith. The four corners of that faith are baptism by water, baptism by the Holy Spirit, the virgin birth, and the resurrection and the return of Christ.

I had to learn the Bible. But because I was still that troublemaking kid that I've really never stopped being, I took issue with the church, criticizing it in a newsletter I began writing and printing on the church's mimeograph machine. I thought the church was not sufficiently involved in the community, and I wrote fiery editorials to that effect. When the pastor found out about my newsletter, she put a stop to it. No matter what I do or what organization I join, I always seem to get myself into some kind of trouble. The pastor's action, though, in no way changed my sense of belonging.

I have always been an agitator, whether playing class clown or speaking truth to power. I challenge authority when I see it misapplied or abused. Rather than changing that tendency in me, my finding a home at a church helped me to focus my efforts on effecting justice. The day I gave my mother her birthday present was a turning point for me. Until then I had been a lock without a key. I'd tried choir, I'd tried being an altar boy, I'd tried all sorts of things, but nothing worked until I went back to church. Now I'd found it. I felt valued and inspired. The seed of a powerful idea had taken root in my mind: I began to believe that with God's help I could accomplish just about anything. I'd always had the energy to accomplish things, but now I had direction. I started hanging out with a different group of guys. We'd go out to the pizza shops at night, we'd walk around the community and talk to the kids, to gang members, about our church. We were doing ministry. I felt inspired to help, and a new and unfamiliar confidence blossomed inside me.

I gave up the gang life I'd fallen into. That kid I'd known from running the streets—the one I had lost track of till I saw him up on the altar—I became him. I stopped all contact with my old friends. I avoided them. I hid. I even gave up baseball. At school I worked hard and paid attention. On my walk home I'd take a different route and I'd enter my building by the back door. I'd shut myself in my room and I'd study. I became a ghost. I didn't want to be confronted by my old friends, I didn't want to be sucked back into that hopeless, aimless, pointless life, and I didn't want to see the effects their choices were having on them. Because that lifestyle was killing them. Quickly or slowly, that way of living brings everyone in it down.

John 3:16 was run primarily by a group of young people who had come through the David Wilkerson Ministry Teen Challenge. The average age of the church members then was between 19 and 21 years, and the church was stocked with kids the city had assigned to Wilkerson. He was well known in New York in those days. The papers would cover him when he went into juvenile court and asked to divert the dead-end kids from detention to his ministry. And now here were those reclaimed juvenile delinquents, making a difference in their community and having a real impact on me. We would hang out at diners and restaurants and we'd talk. All my old friends and I seemed to have talked about little other than baseball or jerking off or screwing or some stupid gossip that was making its way through the neighborhood; we were playing hooky or stealing or fighting. In this new peer group I'd found, we talked about values, and not in the abstract. Those values were changing me. I was hanging out with young men who wanted to be ministers, and even though I didn't want to be a minister when I grew up, I found it stirring to talk with them about how we could be instruments of God. I wanted to get a job in which I could be helpful to my family and my community. I thought I could be a bookkeeper; I could be an accountant.

I found purpose in the faith, and I found freedom in the strict rules of behavior. Smoking, drinking, dancing, and even going to the movies were forbidden. This puritanical approach was perfect for me at the time. I could close myself off from the world and reflect, like an ascetic. Alone in my room, I would think about the church and my faith. No girls, no vices. I went cold turkey on most of my life. I had a new gang.

As I said, I became a much better Catholic when I became an undercover Pentecostal. I also became a better student. My grades improved, my troublemaking ways ended. I continued to speak up against injustices large and small, but I stopped being the class screw-up.

My mother's plan to save her son's soul was working, but she wasn't finished. Chasing me with the bat was part of Step 1, and taking me to her church was Step 2. She had pulled me away from the worst influences in my life. I was off the streets and largely out of trouble, but that meant only that it was time for the next step.

She knew I was still seeing girls and messing around. She knew I was doing much better, but while I may have been on the road to salvation, in her mind, I was not yet saved. She kept at me. In the past, she had beaten me, she'd bullied, she'd reasoned, she'd cried. She'd stopped eating and walked to her room and quietly shut the door. She had told me I was on the wrong path, that I was breaking her heart, that I had to change. These were things I was used to. But when Pastor Ortiz's daughter, Vilma, started coming around, I barely knew what was happening.

For the first time, my mother was encouraging me to pursue a relationship with a girl. Vilma was welcome in my home and she was interested. But I felt forced into the relationship. I tried to break it up many times, but I never quite had the will to go against my mother's plan and Vilma's wishes. Eventually, I would marry Vilma. Our marriage, which would give me children, did help to settle me down, but it lasted only until the children left, and it wasn't very happy.

Still, I had turned a corner. Just as moving from the tenement to the high-rise had been a turning point in my life, attending services at Tabernaculo de la Fé set me on a path to what I believed could be success.

Before that point I had tried and failed and tried again, always becoming disillusioned. But now I was seeing something come of my efforts and from that point on I believed that things could turn out well. This belief has been the foundation of all my successes. In every new endeavor, I've carried a faith that I can accomplish something, because God can make anything possible. I have taken many leaps and have tried many things even though at first I was afraid to try. I stopped wasting time with worry about whether I could complete the new task I had set for myself. In short, my faith gave me something stronger than my fear. I welcomed new endeavors and I took on new assignments and appointments, some of which had never been done before. My faith assured me that even if I failed, I would be all right. And I have never been wrong to believe that.

My faith helped me turn around my academic career. After a bumpy start (we will meet Brothers Otto and Leahy in the next chapter), I graduated with honors. Then, keeping to my plan of becoming an accountant, I enrolled at St. John's Junior College. I loved accounting. I loved working with numbers. They are absolute values. There is no need to wonder how much $100 is worth. It's the same no matter who is holding it. In a society full of complicated rules and shifting values based on differences both real and imagined, numbers and mathematics had a comforting solidity for me.

I did well at St. John's, first in the junior college and then in the university, and during my last semester, I set up interviews with the top 10 accounting firms in New York and began applying to MBA programs. At the same time, I learned that, unbeknownst to me, I had been recommended to an organization that helped minority students get into law school. What did I know about the law? Very little. Why would I want to be a lawyer? I couldn't have told you. But I applied to Temple University Law School in Philadelphia, and then I was accepted. I enrolled and, with the best intentions, moved to Camden, New Jersey, and began my studies. Newly married, with a young family living across the Delaware River from school, and with no means, I had a hard time adjusting to the study of the law and the culture of law school. Temple was not a supportive environment, and I often felt more like cannon fodder than a student. The school was not set up to support its students; it was set up to weed out the poorer performers and graduate one-third of its initial enrollees.

Making it through Temple Law School was one of the most difficult things I have ever done, and without the support of classmates like Carl Singley, without the support of professors like Peter Liacouras, and without my faith to strengthen me, I would never have succeeded. But I did. I persevered, and along the way I helped to change the law school for the better. And I came to see the law as an opportunity, a tool with which to create a more just world. My faith showed me what to work for, and the law provided a means. I jumped into the struggle for greater justice for minorities and the poor. I believed that a just world was possible and worth fighting for. And I had faith that with God's help any fight was winnable.

Faith led me to run for the bench in Philadelphia. Faith, and a little encouragement from then district attorney Ed Rendell, who approached me in 1980 and told me I should run. Thirty-three candidates were running in the Democratic primary for 10 judgeships. And it was there that the election really happened. Philadelphia is a Democratic machine town, and a Democratic primary win in the spring makes a candidate a shoo-in in the autumn general election. Republican candidates can occasionally break through, but they can do so only with strong ties to the Democratic power structure. Rendell and I did some calculations of what my strengths were and how I could actually win, but we both knew I was never anything more than a long shot. I had good relationships with some connected people, such as my mentor Howard Gittis at Wolf Block, who would be able to work with Buddy Cianfrani in South Philadelphia; Charlie Bowser; and others. But I was not a party insider.

Yet run I did, and though I had to fight just to get my name on the ballots, I won. I had made a promise to God in the days before the primary that if I won, I would dedicate three-quarters of my time to helping minorities and the poor, to use the law as the instrument of social justice that I recognized it to be.

And when I came to serve on the bench, I remembered that promise. Throughout my time as a judge, I dedicated most of my time to service of the poor. I worked with the Salvation Army, and I served on economic and community development boards with Philadelphia's economic development guru Walt D'Alessio. I founded the Hispanic Association of Contractors and Enterprises (HACE) to undertake housing and community development. I helped develop the Bloque de Oro on Fifth Street in North Philadelphia. I raised money for the homeless. I worked with churches and individual residents in poor neighborhoods. I offered just about every Latino organization in the city financial support and guidance—and those organizations are today some of the strongest agencies in the city.

Shortly after I became a judge, I met Jeff Comment at a prayer breakfast in Harrisburg, Pennsylvania, where I had been asked to lead the closing prayer. He was a senior vice president at John Wanamaker in the early 1980s. He would later become president and chief operating officer, but he was already a giant in Philadelphia. Late in the decade he would move to Kansas City to lead Helzberg Diamonds, which he would take from a midwestern business to a national one that eventually became a subsidiary of Berkshire Hathaway. Jeff, like me, was a man of deep faith. After the breakfast, Jeff and a few others offered me a ride back to Philadelphia. No, I said. I have a car. I did not pick up on the invitation to talk, but lucky for me they persisted.

"Well," said Jeff, "then why don't we ride with you?"

On the two-hour drive back, Jeff asked for my help in putting together a prayer breakfast for business and community leaders in Philadelphia. He said that between his business relationships and the community contacts I had in my Rolodex, we could make it happen. It struck me as a powerful idea, especially when he said he wanted it to be a civic function, not controlled by the clergy. The ministry would be a part of it, but Jeff's vision was of a gathering for people who were not normally or officially involved in religious activities. Neither of us wanted to have it appear like a church outreach or an evangelizing effort.

Two pillars of our endeavor who had a hand in our success were Lin Crowe and Russ Cadle. When I met Lin, he was based at the 10th Presbyterian Church at 17th and Spruce Streets, doing prison ministry, as he is today. He helped develop the Leadership Foundation that guided the Philadelphia prayer breakfast, which became known as the Mayor's Prayer Breakfast. Russ, a pastor at the Church of the Savior in Radnor and chaplain to the Philadelphia Eagles and 76ers, had ministered to Jeff personally. He joined us and helped us bring people in as speakers and as regular attendees.

Right from the start, the annual prayer breakfast was a success. The first one was held in 1982. Our guest speaker was the astronaut James

Irwin, who had been to the moon on the Apollo 15 mission in 1971. He was the eighth person to walk on the moon, and he spoke to us about the "Genesis Rock" that his mission had brought back, and how much more real God became to him after he returned.

The annual prayer breakfast gave like-minded civic leaders a chance to come together to renew their faith and explore ways to put that faith into action. It was run just the way we'd planned, by business people, and it was well attended every year until Jeff left for Kansas City. He was the driving force, and he seemed to take a lot of that energy with him. He was a dynamic and inspiring presence, and he was someone people wanted to work with. I understood that two minutes into the two-hour drive from Harrisburg.

I've always made plans. And I've almost always had to scrap them because they didn't work out. But I've kept trying because the unplanned developments that kept them from working out always kept me occupied. My life is a testament to the blessing of the unforeseen consequence. If I had stuck to what I thought I had to do, I might have been rewarded by settling into the quiet life of an accountant, secure but surely unfulfilled. But it has been far more interesting to be flexible and to take the opportunity that suddenly crops up. One thing has led to another, and I have been rewarded by a life full of interesting people and deep connections. I may not understand what's happening as it's happening, or why, but my life has never been dull or devoid of meaning. This is the power of faith, to allow the unexpected, the uncomfortable, and the exciting thing to happen because you believe that what awaits you will turn out all right, and that you will turn out all right, too. One thing follows on another.

My involvement with the Mayor's Prayer Breakfast was one such turn. It granted me entrée to an exciting opportunity, when members of the Philadelphia clergy got together to invite the renowned evangelist Billy Graham to bring his crusade to Philadelphia. These events were much like tent revivals on a grand scale. He had done them all over the country, but no one had yet been able to bring one to Philadelphia.

The Mayor's Prayer Breakfast has been held every year since Jeff Comment left, though the aim and the tone are different now; the breakfast functions as an outreach from the clergy rather than a gathering of business and civic leaders of faith. Thus brought together, a few persistent church leaders I knew from the prayer breakfast, including Lin Crowe, had secured a meeting with Graham's people. At that meeting, Graham's team had agreed to do a crusade in Philadelphia as long as the invitation came from all denominations and faiths.

No crusade had yet happened in Philadelphia because members of the black clergy who had participated in the civil rights movement in the 1960s had reservations about Graham's response to the movement. Though Graham had never been antagonistic to the cause (he famously hosted Martin Luther King Jr. at one of his crusades in 1957 and even posted bail for him in the early 1960s), in that time of great social upheaval and urgency, rather than calling for civil disobedience, Graham had called only for caution and patience.

The small organizing team had called a meeting of the Philadelphia clergy and announced that they would have to send an invitation with one voice, across creeds and colors. I was a great admirer of Graham's, but I knew that hosting him in Philadelphia would require hashing out a few things first. And so we did. Those black clergy members with doubts pointed out that Graham had been just the figure King was speaking of when he complained that the enemy of progress is the moderate who says wait. But they were willing to hear more from Graham's camp, and because, despite these doubts, there was also some real enthusiasm for the crusade, they called another meeting, this one with Graham and his people.

I remember that meeting. It was held on a Saturday afternoon in my judge's chambers. I was the only layman in the room. Billy Graham was there to address the misgivings the leaders of the black clergy had put forth. The discussion was frank but warm. It was honest and earnest, and we worked to get through any issue that might hold us back from making the Philadelphia Crusade a success. Rev. Gus Roman, a towering intellect in the theological community, brought up the crusade Graham held in New York in the 1950s. Martin Luther King Jr. had been asked to lead a prayer. A few black people were in attendance but no black leadership was involved and the stadium in which they met to pray was segregated. The situation was much the same in the 1980s when Graham led another crusade in New York. When Roman spoke, he spoke with authority. In the 1960s, Roman had been the right hand of the civil rights titan and social activist Rev. Leon Sullivan. Bill Moore, who had been chief of staff to U.S. Representative Bill Gray, spoke too. And though the atmosphere was tense, we all thought that Graham responded beautifully. He admitted that he had not handled the issue of race well at those crusades. I remember that he stood up and apologized, personally, to everyone in the room as representatives of their faiths and their communities. He apologized for not having been more involved in or more supportive of the civil rights movement. He promised—and he would keep his word—to help us assemble a majority-black leadership team for Philadelphia. The team would include Bill Moore, Bishop Ernie Morris, Gus Roman, and Rev. Benjamin Smith, pastor of Deliverance Evangelistic Church, the largest church in the city at the time, built on the site of old Connie Mack Stadium in North Philadelphia.

I don't know whether I have ever felt anything quite like what I felt in that room when Graham spoke. He accepted what we said to him and addressed us with humility and grace. I think we all took him at his word. The roadblocks had been cleared and we were ready for the next step.

That next step was a comprehensive outreach to every house of faith and every clergy member in the Philadelphia area. I visited more than 500 houses of worship, including Buddhist temples in Chinatown, and I talked to people of every denomination, including Mennonites in Lancaster. The Graham crusade may have been the first religious event in Philadelphia history to bring together church leaders of black, Hispanic, white, and Asian backgrounds.

It was a long campaign, and there was always another meeting on the agenda, another retreat on the horizon. It was not easy getting consensus among so many Philadelphians of different faiths, with so many different histories, and we worked hard to make the crusade something everyone would be proud to be a part of. It took organization and dedication and the humility that comes with true faith. Strong belief had to be tempered with meekness. In the lead-up to the event itself, Rev. Bonnie Camarda, who was a member of my church and whom I had mentored in community involvement, recommended me to chair the board. The leadership group was aware of the balance of races and felt that a black or a white chair would give it the appearance of being a black or a white initiative. Maybe I was the perfect candidate. With me at the helm, their crusade could be neither, or both.

The planning meetings continued. Some were held in Philadelphia, others during weekend retreats in places such as Cannon Beach, Oregon, and Harvey Cedars, New Jersey. I was moved and inspired at these gatherings as I watched people of deep faith work together for something as worthwhile as I believed this to be. I saw our work as faith in action and I believe it changed me, as it did others. I was chairing the crusade at the same time that, in my role as an administrative judge, I was working to clean up the backlog in Philadelphia civil and criminal courts. I was exhausted, but I didn't know it. I discovered how much it had taken out of me only when I saw the pictures of myself at the time.

Planning moved ahead, and in July 1992 we held a press conference with Graham at Veterans Stadium and then moved on to make two stops in depressed Latino communities in the area. Our first stop was just across the Delaware River in Camden, New Jersey, at a drug and alcohol recovery program. My job was to greet the crowd and introduce Graham. I meant to keep my message brief, but just as I began to speak, a young man from the rehab stood up, pointed at me, and called out, "You're the one!"

Stunned, I asked him what he meant. What had I done to him? He said, "You're the judge who put me in jail for five years!" As I tried to work out how I could explain to him what my job was or how the justice system worked or what my hopes were for his rehabilitation, he continued.

"Thank you," he said, "for what you did."

He went on to say that if I had not given him a prison sentence, he would never have come to this rehab center, and he most likely would be dead. His sentence, he said, had saved his life. It was a very powerful moment for me, and it reinforced my belief in justice as a way to set things right. The criminal justice system is more than simply a means by which society metes out retribution. A structure that only punishes is inhuman. I have never wanted to have any aspect of my life lie outside of my faith in God, and that faith means having faith in his children, too. This man reinforced that faith.

When Graham spoke, he was just as impressive as he always was. We spent the rest of the day touring the city and meeting with people, including clergy. I got to show him the Bloque de Oro, on 5th Street in North Philadelphia, where I directed a Latino merchants association along a corridor that ran through the barrio. I remember seeing how much time and effort it took him to shuffle up a few steps as we took our tour. It was apparent that he had Parkinson's disease. But when he was at the podium or interacting with people, he was still so powerful, so resplendent. It was remarkable to watch him reach inside himself and flip an invisible switch to "ON."

Graham was a remarkable person to watch. Often he would come into my office for a meeting looking as though the wind had blown him there. His hair would be disheveled and his coat a little rumpled. He was tall, and his eyes were intense. In person, he was very quiet. He had an air of real humility, and as he sat in these meetings, everyone knew that he was listening. He sought counsel far more often than he gave it, and when he did speak, he spoke softly.

Few times in my life have I been happier. I was heading up a leadership group of more than a dozen black and a few white ministers. We reviewed all suggestions and approved or vetoed each one. I remember that we voted down having Johnny Cash sing at an event, and instead agreed to hire the Brooklyn Tabernacle Choir to appeal to our audience. Between my professional efforts, which involved working on court reforms and dealing with picketing Teamsters, and my work as chair of the crusade, my workdays extended long into the night, and my weekends were spent visiting churches and getting as many people and congregations involved as I could.

The crusade was a great success. It was held for four nights that summer at Veterans Stadium. More than 50,000 people attended each night, including Mayor Ed Rendell and Everett Koop, director of Children's Hospital of Philadelphia. I remember one very dramatic evening. Reggie White, all-time great defensive end for the Philadelphia Eagles and a man of deep faith, was scheduled to speak. It was June 25, 1992, the day that many Eagles fans will remember as the day that Jerome Brown, a well-liked and talented defensive end on the team, had been driving fast with his nephew in the car on a wet road in Florida when he crashed and they both were killed. Not long before he was supposed to speak, Reggie got the news that his friend and teammate had died. He went to the podium and after a prayer, he opened his heart and spoke his testimony. It was as poignant a moment as any I witnessed during the whole crusade, and it seemed the crowd was stirred as well.

Nearly 250,000 people attended the four evenings of the crusade without a single report of trouble in the neighborhood. Close to 2,000 people converted and were baptized, while countless others approached the altar in support and faith. Some of those new converts came to my home church and today are leaders in the congregation. All these years later, I still run into people in Philadelphia who tell me what a powerful experience the crusade was and how it changed their lives. We had wanted to knit together a tighter community of faith, between denominations and races, in the inner city and the suburbs, and we did. The crusade inspired a greater spirit of cooperation in Philadelphia that lasted for years.

I had a humbling moment during the crusade after I made a major mistake I would be remiss not to mention. In my role as chair, I often

*Clasping hands at the Billy Graham Crusade: on the far left,
the Reverend Ben Smith, pastor of Deliverance Evangelistic Church in North
Philadelphia; on my immediate left and right, respectively, Bill Moore
of Tenth Memorial Baptist Church in North Philadelphia and
the Reverend Billy Graham.*

fielded calls from journalists. I took one phone call from a reporter in North Carolina who asked me about Graham's health. "How is Billy doing?" he said.

"He gets on stage and the glory of the Lord shines all over him," I said. "One could never tell that he has Parkinson's." I thought I was paying Graham a great compliment, but instead, I was revealing a closely held secret. When the call came from his ministry, I realized my blunder. Feeling deep shame and regret, I wrote a letter of apology to Graham and asked him to forgive me. I will always treasure the letter he wrote back to me. He was kind and generous and somehow managed to forgive me without acknowledging that I'd done anything wrong. He even said that he felt relieved. He was a man of grace and kindness, and I will never forget my time with him. I was struck by his humility. In our meetings, he rarely provided counsel but regularly sought it. And I will always remember his hair. There was something endearing about it. In private moments it was almost always a little mussed from his hat. In public he

BILLY GRAHAM
MONTREAT, NORTH CAROLINA 28757
July 27, 1992

My dear Nelson,

Bless your heart! Your letter of July 2 has
caught up with me here in Europe where Ruth and I
have been trying to put in time each day on my
memoirs. (Sometimes I wish I had never agreed to
tackle this horrendous project!). We both feel a
lot stronger and more relaxed after several weeks
away from the pressures at home and the telephone
--and with opportunity to rest and get exercise as
well as work without the distractions of the
office.

I was appalled that you were embarrassed by the
Charlotte Observer story. Naturally, I realized
that you would not have approached them with a
story! I have had enough experience with
newspapers, and especially with my hometown
Charlotte paper, to know how they go about things.
Therefore, do not give it another thought.

I had been reluctant to issue a release or talk
about my own personal health--but now that it is
public knowledge I feel a great relief and perhaps
people will be more understanding if I move a
little slower or turn down their invitations in
order to keep a more realistic schedule. Our
office in Minneapolis has apparently received some
wonderful letters and phone calls of support, so I
think it may increase people's burden to pray for
me and the ministry--which is wonderful.

I will never forget my times of fellowship and
prayer with you, and am certainly counting on all
of you to pray for me in Portland just as you did
during our time in Philadelphia. Thank you again,
dear brother, for being such a blessing to me
personally.

With warmest Christian affection, I am

Cordially yours,

Bill   *Love To The Brother.*

The Honorable Nelson A. Diaz
Administrative Judge of the Trial Division
Room 516, City Hall
Philadelphia, PA 19107
USA

*Letter to me from Billy Graham—a very kind man
and someone I greatly admired.*

would make sure that he was put together, combed down and buttoned up, because it was his job to present himself as a voice of faith and a man of God. But in private, I think his humility grew right out of his scalp, a little messy, and just a bit amusing.

What a life I have been given. I don't know how to look back on it and not see the hand of God pushing me along, taking care of me. Sometimes that hand came in the form of an opportunity I didn't quite understand, that only later revealed itself as a blessing. Other times, it took the form of my mother, chasing me home with a baseball bat.

I was a little brown child raised in tenements and high-rises. My first bed was an old sofa in the living room. At five I was sexually abused. I ran with gangs and feared the police. I spoke no English when I went to school; I learned it only little by little over the years. My household was often filled with strife and recrimination, and the arguments between my parents sometimes ran long into the night and rang off the walls.

But my mother loved me, and my stepfather did, too. I thank God that at 10 years old I was rescued from the tenement, and at 15 I found my faith. I thank him for the strife. I thank him for the tribulations I've endured. I have a family who loves me. I have friends who support me. And I have stories. I have a lot of stories.

I sometimes see my life in terms of the ambition that drove me to be more than I thought I could be, and sometimes I see it through the lens of my desire for something simple and understandable. I wanted a humble life and I wanted a grand life. But how I came to live the life I have led I owe to my faith. Without the steadying hand of my belief, I would not have had the courage to do all I have done. I would not have been optimistic enough to believe that though I'd never been a good student before, I could become one. Or optimistic enough to believe that though a Latino had never served on the bench, I could.

My faith helped me, buoyed me, and saved me. I believe faith can do that for anyone. What it did for me it can do for anyone. And it was never more embodied by anyone than it was by my mother. Thanks to her, I am the man I am.

4

TEENAGE YEARS

OMING TO MY FAITH was another turning point, another of the before-and-after moments that punctuate my life and provide its texture. At 15, I experienced the second great shift in the trajectory of my teenage years and my scholastic career. As a Puerto Rican kid from West Harlem who spoke only Spanish, I had struggled with the obstacles placed before me. I had lost years at school stumbling through lessons taught in a language I barely understood. If I had hoped for a smooth ride through life, I had clearly been born in the wrong place at the wrong time.

I grew up in a Spanish-speaking household, with Spanish-speaking friends and neighbors. I spoke no English as a young child, and yet I was placed in an English-only school with teachers who spoke no Spanish. And I was not just one child in a new school but part of a massive influx of Spanish-speaking kids. I was part of a seismic shift that would forever change the ethnic makeup of New York City. Whatever tenuous equilibrium the previous waves of immigrants had achieved was gone. We were moving into neighborhoods that had been claimed by Irish immigrants who, even with a 100-year head start, still felt unwelcome in America. From the start, the Irish were stigmatized and portrayed as subhuman, but they fought to remain; they were in America to stay. They found niches, they assimilated as quickly as possible, and they worked very hard to become Americans. By the time we arrived, many of the positions of ground-level authority had been taken by the Irish. The teachers at the Catholic schools in New York were predominantly Irish, as were the Catholic priests. The police also were predominately Irish, to the extent that in the Puerto Rican community we called the police *la jara*. Only years later did I realize that *la jara* is a corruption of "O'Hara."

The Puerto Rican migration to New York, which continued throughout my childhood, brought so many of us to the city that we formed enclaves. Block upon block of new people moved in, bringing their own shared customs and speaking a foreign language. To the Irish residents of these neighborhoods—who had endured insult, injury, and incarceration to establish themselves there—these new arrivals did not seem to be interested in becoming Americans, but they were helping themselves to what small piece of America the Irish had fought so hard for. The Irish had earned their place, and they were fiercely patriotic. They believed in citizenship and democratic participation. But now these newcomers, who wouldn't even bother to learn the language, were snatching away their hard-won territory. Crowded schools became more crowded, making things harder for the administration, the teachers, and the Irish students who already spoke English. Streets that were already crowded became more crowded.

Outside of school I heard and spoke only Spanish. It was not until third grade that I could speak any English at all. And the English I learned, growing up in a section of New York that also had a large number of black residents, had a lot of black lingo in it and was mostly curse words. I passed those first few years of grammar school, doing my best to learn to read and write a language that I could not speak, on the strength of my facility in arithmetic. My teachers saw my problems not in terms of a language deficiency but in terms of behavior. I would talk to my classmates and act out in class because I was bored. My report cards during those years showed a steady output of Ds in discipline.

I was a kid who always tried, though. As the years went on and I gained some proficiency in English, I didn't trust my vocabulary or my command of the language, so I memorized facts and I memorized concepts so I could parrot them back on tests without having to rely on my own ability to form coherent and correct sentences.

By the time I was 10, I could hold a conversation in English. I could listen and respond in class, and while I wasn't what one would call literate, I felt confident enough to communicate. By the time I was 14, I felt stronger in English than in Spanish. I could think and write in English, and I used it exclusively in school. But while my proficiency in English was growing, bit by bit I was losing vocabulary in Spanish. At home we still spoke only Spanish, so I never lost the ability to comprehend it, but my command of Spanish was suffering because I wasn't using it to communicate the concepts I was learning. After I joined the church, where services were conducted entirely in Spanish, and I began to express substantive ideas in Spanish, I felt that I was coming closer to being truly bilingual.

Years later as I became involved with drafting legislation on bilingual education, I gained a new perspective on my own experience as a child. According to the research on language acquisition, by the age of eight, a person has acquired half of all the knowledge he or she will learn in his or her lifetime. Fluency in a language is achievable after this age, but it is much more difficult; so too is being comfortable—being, in a sense, "at home"—in two languages. I came to understand that being taught in English had made it harder for me to learn the concepts. A sophisticated or nuanced idea cannot be translated into a basic vocabulary. But English immersion was the model at the time, and it was accepted by the many German immigrants who had preceded the Puerto Rican migration. Learn English as fast as you can, they believed, and go from there. But one thing that had changed between the time of the great German immigration and the Puerto Rican migration was the job market. For those German immigrants in the early days of the 20th century, a job as a factory worker or as a laborer could sustain a family. That was not so when the Puerto Ricans arrived.

There is ample evidence that a different approach can be effective, too. After Fidel Castro came to power, the Cuban immigration to Florida flooded the schools there with Spanish-speaking students. The Cuban immigrants insisted that the schools provide Spanish-language classes in Cuban-only classrooms until the students had learned English well enough to be taught in it. Students, according to this concept, would continue to learn complex concepts in Spanish until they had gained enough of a command of English to translate ideas into a new language sophisticated enough to accommodate them. And by continuing to learn ideas in their native tongue, they would continue to have a command of Spanish, while not falling behind in ideas. Once those students had reached a high level of proficiency in English, they could be taught those concepts in English.

For me, grammar school was an eight-year game of catch-up, and while everyone else seemed to be running the 100-yard dash, I felt as though I was blindfolded, hopping along in a potato sack. I worked hard to pass tests in grammar and reading, and my struggles in those subjects continued well into high school, where more complications developed. I not only struggled with English when I went to Rice; I also got off to a rough start with the faculty. Yet the fact that I'd made it to a Catholic high school at all would have been a big surprise to anyone familiar with my grade school performance.

All Catholic school students took a test in eighth grade to determine where they would go for high school. Students who did poorly on the test washed out to public school, and if you had polled the faculty at Annunciation about where they expected to find me come freshman year, the answer would likely have been the detention room at East Harlem's Benjamin Franklin High School, where all the Catholic high school washouts in my part of New York ended up. But to everyone's surprise, not least of all my own, I did very well on the placement test and was given the choice of three Catholic high schools: DuBois, Cardinal Hayes, and Rice.

The teachers at Annunciation didn't know me very well, and I never felt they had much faith in me as a student, or perhaps even as a person. They didn't seem to consider me a child to try to reach or to figure out. I was opaque, to be taken at face value, like a rock sitting in the middle of the road, an obstacle to the other students' progress. I was a Puerto Rican kid who didn't speak English very well, who acted out in class and distracted the other students, who made the teachers' day harder. I was the kid who had drunk the wine in the sacristy after communion. Why should anyone bother with me? And yet here I was with test results that must have been a mistake. They advised me to go to Rice, perhaps because it was closest. I don't think any of them thought I had a chance to succeed at a Catholic high school. And while their advice might have been hasty or dismissive, it was the only advice that I was going to get. I had no other counselors.

Had they known me better, they might have given me different guidance. If they'd known that I played baseball, for example, they might have steered me to Cardinal Hayes, which had a good baseball team. Playing on a team like that might have helped me win a scholarship to a good college. But they didn't know, and I didn't know to ask. So I did as they said and enrolled at Rice, right in my neighborhood. It offered

A pensive picture of me at age 15.

two tracks: commercial and academic. I was put on the commercial track, because no one expected me to go on to college.

Rice High School, founded by and named after Edmund Rice, was run by the Irish Christian Brothers. They were big on discipline and did not tolerate any messing around. Most of them carried blackjacks, which they would use to hit students across the shoulders at a moment's notice. Brother Otto, however, carried a thin little stick, like a switch, and he'd beat students with it for every wrong answer on his frequent pop quizzes in American history. He was not a skilled educator; the full panoply of his methods of motivation consisted of that switch across your backside. I did poorly enough on those quizzes to remember the feeling of that switch to this day. I failed American history my freshman year.

Brother Otto and his infamous stick were to be avoided at any cost, and so rather than retaking the course with him, I took it during summer school and passed the regents exam. But he was not the worst teacher I encountered at Rice. That honor belongs to Brother Leahy, a counselor and teacher with whom I took three classes my freshman year. I received a 69 in each one. If you got off on the wrong foot with Brother Leahy, there was little chance of ever recovering. And thanks to my naïveté and my tendency to talk in class, I quickly earned his eternal antagonism. Early in my freshman year he lectured us about the boys in class who had their hands in their pockets. He was talking about the boys who played with themselves all the time and didn't bother to hide what they were doing. Not having a great command of the English idiom, I thought he meant the boys who were too lazy to take their hands out of their pockets and do something. I thought it was a comment on our poor work ethic, or maybe our posture. I responded, "But Brother Leahy, you always have *your* hands in *your* pockets."

So after those three Ds in those three courses with Brother Leahy, I made sure never to take another class with him again. The damage to my overall average was profound, and it took all of my four years there to overcome it. Despite my being on the commercial track and despite my early experience with the harsh grading of Brother Leahy, I took as many academic courses as I could and I made the honor roll. I was being pushed away from the academic track and toward a life in the trades, but I knew that I wanted to go to college. I never talked to anyone about my aspirations for higher education, because doing so would most likely have put me right back in the crosshairs of Brother Leahy in his capacity as a student counselor, and I was giving him as wide a berth as I could. I thought it best to keep that dream to myself, working hard and keeping my head down.

Even though I had found religion at age 15 and aspired to college, I did not suddenly transform into either a saint or a scholar. Nor were all the teachers at Rice terrible. Take Mr. Tobin, for instance, a lay teacher who worked construction in the summers. Mr. Tobin's demeanor was a little rougher than that of the other teachers at Rice. He taught me English for two years, and he used me as a kind of cautionary tale for the class. When I did poorly on an assignment or a quiz or I'd answer a question wrong in class, as I often did, he'd have me come up and kneel. We developed a kind of routine, like a comedy sketch in which I'd beg forgiveness for my terrible grades or my lack of understanding of the material. I was both the butt of the joke and part of the routine. It may seem like a humiliating experience, but our routine was always a big hit and Mr. Tobin seemed to like me. Moreover, I felt I was contributing to the class and keeping things interesting. Mostly I felt that he didn't resent my being there, and the times we'd perform our little skit were some of the few times I felt I was welcome, or that I could be of use. Mr. Tobin was gruff, and this was his rough way of keeping the class interested and letting me know that I was a part of it.

Brother Smart was a young teacher and well-liked by the students. He was handsome and he was cool. He was a chaperone on a class trip to Washington, D.C. We stayed in the American Hotel, and we had heard that students from a girls' school were staying on the floor above us. Apparently Brother Smart had heard the same story, and he caught me in the stairwell after curfew, on my way up to see what I could see. But he didn't report me. He just sent me back to my room.

Years later, in Denver, I ran into an Irish Christian Brother from New York and I asked him about some of the brothers who taught at Rice. He told me that Brother Smart had left the order and was now married. He said that Brother Otto had been an alcoholic, who eventually could no longer teach but had been looked after until his death.

Freshman year I was a D student in large part because of the leathery, humorless heart of Brother Leahy. I still struggled throughout high school, but I did much better when I no longer took any classes with him. From sophomore year on I got steady A's and B's. English and social studies were always challenges, and not just because of the language barrier. Mr. Reilly taught social studies and was the most boring teacher, and perhaps the most boring person, I had ever come across. I often wonder how well I might have done if I'd never come to Brother Leahy's attention.

Toward the end of every summer, around Labor Day, I went to Puerto Rico to see my people. I usually stayed with my uncle Diego and his growing family. Diego and his wife made a good Catholic couple and wound up with 10 children. Every day I'd go into Vega Alta and stand around at my father's store, watching the merchants and customers come and go. At lunch he and I would go to a cafeteria together, and sometimes he'd take me around to some of his properties or other businesses, or we would just travel around, looking at landmarks.

"You have a father," my mother would always say. She wanted to make sure that he and I kept in contact, that I felt a connection to the man whose blood was in my veins. She also hoped that I might inherit something from him when he died.

Luis Díaz was born on the island on October 14, 1901. (October 14 is a powerful date for me: my mother died on that day in 2016.) Luis grew up in Manatí and served in the military during World War I. One day he drove me into Old San Juan to see San Cristobal, the hospital where he had been stationed as a guard. After the war, he went to work in his father's little store in Vega Alta, and in a short time he turned that little store into a big deal. He was very much the big man in that city of 35,000 with a Levi-Strauss factory and a sugar cane refinery.

My father had a big personality, and he had a head for business. He greeted people on the street everywhere we went and seemed always to have a quarter for the beggars. Right up to his death he seemed vital and strong. He was impressive to me, and I wanted to make him proud to have me as his son. The house he lived in was so big that after he died, it was sold and converted into a medical clinic. I had heard of his other children—the three sons, one of whom was a dentist, another an engineer, and the third an optometrist; the daughter who owned a dance studio and the daughter who was a prominent member of the community—but I had not met them. I had seen his son who worked in his store, but we were not introduced and never spoke to each other until years later. I would not officially meet any of them until later, for reasons I never discussed with my father but always felt had something to do with his taking a wait-and-see position with me, his poor son from the New York ghetto. The only half-sibling I spent any time with before graduating from high school was his youngest daughter, Ana Luisa, whom everyone called Wilfa. She was six months younger than I and a grade behind me. She was also the child of a woman other than Luis's wife.

I wanted to be as impressive to my father as he was to me. Because there was no real affection between us, I turned to the idea of respect as an acceptable substitute. I did not see how I could win his love, so I would try to impress him. I visited him out of obligation, and most of the time we were together I watched him work or listened to a lecture from him about his business or his properties, about how he moved his money around to avoid taxes, or about the history of the island. I learned about his business philosophy and his values, and I learned about his political views. He was a statehooder who had no time for the political left. He said that Puerto Rico would have sunken into the sea long ago if not for the United States. He was always cordial to me. But I was a once-a-year visitor and he never came to the mainland. I would invite him to school events, to my graduations, even to my wedding, but he never came. I never felt that I had a place in his heart. When he died,

I learned beyond any doubt that I did not; I was the only child of his not included in his will.

I did, however, get close to Wilfa. My father had set up her mother, Luz Maria, with a big house and a farm and a dress shop in Dorado. She and Wilfa were kind to me. Wilfa went to an all-girls Catholic boarding school in Manatí. My father took me with Luz Maria to visit Wilfa at her school, which felt like going to visit someone in a jail where all the guards are nuns. We were permitted to break Wilfa out and take her to lunch. I remember that lunch well, because I got a drink that had rum in it. I had never had rum before and didn't know what I was ordering, but I guess I sounded confident, because no one warned me. It had been a long day of running around and being out in the sun, and it was mid-afternoon and I was hungry. I took a few sips of my drink, which was delicious, and fainted. That was how Wilfa met her half-brother.

That weekend, my father took me to Dorado to stay with Wilfa and her mother. Wilfa's mother had adopted the daughter of a man who worked on her farm. Her name was Grisette, and she and Wilfa and I spent a few days together in that big house when a big storm came through. It was the season for big storms. We listened to records and learned the dances and had a good time. I don't remember seeing Grisette again much after that, and she died young.

Wilfa and I were the two bastards that my father recognized. My mother always maintained, however, that there was at least one other, a girl who lived in Vega Alta and called my father "Uncle." Wilfa was very much like my father. She looked like him and thought like him. She would go on to Catholic University in Puerto Rico and then to law school at Interamerican University of Puerto Rico. She spent part of the summer after she graduated from Catholic in New York learning English in a program at Columbia University. She came to my wedding, and I have a picture of her in a miniskirt, sticking out amid all the modestly dressed parishioners of my congregation. She didn't go into the law full time but has done very well in business, as I would expect from her father's daughter.

Puerto Rico was such a different world for me. There I saw big houses everywhere and had time to relax. Luz Maria would take me into Vega Alta and tell me to take whatever I needed from my father's store. I never did. She offered to take me in, to let me live with her and Wilfa. I told my mother about it. To my young mind, the offer had a certain appeal. It would have meant a different life, living in a big hacienda. But not surprisingly, my mother opposed the idea. Moreover, she was angry. I was her boy and I was living with her. We may not have had much, but she certainly wasn't going to pawn me off on some rich lady in Puerto Rico. Nice as that life seemed, I was going back to New York.

Wilfa and I remain close, and I will always be grateful for how welcoming she and her mother were to me. They were always kind to my mother and stepfather, too. And when my stepfather was in the hospital in 2017, Wilfa came to see him.

Life in New York, compared with life in Puerto Rico, was hardscrabble. My mother watched children during the day for neighbors, while my stepfather worked as a doorman or in a restaurant. My uncle Paulino, the oldest of my mother's brothers, who had been one of the first to migrate to the mainland and had served in the army, struggled after his retirement. Paulino was a proud man. He was tall and strong like his father, who had cut such an impressive figure, riding his horse across Puerto Rico working the sugar cane. But he had come up against some hard times. He had three children and a wife, but he had some very bad habits, too. He gambled and he drank. And living in East Harlem, if you were looking for a fight, you never had to look far. One night, coming out of a barber shop after an evening of drinking and shooting crap, he got into an argument over the game. The argument quickly turned into a fight, and Paulino stabbed a man with his knife. He was convicted and sent upstate.

One weekend Pop drove Mom, Cookie, and Paulino's wife and kids in my mother's 1957 Chevy station wagon up to see my uncle. I stayed home to go to church. On the drive home on Sunday night, as they came down the Saw Mill River Parkway through Westchester, heading for the West Side Highway, another car bumped them and ran them off the road. They went down an embankment, and if they hadn't crashed into a tree, they probably would have gone right into the river and all died. As it was, Cookie came away with a minor head injury and my mother with bruising on her chest. There were other injuries too, but not serious enough to remember. The car was totaled, and they never recovered any money from it. It took my mother a long time to recover from her injuries, but it could have been a tragedy.

I often stayed home from trips like this one. My life in those days consisted mostly of school, work, study, and church. But in my free time, one of my favorite things to do at Rice was to watch our basketball team play. Rice's team was strong. Our star player was Dean "The Dream"

Meminger, who went on to be an All-American player at Marquette University and later to win an NBA championship with the hometown New York Knicks in 1973. Our rival school was Power Memorial High School, but if we were honest, we would have acknowledged that Power had no rivals outside of the perennial powerhouse DeMatha High in Washington, D.C. Power had Lew Alcindor playing for it. Alcindor would go on to win championship after championship playing for John Wooden at UCLA and then, as Kareem Abdul-Jabbar, play for the Los Angeles Lakers in the NBA. New York was a great city for basketball, and Catholic high schools were basketball crazy, as was I.

When I wasn't in school or studying or at church, I was hustling. As a student in the New York City school system, I had a bus pass to get me to and from school and I used it to make a little extra money. I had a job making deliveries out of Grand Central Station for National Messenger, and when I had a package to deliver to the airport, I would take public transportation and then put in for reimbursement for a cab ride. Taking the subway out to the airport was free for me and the fastest way to get there, certainly faster than taking a taxi. A few extra dollars at that job was helpful, too, because if I could take care of all of my own expenses at home, I could help out my parents, who were always struggling to keep up with their bills.

I had a job at Gimbel's Department Store, too, working in the office as an executive trainee, and I'd come in on Saturdays, when I had the office to myself, and do bank reconciliations. During the week I'd help in the accounting department doing whatever needed doing, and I worked with Leon Vestyck, the senior vice president in accounting. They taught me a lot about the retail business, including how to develop loss leaders. Later, as director of the Spanish Merchants Association, my experience at Gimbel's led me to develop a deal with the Milk Control Commission of Pennsylvania for businesses along the Bloque de Oro on North 5th Street and other grocery stores in Philadelphia.

The most lucrative job of my youth was caddying. My cousin Papo Figueroa worked at the golf course at Lake Success Golf Club, out past Queens, in Great Neck, Long Island, and when I was old enough to handle it, he got me a job there, too. Lake Success was a very nice place with a beautiful course, especially to a kid from West Harlem, and it had some prominent members, including Yankees pitcher Whitey Ford. Caddying wasn't very difficult: just walk the course, lug the two bags, stay quiet, and offer the right club when necessary. When I first went

My high school photo.

out, I knew nothing about golf, and sometimes I offered the wrong club. But mostly it was easy: driver to start, putter to finish, and in between maybe you hand them an 8-iron when they want a 9, or a 7-iron and they want an 8. Anyone can fudge a lot of it. I quickly learned to offer general advice when asked—slow down your backswing, keep your head still—because no golfer wanted to hear "I don't know" in response to "What am I doing wrong?" The worse the golfer, the harder the caddying job was, because they all wanted hand-holding, they all wanted advice and only so many times in 18 holes could I say, "Your feet. Your feet are all wrong."

On Saturdays and sometimes on Friday afternoons, I'd caddy a couple of rounds of golf and leave with $50 in my pocket. Eighteen holes of golf was what we called a loop, and a loop consisted of carrying two bags at $10 each. The standard tip was $5. That job paid for my college, for my wedding between college and law school, and for a down payment on a house for my parents in Puerto Rico.

I developed the habit of keeping myself busy in those days. I had disappeared from the streets and my old life and my old friends. I would go into my building through the back door and hole up in my room to study. I stayed involved with my church and stuck with my friends in youth ministry. I sang in the choir and taught Sunday school to 35 kids I'd round up and bring to church. I served as treasurer of the youth society and wrote articles for the church newsletter until my style of firebrand journalism got the newsletter shut down. I did parishioners' income taxes for free. I loved that church and those people. For the first time in my life, I felt appreciated. For the first time, I was treated with respect and welcomed as a leader.

My mother was happy, too. She had brought me back to God and had put me in a place where I was supported by friends rather than being led astray by them. And now, she wanted me to get away from those skinny girls she'd heard about and to find a nice devout girl to marry. And that girl, as far as my mother was concerned, could be found every Sunday playing the organ at her mother's church. That girl was Vilma.

Vilma was a couple of years older than I. She was smart, studious, and musical, but she already had a boyfriend. He was in the military and often came to visit her when he was back in New York, but my mother didn't see that as an obstacle. She started regularly inviting Vilma over for Sunday dinners, and from then on, we were together. I didn't have much interest in having a steady girlfriend at 15 and had never before stayed with the same girl for more than two weeks. When I wasn't studying or working, I wanted to play baseball and hang out with my new friends, but Sundays were for church and Vilma, either at our apartment or at Vilma's family's place.

Vilma soon broke up with her army boyfriend and started to see only me. She seemed happy enough to have me as her boyfriend, though she never liked my family very much. I always felt that she looked down on us. Her parents were people of standing in their church. Her mother was the pastor and her father was a leader of the church. My mother and stepfather were humble parishioners who didn't make much money or have any such status. My father never left Puerto Rico. Although my mother was happy to have Vilma in my life, she never enjoyed a warm relationship with her. Throughout our marriage and our childrearing, my mother and Vilma never became close. Later I learned that Vilma was often disrespectful and unkind to her.

I felt trapped in my relationship with Vilma—trapped in a web of the hopes held by her and my mother, trapped by pressure from Vilma's parents to get married before I started college. But Vilma was also supportive of me. She helped me with my papers in high school, and some of my success at Rice I owe to her, and because I did well at Rice, I was presented with options for college. I graduated at the top of the commercial section and hoped to go to college for accounting. I could attend a community college in the New York State system, Iona College upstate or St. John's Junior College, which was part of St. John's University. I chose St. John's, which had just moved their main campus to Queens, because I could live at home and attend. I was also a huge basketball fan and St. John's was a basketball-crazy school. They had a great basketball team, though they almost lost their accreditation in 1969 because they built their gym at the new campus before they built the library.

I didn't have the money to pay $600 for tuition for my first semester. Once again, while there were better options available to me, I didn't know what they were and nobody told me, so rather than borrowing money from a federal program, I got on the school's own tuition plan. It was a terrible arrangement with high interest, very much like what a street-level loan shark might have charged me. Every month I had to pay off the interest, and so I kept working whenever I wasn't in class—at National Messenger, at Gimbel's, at the golf course, anywhere to make a little money. Eventually, after that first year, I earned enough money to pay the tuition up front and stay ahead so there was no loan to pay off.

The campus in Queens was beautiful. It took me an hour and a half to get there, by two subway lines and a bus. It looked like a real college campus. There was grass and there were gathering areas in front of the buildings. There were trees that you could sit beneath and study, though I never did. I was too busy rushing from class to class and then from campus to one job or another.

I was part of the Economics Honor Society. I started the St. John's Accounting Honor Society. I participated in the glee club when I could, but I didn't get involved in campus life. I took no part in fraternities or sports. I do remember hearing music blaring out of St. John's Hall, where the fraternities did their activities. I didn't know what I was hearing, but it turns out it was the Rolling Stones.

A lot of middle-class kids went to St. John's. They'd drive there and they'd join fraternities. I didn't understand the fraternities. I'd see them doing their hazing of pledges and I knew that they held wild parties, but I was in college for an education. It seemed like the young men who joined the fraternities were there to do a whole list of things that I suppose added up to "the college experience," with academics coming in a distant last place. I just could not understand those priorities.

I did, however, have one true spring break–style vacation of fun in the sun in Puerto Rico in my college years. A friend of mine who went to St. John's, Arthur Fierman, and I decided one year that we should go there during the three-week break between semesters. Arthur lived in East Harlem on 103rd and Lexington Streets, and he had a car. Sometimes I'd ride in with him when our schedules matched, paying the quarter toll as my contribution. He was half German and half Puerto Rican, and he worked at a bank, which meant he could afford a car. Since I had never done a lot of beach activities when I had gone to see my family, the idea of a beach vacation sounded novel. It would allow me to fill in some of the gaps from my childhood.

I found a perfect hotel called El Toro that was cheap enough to allow us to stay in Miramar. We took 20 friends from St. John's and arranged to meet my sister Wilfa and 20 of her friends from Catholic University. We would gather at Rincon, Ponce, or Las Palgueras, resort towns on the ocean in the southern part of the island. My friends would surf all day and we would laze around. Once we went to the bioluminescent lake Las Palgueras, which glowed at night because of the exotic bacteria that thrived there.

One night we found a man with a boat who agreed to take us to a little unpopulated island to the southwest where we could hop a fence and have the beach to ourselves. It was called Isla de la Gata. We asked the man to return for us in a couple of hours. The evening seemed to get off to a great start, but we were with 21 good Catholic girls who were not inspired by the clandestine nature of our little escapade. After a few hours of good clean fun, we started to wonder where the boatman was. He didn't come back. Out of boredom I decided to take a dip in the beautiful surf and swim a little. I swam and splashed around, the night wore on, and the boat still didn't come back. Day broke and still no boat. The boatman never came back. Finally, the Coast Guard found us and took us back to our hotel. On the way, we learned that the beautiful water I had been swimming in was a shark preserve.

I had one solo misadventure, too, when I rented a little motorboat on Isla Verde, a tiny dot in the sea east of San Juan and just north of the airport. There's almost nothing and no one there, and I flooded the engine. I was too far from shore to be seen, so I just floated there until luck brought me a passing yacht from the nearby marina, which towed me in to shore.

When we got home to New York after three weeks on the island, my surfer friends, who had been up every morning at 5:00, had to go to the hospital to be treated for sun poisoning.

It was also during my freshman year that my family suddenly and unexpectedly gained a new member. I say "unexpectedly" even though my mother had been waiting for almost 20 years for him to arrive. Ever since she'd delivered a stillborn son and the staff at the hospital had blamed her for the death, she had carried a wound that never fully healed. She always said that God was somehow going to give her another child, to make up for the one who had been taken. Which is why, 20 years later, she went through all she did to adopt my brother Noel. Throughout my childhood and beyond, my mother made a little money watching neighborhood kids for the day. In the mid-1960s, my mother's good friend Gineta, who had been matron of honor at her wedding, recommended her to a friend of her family back in Puerto Rico who had asked about someone who could babysit her infant for the day.

I was 18 then, still living with my parents, and I remember when the woman brought her baby over. She was known in the neighborhood to have a drug problem. Having a drug problem was not uncommon at the time. What was uncommon was that the woman showed up at our apartment with a very tall white man. White men were a rare sight in West Harlem in the 1960s, and in my home, even rarer. My mother watched baby Robert for the day and into the evening. And when Robert's mother did not come back, my mother kept him overnight.

What else could she do? My mother cared for him, and that day was followed by another day and baby Robert's mother didn't come back. My stepfather asked around our neighborhood, in Gineta's neighborhood near 135th Street, but no one knew where she was. Days became a week, and then a month, and the months followed one another as my stepfather kept searching, kept asking, kept walking the streets. One day, after three months of searching, my stepfather was walking down 137th Street in West Harlem, when he saw a very tall white man—the very tall white man who had come to our house with Robert and his mother. It turned out that the tall white man was not Robert's father and that Robert's mother was in rehab. When my stepfather went to the rehab hospital to find her, he learned that she was registered under my mother's name, Maria Rodriguez.

By this time, my parents had begun the process of adopting the little boy. My mother had been waiting for another child since 1949 and wanted to bring this boy up as her own. After Pop found his mother, he went to family court and asked to have her arrested for child abandonment. If they could compel the boy's mother to appear in court, she could give consent to the adoption and they could complete the legal process. No one knew who baby Robert's father was, so his mother's consent was their only chance. The mother appeared, and she consented. The adoption was soon made official. We would rename him Noel, because we would learn that he had an older brother also named Robert. With us he would have his own name, and after the adoption Robert's name was legally changed to Noel.

We lost track of Noel's mother after that but found out many years later from Noel's biological brothers that she had died in Philadelphia in 1972, the week I graduated from Temple Law School. Noel tracked down his brothers decades later, in Texas. They had been raised by their mother's mother in Puerto Rico, the one who was friendly with Gineta. It turns out we were all in Philadelphia on the day that Noel's mother passed away in 1972, but we had no way of knowing.

In the two years I spent at St. John's Junior College, I got good grades. My worst grade was a D, which I received in an introduction to biology class of 500 students, taught by a professor who was projected on a screen. From there I matriculated to the university and continued my studies. During the next two years I kept my head down and plowed through. I worked; I studied; I went to class; I went to church. By the time I graduated, I was second in my accounting program and first in my class in economics. The top accounting student was Susan Webber, who went on to become a professor at Columbia University. Sometimes, if we were both on campus at night, we'd have dinner together at a nearby restaurant. We got along well. We were becoming friends when, one day, Susan made the mistake of calling my house. My mother answered and gave her the same treatment she'd give any girl who called for me who wasn't Vilma. Who was she? Did she know that Nelson had a girlfriend? And Vilma was a good girl. Susan never called again. We remain good friends, and I remain proud to have finished second to such an accomplished and meticulous accountant.

Although I could pack the back of a plane with young men I knew who were eager to vacation in Puerto Rico, besides Arthur Fierman and Susan, I didn't count many of my classmates as friends. I just didn't have time to be sociable. Before I left each morning, my mother would make me a sandwich, which I'd often eat in the library while I studied. I enjoyed talking with Arthur on the days that he drove us to school. He went into marketing and lives in Florida now.

As my college career wore on and my graduation became more and more likely, I felt that my father was beginning to accept that I could make something of myself, because during those summers I began to meet his other children. Over the years I'd often seen Eddie, who managed the store, but had never been introduced to him, a situation that had made for some awkward moments in the store. At times the two of us would stand on opposite sides of the counter, not speaking, not acknowledging each other, and assiduously avoiding eye contact. I also met Angel Luís, the optometrist; Víctor, the engineer; and Fernando, the dentist.

My father introduced Fernando and me on a boat. Out on the open water things got a little choppy, and I spent most of our voyage below decks, throwing up. Fernando and I stayed close until our father's death, and he kept in contact with me and made me feel like part of the family. We had a falling out when he assumed control of all of our father's properties, and I took him to court. All that came of that was acrimony, really. But I'll always remember Fernando's kindness to me.

I made plans. I had a clear idea of what I wanted to do. But see what happens when you put your plans in the ring against fate, and fate wins in a knockout every time. I offer the story of my little car in illustration.

I got my driver's license on my 18th birthday, and three or four months after that I went to the Reedman dealership in Langhorne, Pennsylvania, on the recommendation of young man from my church. I bought a little Renault for $600 and put it on my mother's insurance. Buying that little car set in motion a string of events that would determine the course and quality of my life for decades to come.

Not six months after buying my car, in early December, I was driving Vilma and my stepfather up Broadway to church, where Vilma was the organist. As we crossed 135th Street, we were broadsided, and my little $600 Renault from the Pennsylvania dealership was thrown into the air and tossed onto the median by a big New York Buick, an absolute boat of a car, that had run the red light. My stepfather took the brunt of the impact in the back seat—no one wore seatbelts in the

1960s. Vilma was in the passenger seat but came away with only minor cuts on her legs. I came away unscathed. We took my stepfather up to Columbia-Presbyterian Hospital, where they told us he had five broken ribs.

My stepfather worked as a doorman at an apartment building called the Wesley Towers on 89th Street between Amsterdam and Broadway, and during the holiday season he made most of his money in tips and gifts. But there would be no manning the door for him that year, not with five broken ribs, not when just standing was almost unbearable, when breathing was almost unbearable. The timing was disastrous. My family needed that money; we had budgeted for it. So we decided to see whether I could fill in.

We asked the superintendent, and he agreed. I put on the uniform and worked a shift from 3:00 P.M. to midnight while I was going to college. The timing was tight, but it worked out with my schedule. I'd go to school in the morning and stay till early afternoon, then take the train back to Manhattan and run over to the building and man the door for nine more hours. The superintendent knew my family was in desperate straits, and while I was grateful to have the work, he took advantage of a young kid who didn't know any better. He gave me an added duty that was not part of a doorman's job—sweeping the stairwells of the entire high-rise building from top to bottom. It was a huge task. Judging by the amount of dust I swept up, I may have been the first person ever to sweep them. It certainly felt as though I was. The dust from all that sweeping landed me in the hospital with bronchitis. And the bronchitis brought about the return of my asthma.

In the summer of 1969, while I was studying in a summer program in preparation for law school in the fall, the draft board called me to take my health exam. I failed because of my asthma. I had wanted to join the army, to follow in my uncle Paulino's footsteps. It seemed like a great way to get away from West Harlem and, frankly, a looming obligation to marry Vilma, my girlfriend of seven years.

So, because of that little car getting hit by that big one and breaking my stepfather's ribs, which led to my working his job, sweeping all those dusty steps, which caused my asthma to return, in turn flunking me out of the army, I married a woman out of a sense of duty.

I had not married for love, and I couldn't join the army, but I had made it through my youth. I hadn't died or been incarcerated. I had a college degree and I had a future. The world awaited, and I had a plan, useless though it was.

5

LAW SCHOOL

IN 1969 I GRADUATED second in my class at St. John's with a B.S. in accounting. I wasn't sure what to do next, but I felt optimistic. I applied to MBA programs. And most promising of all, I had a job interview set up with Arthur Young and Company, a big New York accounting firm. My future seemed to be unrolling before me beautifully. Opportunities seemed to be laying themselves out before me. One such opportunity came from the chair of the accounting department at St. John's, who recommended me for inclusion in the newly founded Council on Legal Education Opportunity, known as CLEO, an organization that helped minority and low-income students apply to and attend law schools. I wasn't interested in law school or a career in the law beyond considering it another possible good and stable profession in which I could make good money and live an easy and predictable life. I marveled at where I found myself when I thought about where I had started. No one, with the possible exception of my mother, could have predicted it. And no one, least of all me, could see where things were going.

The CLEO program accepted me into its Pre-law Summer Institute. For six weeks during the summer I would live in a dormitory at New York University, work on law school applications, and learn the basics of what law school would require. I knew little about the law profession beyond what I'd seen on the TV show *Perry Mason*. Numbers were my strong suit. Also, I had a plan. It included a new apartment in the Bronx and a wedding only weeks away. Now that I had graduated from college, Vilma and I were getting married. But the program's six weeks encompassed our wedding date. If I were to join the program, I'd be spending half of the summer living in a dormitory with a roommate.

This was not the plan. I had been doing a lot of work and sinking a lot of money into repairs and improvements to the apartment Vilma and I were going to move into. I was formulating a plan, and in it accounting featured prominently. All I had to do was stick to it. It was becoming clear, and it seemed solid. But I never got to find out whether it would have worked.

I made a hard right turn. I took a leap. Vilma was unhappy about my decision, and almost every night when my roommate brought girls back to our room, so was I. Vilma and I still got married that summer, on a Saturday, but on Sunday night I headed back to the dorm and to my roommate and his dates. Vilma moved back in with her parents for the rest of that summer and waited, her marriage and her new life put on hold, and I went home on the weekends. There would be no honeymoon. In all, we spent one month in that newly refurbished apartment in the Bronx, one month with that coherent and workable plan, and then it was time for a new plan and a new path.

The CLEO program, which had contacts with law schools in the region, provided us with applications and coached us through the process. The only New York school interested in me was St. John's, but I did not want to return there. For one thing, I thought I might come off as provincial if I attended the same university for undergraduate and law school. For another, despite the school's involvement in the CLEO program, my experience at St. John's left me with the impression that the school was not committed to admitting and supporting minority students. In response to the acceptance, I sent a letter explaining in detail why I was turning down the offer. In one of my life's many ironic turns, the law school I later attended had a worse record of supporting minorities, and women, than St. John's. I learned after I arrived that only four African Americans had graduated from the law school in the previous eight years. In my class we counted five women, and I was the lone Latino.

I applied to Rutgers Camden and American University in Washington, D.C. My roommate had an application for Temple University's law school, but he wasn't interested. As something of a lark, I took it and filled it out, thinking it would not come to anything. But it caught the attention of a young professor who was running a pilot program there. His name was Peter Liacouras, and he would go on to be the dean of the law school for eight years, and from there head the university for almost 20.

Temple, Rutgers Camden, and American all accepted me. American was a good program, but D.C. was too far from home. Rutgers Camden offered me a scholarship, but its law school was brand new, and Temple had a good reputation in tax and corporate law. And Temple also had Peter Liacouras.

Peter was a champion of minorities at Temple and, for lack of a better word, I would say he bamboozled me into going to Temple Law School, where I would be the first and, for a time, the only Latino student. Peter had a plan, and he wanted me to be part of it. He saw something in me, and whether or not I saw it myself, I wanted it to be true. My relationship with him would change the course of my life.

I sometimes think that I should never have listened to him, that I should have stuck to my plan of living a predictable, low-stress, stable life with few headaches and no surprises. But he was hard to ignore. He would call me and campaign. He'd say he knew I was considering other law schools, but he hoped I'd come to Temple. He'd tell me about the large and growing Latino population in Philadelphia, about all the things he wanted to do at Temple Law School. My interest in being a lawyer at all was lukewarm at its warmest, but he was relentless. He called me sometimes daily and wouldn't let me get off the phone. You should come, he would say. He could be very persuasive. Despite my misgivings about the law as a career, about Philadelphia as a city, and, after a stay in a fleabag hotel near campus and an unimpressive tour, about Temple itself, the unrelenting charm offensive of Peter Liacouras worked. And so I decided on Temple University Law School. Temple would pay for my tuition, and the CLEO program would pay for my books.

That left the housing expenses to my unemployed wife and me. Campus housing was too expensive for us, especially since I'd thrown all that money away fixing up the apartment in the Bronx and I had paid for a wedding. We couldn't find anything near Temple's North Philadelphia campus and our search for housing began to get desperate. Vilma's father, however, had a good friend, Ralph Franco, who was a minister in Philadelphia but who lived in Camden. Ralph and his wife offered us space in their attic for two months, and we took it until we could move into a little house for $110 a month, right on the Francos' block. Temple was just a manageable drive over the Benjamin Franklin Bridge.

We were set up to live, but I was not ready for law school. My first semester was very difficult. I was unprepared for both the culture and the curriculum. As a kid who'd grown up poor in a Harlem high-rise project, I found many legal concepts foreign. Learning the law was like starting over in grammar school, trying to master the new concepts while learning a new language. My parents never made more than $50 a week, and we owned next to nothing. My experience with property and ownership was limited, and it was complicated. No one I knew owned property or real estate. Many of my parents' financial transactions were decidedly below board. New York housing was a racket, and my mother had to pay $700 just for the privilege of obtaining a lease. Little in my experience was relevant to what I was studying, and street smarts were no foundation for learning such concepts as a fee simple, a fee simple divisible, and the common denominator of community expectation. I was not prepared to do the hundreds of pages of required nightly reading or to spend most of that study time looking up terms in *Black's Law Dictionary*. Most nights I'd stay in the library until 2:00 A.M. trying to keep up. I did not really know how to study, and even though there were concepts I came to understand well, such as criminal law, contracts, and torts, my knowledge wasn't translating to the exams. I had studied numbers and had tested well in pursuit of my degree in accounting, so I was surprised and troubled to be failing exams and struggling academically. We had moved and started a new life here. I was in law school, not grammar school, and I could not afford to flunk out. I worked hard not to panic.

The basic difference between an exam in law school and ones I'd taken in my undergraduate years at St. John's was that the law school exams did not so much want an answer to the problem as a thoroughgoing discussion of all the issues that surrounded it. My first year was miserable, and every time I saw Peter Liacouras, I asked him what he had against me that he'd bring me to this hellhole of a school.

I found much at Temple to dislike, and my education-by-disillusionment at Temple Law School went far beyond the classroom. I was in a place that had few minority students—my class had nine African Americans, in addition to the five women and me, the lone Puerto Rican—and was either unwilling to support them or incapable of doing so. I began to chafe at the injustices I perceived, and then I began to fight. Once I began to understand the school's admissions practices, my response was almost instinctive, but my years at Temple Law School forced me to hone my innate resistance to the impositions of authority. I had to learn how to respond appropriately to rules made without taking into account those they might affect, to the requirement that the aggrieved give assent, and to the expectation of their gratitude. At Temple, I learned how to protest.

My faith had given me a backbone and inspired in me the desire for a better world with a moral imperative. I wanted to see a more just world, and I had been inspired to help bring it about. At Temple I was able to put my faith into practice and fight for greater equality and representation of minorities and the poor. I knew that I faced certain impediments not only because I was the individual Nelson Díaz but also because I was a Latino and a Spanish speaker. It was no coincidence that my advocacy and activism blossomed when Carl Singley, who would become a lifelong friend, returned to school. Carl had come to Temple Law School from Talladega College in Alabama with the previous year's incoming class but had then been drafted. He returned for the second semester after he, like me before him, failed the draft exam. It felt like the return of a good friend from the old neighborhood.

My first semester had been a disaster, and by the time Carl returned, I had flunked three exams and been placed on academic probation. Studying was difficult for me, because I had never really learned how to study, and the social aspect of law school was overwhelming. I had not been prepared to sit in a class with 250 students or to be the only Puerto Rican among them. Peter had recruited me and he supported me and he had a plan, but there were so few minority and women students, and he was just one professor working in opposition to the policies of the school. Carl helped me.

Carl was brash and confident, and he carried himself with a youthful swagger that put some people off, but being around Carl gave me a reprieve from all the strange new foreignness I had been steeping in. For the first time since moving out of New York, I could feel at home. Talking with Carl about the law was like talking smack in the park with my Harlem brothers. He was unlike the other African American students, who were meeker and more intimidated by the numbers and less willing to speak up or speak out. Carl and I became a study group of two. We staked out seats in the library that would be ours for the rest of the year.

Carl knew how to study, how to take an exam, and how to read a book to glean the specific information the professor was looking for. He taught me to look through the table of contents to identify what I needed to review for a test, rather than wandering through a textbook as though I were reading a novel, reading every word from start to finish. My grades immediately improved. I never flunked another test.

In short, Carl provided me with something no professor or administrator had thought to supply. The dean of Temple Law School, Ralph Norvell, believed that the struggles almost all of the minority students were experiencing could be addressed with a remedial reading class, as if the issue were a grade school problem. Some professors offered tutoring sessions during which they simply repeated what they'd already said in class. And when the minority students started flunking out, the professors and administration merely shrugged and said they had done all they could. Flunking out was part of the process, the winnowing down many law schools used to pare a class of 250 down to one of about 80 by graduation. And that failure was ascribed only to the students who had failed, not to the school.

A core of students that included Carl and me, as well as Dorothy Moore, Ernie Jones, and Charles Duncan, recognized that the issue was far deeper than the natural process of thinning the herd: this was an issue of unaddressed cultural differences. We decided to address it, and in year two, Carl, Dorothy, Ernie, and I became the leadership of a new group that we called the Black Law Student Association.

Carl was elected president, Ernie Jones vice president, Dorothy Moore secretary, and I treasurer. Sometimes I cringe and sometimes I chuckle when I think back to what we were doing and what we thought of ourselves. As radical as we believed we were, we still made the one woman in the group the secretary.

Ernie Jones had served in the military and become a Black Panther. He had a fireman's coat that he always wore and he sold the Black Panther Party's newspaper. He was a very pragmatic student, and he was in law school, it seemed to me, just to get through it. He would put in exactly as much work as he thought was required to get by. He took shortcuts when he saw that he could. While I was plowing through the cases we were assigned, he'd read the headnotes. And he managed to get by that way.

Dorothy Moore, who was from North Carolina, was one of the most level-headed people I ever met. I remember the sound of her southern accent staying calm and reasonable amid the rising voices of the hot-headed men, keeping the peace in a room full of testosterone.

The Black Law Student Association, known as the BLSA, was founded primarily as a way for us, as minority students, to support ourselves. We agreed to study with no one but the other minority students, to help each other when no one in the administration or on the faculty seemed able to. Our plan helped our grades, but still some of the students washed out after their first year. Back when Peter Liacouras was recruiting me to come to Temple, we'd agreed that I would be able to recruit students for the law school and weigh in on the admissions process. In my second year, a few students I'd recruited entered year one and joined the BLSA.

Peter was on sabbatical in my second year, but a few other professors supported us. Joseph Passon, who sometimes co-taught property courses with Norvell; Herman Stern, who would chair the reconstituted admissions committee when the new administration was installed; and Joseph Marshall all believed in what we were doing and saw the need for change.

Because of our study groups, my grades improved greatly. I received A's, including one in a five-credit torts course, and had a chance to re-take the three exams I had failed in my first semester. I passed out of academic probation and never looked back. The BLSA also offered us a social outlet. Carl had gotten married while away in his first semester and lived in a big house in Mt. Airy. We'd sometimes have parties in his basement. We stuck together and supported each other and sought to support other initiatives at other law schools and on our own campus.

While the BLSA was taking a stand for minority students in the law school, elsewhere on Temple's campus, the undergraduates were staging a revolution of their own. Several black student groups held a summit meeting and invited the BLSA to join them, and we did. We all sat around the room, but the leaders wouldn't start the meeting. They just waited. It wasn't paranoia that made me feel that several of the students there were staring at me. They were. Finally, one of the leaders said that they were waiting for the enemy to leave before the meeting could begin. They meant me, with my fair skin. The other members of our group stood up and vouched for me, and the meeting began.

I was very concerned with increasing the enrollment of Latino students at Temple. During this time, when there were only 35 in the entire university, I had my first contact with Aspira, an organization founded in the 1960s by Antonia Pantoja to promote Puerto Rican enrollment in college. Aspira worked with high school students to help them apply for admission, financial aid, and scholarships. Aspira clubs in high schools offered this support as well as training in leadership and Puerto Rican culture. While we were organizing the Federation of Puerto Rican Students (FPRS) at Temple and helping them find ways to increase their numbers, we had a great ally on campus, Epifanio DeJesus. Epi counseled and recruited minority students at the Temple Opportunity Program. Throughout our struggles with the administration, Epi supported our efforts and even reached out to Aspira to bring more students to support us when we picketed.

I was still at Temple in 1971 when Epi, as executive director of the Philadelphia chapter of Aspira, asked me to chair the board. Epi would serve until 1975, when he ran for City Council. I stayed on and became secretary of Aspira's national board, where I worked with Luis Alvarez, whom I had known since he and I worked together as stock boys in a little store in New York. Luis had gone on to union organizing and was now a charismatic leader and fundraiser for Aspira.

Aspira had grown under Pantoja's leadership. She started it as a local youth organization, but by the time I joined the board, it was a strong program that provided educational opportunities to Puerto Rican kids all over the United States, with chapters in Puerto Rico, Chicago, Philadelphia, and Cleveland and in many other towns and cities, including in Connecticut, Massachusetts, and Florida. Aspira, which now runs several charter high schools and other educational projects, is the largest organization for Puerto Rican youth in the United States. I had admired Pantoja for a long time, but it was only in 1994, when I was general counsel at the Department of Housing and Urban Development, that she told me we are related through my grandfather Pedro Cancel Pantoja.

Back at Temple, the BLSA was gaining attention from other community and activist groups, including the Young Lords, a leftist Latino movement that stood for Puerto Rican independence, human rights, and freedom. The group, which got its start in Detroit, was modeled on the Black Panther Party. When the undergraduates started planning their protests at Temple, I met a young man from the Young Lords who called himself Yoruba. He had sought me out to discuss what actions we could take on the campus to ensure that our people were better treated. He told me about other things the Young Lords were doing in Philadelphia. It seemed as though every time we spoke, Yoruba—whose

With President Bill Clinton and my cousin Antonia Pantoja, circa January 1997, after I nominated her for the Medal of Freedom while I was working at the Department of Housing and Urban Development. I was honored to escort her to the ceremony at the White House.

real name was Pablo Guzman—would tell me about one or another member who was in trouble with the law.

The Latino community considered the Young Lords a communist group. They offered things like a lunch program and education services. They also knew how to make a splash and sometimes they showed a subversive sense of humor. In New York, they took over a church to call attention to the poverty of the Latino community there. They even stormed the Statue of Liberty and hung a gigantic Puerto Rican flag from her torch.

Yoruba and Juan Ramos, the leader of the Young Lords in Philadelphia, offered the FPRS support that was very helpful, though sometimes I worried that the demands they persuaded us to bring to the table would end the negotiations.

The summer between my first and second year was tough. Vilma was pregnant and we had almost no money. I never felt more homesick than I did while facing the thought of raising a child so far away from family. Because we lived in New Jersey, we did not qualify for public assistance. Lucky for us, Marvin Wachman stepped in to help. Wachman was Temple's vice president of academic affairs, and he used a fund that allowed Vilma to see an obstetrician at Temple Hospital. Vilma had gone the first two trimesters without seeing a doctor, so Wachman's help was critical. Vilmarie Díaz was born healthy in the summer of 1970.

Fall of my second year was busy. I was taking more business law classes and assuming my duties as treasurer of the BLSA. I was still hoping to return to New York, where I could land a job at a big accounting firm. Vilma stayed home with Vilmarie, but she had applied for a bilingual teaching position in the Philadelphia School District and had been admitted to a summer program for temporary certification. I attended all the classes for her and related the coursework to her as best I could. She began working that fall while the Francos watched our baby. Between her job and mine at Camden Regional Legal Services, we finally had a little money coming in. We could afford diapers and a finer selection of meatballs and spaghetti, and we could put a little money in the offertory plate at church.

The Camden Regional Legal Services office was by the Greyhound Bus station, off of Broadway, and not far from our house. Pete O'Connor ran the office, and two longhairs rounded out the staff: Sandy Zeller and Gordon Lewis. I worked there in the summers along with two Rutgers law students: Ron Freeman, who had come to Rutgers through the CLEO program and is today a New Jersey Superior Court judge, and Wayne Bryant, an African American law student who would go on to become a New Jersey state senator and later be sentenced to four years in federal prison for fraud. Working there put me in front of a lot of fair housing cases.

I worked with Lewis, who was one of the top landlord/tenant law litigators. He threw me right into the courtroom, where I did my best to represent tenants in suits based on breach of habitability and other violations of the 1968 Fair Housing Act. There was never a shortage of these cases, and O'Connor thought that we could file a class-action lawsuit against Mt. Laurel, demanding that municipalities do their fair share to provide affordable housing. So we did, in 1971. We, the law students, helped with research, and that summer we filed the case on behalf of the Burlington County NAACP.

In 1975 the New Jersey Supreme Court would decide unanimously for us. In the decision, the court said that each New Jersey municipality had to "make realistically possible the opportunity for an appropriate variety and choice of housing for all categories of people who may desire to live there, of course including those of low and moderate income."[1] The money the state had to put out to comply (with this as well as a second unanimous decision that came down in 1983, known as Mt. Laurel II) set back a development plan for Admiral Wilson Boulevard for 20 years. I drove that route countless times from New Jersey over the Benjamin Franklin Bridge into Philadelphia and back again. The Admiral Wilson was in terrible shape and lined with seedy motels and strip clubs, but I never complained. That money was going somewhere far more important. That case taught me the power of the law.

My third year of law school was monumental. After two years of fighting over the same issues for minority students, we decided to go see Dean Norvell about how we were being treated. As an action of the BLSA, about six of us went to talk to him, but when he saw us coming, he retreated to his office. Carl pointed at him and demanded that he speak with us. I wedged my foot in the door as he tried to close it.

Clearly he was scared of us. Rather than considering us students first, coming to him to discuss ways in which the law school could better support us, he saw us as threats. Surely he had engaged in heated debate before, with colleagues, with superiors, or with students under his charge. But he would not hear us out. He called security, turning a strained relationship between minority students and the faculty and administration into an adversarial one. We went on strike against the law school. We picketed on the sidewalk in front of the entrance and stopped any minority student who was trying to enter the school. Many of those students joined us. White students joined as well. Norvell still refused to meet with us, so all the African American students and I resigned and filed a discrimination complaint with the Philadelphia Human Relations Commission. The commission, along with Marvin Wachman, intervened. Wachman, who would soon be appointed president of Temple University, was always a steadfast ally to minority students. Before coming to Temple, he had been president of Lincoln University. The historically black university had been struggling financially,

---

1. Southern Burlington County NAACP v. Township of Mount Laurel, 67 N.J. 151 (1975).

and in under a decade, Wachman had helped restore it to prominence and solvency. Even when some of my associates were making noises about wholesale revolution at the university, even when the Young Lords started to make their demands to the Law School, Wachman remained steadfast.

I had been working with the Young Lords in Philadelphia since 1971, and Yoruba had opened my eyes to what they were facing with the police and the FBI and even in their own community, where they were trying to do some good. When someone set fire to the house they used as a food distribution warehouse, I decided to help them. I appealed to the Philadelphia Bar Association and others to provide representation and support when the Young Lords needed it. For instance, when they wanted to hold a press conference, we made sure they had a hotel room where they could talk to the press and take questions.

They were an impressive group. Juan Ramos had dropped out of La Salle University to run the group. He would go on to become a Philadelphia councilman and today is a deacon in the Catholic Church. Juan Gonzalez was a brilliant young man, and the most erudite of the group. He would go on to become a columnist for the *Philadelphia Daily News* and then the *New York Daily News*. He had left Columbia University to join the Young Lords, something the school seemed to hold against him, awarding him his degree only in the past few years. Wilfredo Rojas— they called him Hawkeye—would become a corrections officer at Holmesburg Prison, then at the city jail in Philadelphia, and he ran the correction officers union.

At those press conferences in the hotel room, the Young Lords made their own demands to Temple University, and perhaps a few threats as well. I asked them not to make threats, because I didn't want their provocative rhetoric to ruin our chances to get something out of this opportunity or to alienate Wachman or the Human Relations Commission while we were presenting them with our demands.

Wachman and the Human Relations Commission read our demands and for the most part, they could see that we were not asking for anything unreasonable. Wachman never wavered, and we stayed civil and focused at the negotiation table. He and the commission could see that the other party involved was a law school administration that had adopted a position of intransigence. They asked Norvell for his resignation.

Norvell was a tall man, who looked like what you'd expect a law professor to look like. He wore tweeds and had the bearing of a man of education. He brought in some brilliant legal minds to teach at the law school, but under his watch, the school did not support its students. The focus was on identifying the weaker ones and weeding them out to get to a final third that could compete for jobs at the top law firms in the country. Norvell, in all his tweedy erudition, wanted to compete with Harvard.

To put it simply, Norvell was the wrong dean for Temple Law School. He wanted our scrappy state school to pump out future partners at white-shoe firms, and his means to that end was to put us in the grinder and remove those who couldn't hack it. According to the school's attendance policy, students who missed a certain number of classes would fail and have to make up the credits. This at a school where students often took night classes to accommodate their day jobs, where students had families, and where they were, in essence and in fact, adults. In the previous four years, not a single African American student had graduated.

Norvell saw law school, and the law itself, as apolitical—a position that is, of course, political. When Norvell caught wind of plans for a moratorium march, from North Philadelphia down to City Hall, in protest of the Vietnam War, he told all the law school professors that if he heard about any of them marching, they would be immediately dismissed. Temple Law School, his reasoning went, was not to take a political position. Again, every position is political, whether you like it or not. His threat was not heeded, nor was it acted upon. Peter Liacouras marched right alongside me the entire way.

I will never forget the last time I saw Norvell. We were picketing in front of the law school building on Broad Street near Columbia, which is now Cecil B. Moore Avenue. Black students, white students, me. Some of us were milling around, others were on the steps taking it in, doing what students in the early 1970s did. A car pulled up in front of us and Norvell got out of the passenger side. As he crossed the picket line, he looked right at me with such a strange expression. I couldn't quite read it because I could not have had any idea that this was his last day as dean, his last time setting foot in the Temple Law School. None of us knew why he was there or that he had been asked for his resignation or that he had lost and was offering his surrender. It was a look of contempt or disbelief or defeat or all of those things. It may have been how Julius Caesar looked at Brutus on his last day on the Senate floor. It was just a glance though. He looked, but never broke stride, and entered the building. And that was that. He tendered his resignation, which was accepted. Peter Liacouras became the new dean.

Under Liacouras's administration, the law school agreed that Carl and I would be official members of the admission committee and that every incoming first-year law school class would include 45 minority students. Carl and I agreed between ourselves that we would split the number between African American and Latino students. He would fill 35 seats and I 10. Over the years, many prominent public servants came through Temple Law School, including Mayor John Street, Councilwoman Augusta Clark, Ambassador Mari Carmen Aponte, Connecticut judge Ed Rodriguez, and Gil Medina.

Gil Medina's story begins in 1971, when a police officer in Camden, New Jersey, stopped a Puerto Rican driver, pulled him out of the car, and clubbed him in the testicles. The blow killed the driver. This was a very volatile time, and racial tensions were high. The attack sparked a riot in Camden, and Guadalberto Medina, a student at Rutgers Camden at the time, helped to lead the rioters. He was arrested. I was working at Camden Regional Legal Services at the time, and for most of that summer, we tried to get those arrested out of jail. Medina was a good student. He had a 4.0 average and a lot of promise. We helped secure his release and I recruited him to Temple Law School. While he was a law student, he was put on trial for an earlier firebombing of a bank in New Jersey. I tried to find a way to assist in his defense.

By coincidence, I'd helped Joe Rodriguez in his bid for selection to a federal judgeship. Rodriguez was a good federal judge until his death in 2018. Though he was a Democrat who had served only Republican governors, he had pull, he was president of the New Jersey Bar Association, and he was highly respected. As it turned out, Rodriguez's neighbor was the presiding judge on the case. Rodriguez wrote a letter of recommendation and helped Medina get a deal and plead to a misdemeanor. Medina made it through law school with no further riots or firebombings. He became a lawyer, he would run the Spanish Merchants Association, and then he became a city councilman in Camden. He was a big deal in New Jersey, even though he never went to council meetings. I was shocked when I heard that he had become a conservative Republican and been appointed secretary of economic development under Governor Christie Whitman.

After law school, the leaders of the BLSA all went their separate ways, but we kept tabs on each other. Dorothy Moore went into a career ·

at the National Labor Relations Board, where she served for 40 years, the last 15 of which she spent as the director of the Philadelphia Regional Office, and retired in 2013. Throughout her time there, she recruited from Temple, never forgetting where she'd come from.

Ernie Jones took a job with the Philadelphia District Attorney's Office. I remember feeling betrayed and indignant that, even knowing what he knew, he'd gone over to "the other side" and would now prosecute the disenfranchised. Little did I know at the time how much power he could wield from that position, how much he could do from inside that office. Since I was working in the Public Defender's Office, he and I went up against each other in court more than a few times, often in front of Judge Richard Klein, who knew both of us. Judge Klein would often note that we were friends, or had been, and that we should try to work out a deal.

Just a few years later, Ernie and I found ourselves working together at Temple Legal Aid. They were looking for someone to assume the directorship. At the time I was also working with the Spanish Merchants Association and took myself out of the running. But I stayed around to assist Ernie when he took the role. We were true friends, and our adversarial relationship immediately evaporated when we started working together again.

When Charlie Bowser stepped down as executive director of the Philadelphia Urban Coalition in 1975, his brother, John Bowser, took over. John ran the coalition until his death from cancer in 1983. I helped Ernie step into the executive directorship then, a position he kept until 1998.

A brief aside on John Bowser, who was a great man, a financial development genius, and like his brother, a force for progress in Philadelphia. In the early 1980s he was trying to finish a big development project restoring the historic Uptown Theater on North Broad Street. The Uptown, like the Apollo in New York City and the Howard Theatre in Washington, D.C., was a major venue for African American acts and civil rights benefits. Every big act from Redd Foxx to Stevie Wonder, even a 10-day engagement with the Supremes, came through the Uptown. But, like the neighborhood around it, the Uptown had fallen on hard times. It closed in 1978. John had secured a loan through the Urban Coalition to oversee the renovation, but the project was running out of money as it neared completion. If they couldn't get a quick infusion of money, the whole project could founder. John asked Mayor Bill Green

*Chatting with the great Charlie Bowser at a 2007 fundraiser
for mental health services for the homeless. Charlie, a longtime friend,
had already been diagnosed with Alzheimer's, and this was one
of the last times he recognized me. He passed away in 2010.*

for a guarantee for the money from the Philadelphia Industrial Development Corporation, which could cover a loan, or from City Council, so
the work could be finished. For some reason Mayor Green, who knew
what a dynamic figure John was and what an important project this was,
declined. The project went bankrupt almost immediately. A church
opened there in the mid-1980s but had to move out in 1991 because the
roof was a ruin and the space was becoming unusable. Proposals have
been made, funds have been pledged, and plans have been drawn up, but
today it still stands vacant and has yet to reopen.

Cancer was the official cause of John's death, but his family says it was that unfinished project that killed him. They were so upset about what Green had done to the Uptown, and to John, they forbade him to come to the funeral.

As for my friend Carl Singley, he became a professor at the law school and received tenure. When Peter Liacouras stepped into his role as president of Temple University in 1981 and the university began to look for Peter's successor as dean of the Law School, Carl threw his hat in the ring. He had significant backing, but Peter was reluctant. He didn't think Carl was a good candidate. He was a born leader, Carl was, and no one could doubt that, but Peter thought he was too brash, too hardheaded, too quick to pick fights, and not willing enough to compromise. I disagreed, and at the time I was serving on the board of Temple Hospital. I confronted Peter and helped to persuade him not to oppose Carl's appointment.

Carl served as dean of the law school for three acrimonious years of near constant confrontation with Peter. After three years, Peter had had enough, as had nearly everyone else, and he had Carl removed. I remember it well. Carl did not take his dismissal peacefully, and in a move loaded with irony, he locked himself in his office. In the previous decade, it had been Carl pointing his indignant finger at Dean Norvell, and it had been Norvell who tried to lock himself in his office to avoid confrontation and eventual removal. This time however, I was not around to shove my shoe in the door first.

A locked door, however, does nothing to stop the processes of an administration, and Carl left Temple and went into private practice, where he did very well and maintained good relationships with John Street and Ed Rendell. Street had become a city councilman in 1980, taking the spot left by Cecil B. Moore, who had died before the election. When Temple pushed Carl out in the mid-1980s, he became an unofficial but closely held adviser to Street. Soon his friend Rendell would become mayor, and his friend Street would become president of City Council, and the three of them, along with David L. Cohen, would meet almost daily. Carl's influence only grew when Street became mayor in 2000. But soon thereafter, Carl was out. Very few people know the story of his falling out with the new mayor.

Carl and I were both on Street's transition team during his first year in office, when suddenly Carl was no longer part of the team. Street loved to tell stories, and he could tell a good one. He still can. When I asked him about what happened between him and Carl, he told me this story.

In that first year, as the new mayor, Street was getting up to speed on what was going on in the myriad departments around the city. He asked Carl to go to the board meeting at the Philadelphia Parking Authority and find out what they wanted and how they were doing. Simple really; just get the lay of the land and report back. Carl went, and at the meeting he announced that he was now general counsel for the board of the Parking Authority. After the meeting, Carl got a call from an attorney at Duane Morris, who had just heard that he was no longer the board's general counsel and wanted to know what had happened to bring about this unseen turn of events. This lawyer was also a supporter of Mayor Street's, and when Mayor Street found out what Carl had done, he was furious. Carl did not get to keep his post, and he and Street never spoke again.

I think the split did great harm to both men. Carl was never the same after that. He and I worked together at Blank Rome, but by that time we were no longer friendly. He remains a practicing attorney, but he never enjoyed the level of influence he cultivated with the heavy hitters in the city at the millennium. And Street, who had never had many friends to begin with, lost a valued confidant when he lost Carl.

My falling out with Carl happened not long after his split with Mayor Street. Late in 2001, I became city solicitor. I had gained a lot of experience running an office when I served as administrative judge and as general counsel to the Department of Housing and Urban Development. I felt confident about what I was doing. Carl, in all his brash confidence, wanted to tell me how to do my job. I was always eager for good advice, and while I trusted Carl, I knew that he didn't offer counsel—he dictated. In just about any situation, Carl thought he knew best, and when I pushed back against what sounded like orders, he insisted. I had to tell him to go to hell to get him to relent, and my doing so ended our friendship.

Carl will always be an important figure in my life, and in a very substantial way he helped guide me through law school. He was instrumental in dragging Temple Law School, and the university as a whole, out of ignorance and into the era of civil rights. His boldness, his confidence, his street-corner swagger have always been his greatest asset and the key to his undoing.

6

EARLY PROFESSIONAL LIFE
AND ACTIVISM

CHILDREN ARE A BLESSING, and family is a gift. By the time I received my law degree, Vilma and I had three young children, a boy and two girls—Nelson, Delia Lee, and Vilmarie—and through law school Vilma had been the primary breadwinner on her teacher's salary. Children are a blessing, indeed, but they require a great deal of responsibility, and they cost money. And while I had thoughts of moving back to New York to be an accountant, if I did so, I'd be throwing away the law degree for which we had sacrificed before the ink on it had even dried. I had applied for a scholarship from the Council for Opportunity in Graduate Management Education (which offered support to minority students applying to business school) at the Wharton School of Business and had been accepted with a generous stipend so I could pursue an MBA in finance. Never in my years at Temple Law did I feel that the law was my true calling, but I had always been interested in business and in numbers, and the finance program seemed perfect for me. A law degree and an MBA in finance would open a lot of doors.

But law school had been three years of heavy financial strain, and the thought of putting Vilma and the kids through two more years of that—putting us all through another two years of slowly sliding backward into increasing debt to creditors and indebtedness to friends and family who took up for us—was too much.

Posing with Peter Liacouras in September 1981. Having won the primary, I was campaigning for judge in the general election. From the time I graduated from college until Peter's death in 2015, he supported me and encouraged me to exceed my own expectations.

New York called me back, too. But Peter Liacouras urged me to stay. He hadn't recruited me to Temple and brought me to Philadelphia just to let me wander back to New York with my degree and his good wishes. "Finish what you started," he'd always say. He would tell me that I was going to be the first Latino judge in Pennsylvania. Positions were available at the Defender Association of Philadelphia, better known as the Public Defender's Office. I was interested in the Heber Smith Fellowship at the Philadelphia Community Legal Services office, as was my good friend Carl Singley. The director of the Community Legal Services office, Larry Lavin, said we'd have to decide who between us would take it. Carl was my friend and brother-in-arms. We had founded the Black Law

Student Association together, and more than that, Carl had been the one who had taught me how to study. Without the friendship and support of Carl Singley, I never would have made it through year two. So if Carl was interviewing for the position, I would leave it alone. And there was Peter again, asking me why I was giving up, telling me to finish what I started. I told him I would not interview for a job if I would be taking it from a friend. Carl was offered the position, and he accepted, but then decided to take an instructor's position at Temple Law School instead.

Peter told me to wait while he looked into things at the Public Defender's Office. Vincent Ziccardi was a friend of his, and Peter and he agreed that Ziccardi would interview me for the position. It was the only interview I held after graduating. I was quickly hired. The salary they offered would hardly be better than the nothing I earned while at law school, but they promised that when I passed the Pennsylvania bar exam, my salary would immediately become slightly less meager. It was a deal. I was staying in Philadelphia. And I was never going to be an accountant.

Passing the bar had just become a little fairer and more equitable for minority students, thanks to the efforts of Peter and a panel of legal experts. In 1970, Peter had chaired a committee appointed by the Philadelphia Bar Association to look into the administration and grading of the bar exam and to eliminate racial discrimination in any aspect of the bar's admission procedures. The committee was made up of Peter, Ricardo Jackson, W. Bourne Ruthrauf, and Judges Paul Dandridge and Clifford Scott Green. Its recommended measures took effect in 1972, the year I was able to take and pass the bar exam.

Working at the Public Defender's Office would be a good introduction to the law, and it had a certain appeal to me as a budding gadfly. The firebrand and civil rights legend Cecil B. Moore had been a public defender. The image of the public defender was of a hardnosed and scrappy lawyer who demands respect for put-upon clients and stands up for those who have never had anyone stand up for them. More than that, Philadelphia's Public Defender's Office was one of the best in the nation, and my experience there would teach me how to be a trial attorney.

Vilma and I had to be frugal on my pittance of a salary, but starting a career in the law gave me the feeling that I was putting down roots in Philadelphia. I was in Philadelphia and was going to make a go of it. I gave it five years. After that, maybe we'd go back home to New York. I didn't know it then, but within a year, the idea of New York as home would fundamentally change. My mother and stepfather moved back to

Puerto Rico, where they spent three decades before returning to the mainland to live with me in Philadelphia. My mother's absence shifted the center of gravity on where I thought my home was. New York City without Maria in it was not the same place. Not long after my mother's move back, I arranged for my sister Cookie to move back as well to get her out of New York.

Cookie was in crisis. She had married Ivan when she was 18 and he was 23. Ivan was a warm, gregarious person and full of life. He loved to sing and was just a great person to be around. He'd had a problem with drugs before they met but had kicked the habit and was in recovery. It was around five years later, when he was working with young people in a New York State program that Cookie found marijuana in their house. Then bills went unpaid, and the calls and second notices started arriving. Cookie adored Ivan, and it broke her heart to do so, but she left. She had to. She asked me to help, so I did. Ivan died just a few years later. According to the coroner, he had alcohol and methadone in his system at the time of his death, and his overtaxed liver couldn't handle the strain. So Cookie joined Mom and Pop, and they made a home in Puerto Rico.

Back in Philadelphia, I was making some connections. The Latino community was small and the city roiled with ethnic antagonism. In its way, Philadelphia in the 1970s was very familiar to a Latino who had grown up in New York in the 1950s and 1960s. Huge swaths of the city were a dangerous mixture of dwindling resources to be shared by growing populations of differing ethnicities—too little housing, crowded schools, and evaporating jobs as industries pulled up stakes and fled. Few places were as contentious or as prone to racially motivated violence as Port Richmond and predominantly white sections of Kensington. Black families and Puerto Rican families met with objections from their white neighbors from the moment they moved into those neighborhoods, fueling an active and sustained resistance that escalated as the minority populations' numbers increased. Fights would break out between neighborhoods; gangs would meet on contested turf and rumble. Whites would form mobs and beat their new neighbors, sometimes throwing bricks or firebombs through their windows.

The dividing line between the black and Puerto Rican sections of North Philadelphia and the white section was the Frankford Elevated Train Line, which ran along Front Street. But many of the black and Latino kids weren't able to keep to their side of the tracks because their schools were in the white neighborhoods. And as had happened in the New York of my youth, much of the city's racial tension expressed itself in the schools. Minority kids were targets of white kids' resentment as they walked the halls or sat in class, but even more so as they made their way home through unfriendly neighborhoods. It was so bad at the time that Mayor Frank Rizzo instituted bus service to provide safe passage to and from school for the black and the Puerto Rican students.[1] But after a period of success and a significant decrease in ethnically based attacks, the city suspended the busing program, and the minority kids were on their own again. That decision ended in tragedy.

In June 1973, a 14-year-old student at Penn Treaty Junior High named Julio Osorio began the mile-and-a-half walk to his house off West Girard Avenue. He was just leaving school when a group of white kids from the neighborhood started chasing him. Home lay to the west, but they chased Julio south and east, toward the Delaware River. He ran along the river, went out onto a pier, and either jumped in the water out of desperation or fell in. Either way, the current overwhelmed him and he drowned.

It was a terrible shock and—even harder to bear—an almost inescapable eventuality resulting from the city's atmosphere of racial animus: if it hadn't been Julio Osorio chased to his death, it would have been some other kid. And his death, we knew, would not be the last. We in the Puerto Rican community had grown used to being targets of violence, but this tragedy in which a young man not yet even in high school had been harried, terrorized, and chased to his death, this was too much. We could not simply grieve among ourselves or wait patiently for the next incident, the next exacerbating reprisal. We had to do something.

I was still the only Puerto Rican lawyer in the city at the time, and my work with civic groups and my work on the admissions policy at Temple Law School had gained me a reputation as a willing advocate—and a vandalized house in Kensington. But even as I was establishing a reputation in the community, I was learning how naïve I had been.

As a public defender I was learning how to be respectful of judges and of authority in general without being overly deferential or timid. I came into that job with a strong regard for judges, and if I learned noth-

---

1. Charles F. Thomson, "Rizzo Pledges Bus Service for Penn Treaty Pupils," *Philadelphia Evening Bulletin*, June 23, 1973.

ing else at the Public Defender's Office, it was that judges are just like the rest of us, human, fallible, and sometimes disagreeable and venal. Some of the judges I encountered were measured and wise, and some did not seem to care about the law at all. Others demanded reverence without merit. It was a shock to witness their frailties and faults and to realize that people at all stations and echelons were subject to the same range of foibles and idiosyncrasies. They were, I discovered, much like law school deans. It was disillusioning. The world was being taken down a peg in my eyes. It was being unmasked. Seeing things as they were was a gift, but one that was at times difficult to appreciate. This revelation would serve me well, however, as I worked to hold those in power accountable for injustice.

I was asked to act as legal counsel to a group of leaders in the Puerto Rican community who were going to sit down with Mayor Rizzo to discuss the untenable situation that faced minority students in North Philadelphia. Of course I would. I called out sick at work and 20 of us had an hour-long meeting with the mayor.

The meeting was tense. One of the leaders in the Puerto Rican community was the Irish priest Tom Craven, who for years ran the Spanish-speaking arm of the Philadelphia Archdiocese's Catholic Social Services. I had met him during my first summer out of law school, on Commonwealth Day, celebrating the annexation of Puerto Rico. I walked into the Catholic Services building in North Philadelphia, at 7th and Jefferson Streets, to see all these Irish guys serving Puerto Rican food to the Puerto Rican people there. I'd never seen anything like it. Father Craven was one of a kind, and we became good friends. He'd sometimes invite me to his Friday gatherings at the parish, and he and his Irish buddies would sing the songs of the Irish Republican Army over steaks and whiskey. His passionate advocacy for the people he served did not endear him to the very conservative Cardinal Krol, or to Mayor Rizzo, either.

Here were, in the middle of a rather tense meeting, 20 of us and the mayor and his people, sitting around a table. I sat between Father Craven and the mayor, and as the conversation grew heated, Father Craven got up out of his chair.

"Don't you understand the seriousness of this situation?" he almost shouted.

Mayor Rizzo had been a beat cop and then police commissioner. He wasn't one to shrink from a fight, and he never lost his enthusiasm for throwing a punch before thinking. He was, in short, a confrontational man, and he stood up to answer. So I stood up too, and as calmly as I could I reminded the mayor that the man in the clerical collar who was not quite yelling at him was a priest. I reminded the mayor that he did not want to punch a priest. After that meeting, Mayor Rizzo always called me "Counselor."

It was a tough meeting, but it turned out to be a productive one. We aired our concerns and made several demands and requests. Among them were reinstituting the "safe passage" buses and assigning more Puerto Rican police officers in the 26th District to bring the total to 70. We put forth José Lebron to act as the new vice principal at Penn Treaty. José was a stalwart in the community, and himself a graduate of Penn Treaty. We demanded crossing guards and a greater police presence at school opening and closing times.

Besides standing up with thoughts of belting a man of the cloth, Rizzo also listened intently, and he seemed to share our concerns and to be committed to helping. In all it was a far more productive meeting than any of us felt we had a right to expect. Of our 11 formal demands, Rizzo approved 10.[2] In the end, he said it was impossible to assign 70 Puerto Rican cops to the 26th, because there were only 35 Puerto Ricans on the entire police force. But he came through on the others and asked me personally to follow up with him and let him know whether any of the other demands were not implemented.

The next day when I arrived at work, I found that my meeting had been covered in the *Philadelphia Inquirer* and the *Daily News* and that the *Inquirer* had referred to me as "the community group's attorney." My boss, Dennis Kelly, came by my desk carrying the *Daily News* and showed me my picture right there on the front page. He asked me why I'd called out sick if I was actually meeting the mayor. We had a discussion about the use of my time. I was frankly stunned at how upset he was about it. Yes, I'd called out of work, but it wasn't because I didn't feel like working nor was it to angle for a new job somewhere else or to ingratiate myself to the mayor. The city was—in some cases literally—burning, and I was joining an effort to create a pathway to peace and justice, yet here he was standing on a point of attendance. He seemed to have just as hard a time understanding my point of view. That day I

---

2. Jon Katz and Carolyn Skorneck, "Rizzo OKs 10 Demands of Puerto Rican Group," *Philadelphia Inquirer*, June 23, 1973, B1.

decided I should move on. I was offended and hurt. I felt unwelcome and disrespected. I realize now that Kelly was indeed standing on a point of attendance. It wasn't that I was forbidden from doing anything like what I had done, or that I was no longer an employee in good standing. It was about being professional. But I was young and fiery, and I didn't want to work for someone who couldn't see the forest fire for the trees. When a good opportunity presented itself, I would take it and go.

The meeting with Mayor Rizzo was my introduction to Cesar Miranda, the executive director of the Spanish Merchants Association (SMA), who had also attended. Miranda was thinking about moving on from the SMA. He wanted to go to law school and start his own business. He would do those things, too, graduating from Rutgers Law School and starting a produce distributorship, selling fruits and vegetables to the North Philadelphia merchants he had represented.

We were talking not long after that meeting, and he asked me whether I'd consider joining the SMA. He had told me his plans for law school and the business and, noting my unique position as the only practicing Puerto Rican attorney in the city, he offered me the executive directorship. I wasn't sure I wanted it and was fairly noncommittal. The SMA then sent me a letter with an official offer for the job on a six-month contract. As I thought it over, I saw it was at the very least a way out of the Public Defender's Office. It was an opportunity that I could take advantage of, a way to advocate for my community even if it was outside the practice of law. The Latino community needed help in many areas. Most glaring was the need for a coherent plan in economic development. But was I the man for the job?

The SMA was funded by the Office of Minority Business Enterprise (OMBE), a bureau within the federal Department of Commerce. Miranda had me meet with the OMBE's liaison, who turned out to be as informative as she was blunt. Her office, she told me, had concerns with the SMA and its board and if I didn't take the job and make some changes, the bureau would very seriously consider shutting down the SMA altogether.

She pointed out, for example, that, until recently, the SMA had rented an office out of a furniture store, from which they also rented their furniture. That same store was owned by Candelario Lamboy, the founder and chairman of the SMA. Even though the offices had moved out when Miranda became executive director, the OMBE hadn't seen much progress or evidence of what they would consider a professionally run organization. The SMA had been founded to assist Spanish-speaking merchants in Philadelphia, but there was little to show in the way of meaningful assistance, development, or growth. The liaison told me that she hoped I'd take the position and turn things around. So I did, on the first of my six-month contracts.

Taking the position was an abrupt turn in my career path. I was not going to be an accountant, and now I wasn't practicing law, either. I was the executive director of an economic development organization, the goal of which was to create economic opportunities for people of my own heritage. At this time I still felt that one day I would return to New York. But the executive directorship of the SMA was a job that could have far-reaching repercussions. It made me think about long-term projects and a long-term relationship with the city. It was certainly a big responsibility, and the SMA's very survival depended on giving the OMBE some results it could believe in. Lucky for me that I met Charlie Bowser, the executive director of the Urban Coalition, early in my time at the SMA. Here is the story (please remember that I was young).

I was at a demonstration for Julio Osorio in the Puerto Rican neighborhood in North Philadelphia, trying to make sure things stayed peaceful and within the law. I was in my protest regalia, leading chants, keeping everything orderly, when up walked an African American man. He introduced himself as the executive director of the Urban Coalition and offered his organization's assistance. Young, fiery, and not always wise, I snapped at him. "Brother," I said, "you're part of the establishment. We don't need your help."

"I'm not your brother," he said. "My name is Charlie." He walked away and started asking around, trying to find out who the rude young man in the dashiki was. Charlie decided that if I was a lawyer and was running a community development organization—and after all he had met me at a rally in support of the Puerto Rican community—it was possible that I wasn't as dumb as I seemed. Charlie, ever gracious, always mindful of the bigger picture and the greater need, approached me again. We talked and decided we would meet later to discuss how he might be able to offer assistance. That was how my relationship with Charlie began, and it never changed very much from that: Charlie was always ready to help, and his guidance was always true.

The first thing he told me was that the SMA needed to move. At the time the offices were in a bank building—Philadelphia National Bank, which after countless mergers and acquisitions no longer exists—in Kensington. That was no place for an economic development organization that was serious about getting anything done. Center City was where the players were, where city government was, where all the organizations of consequence met. In Kensington we would always be on the outside, spectators, waiting to hear about decisions that would affect us. But in Center City, we could be a part of making those decisions, and the Urban Coalition could help. In fact, they gave us rent-free space near 16th and Walnut Streets, on Sydenham. It was small, but it worked. Very quickly we grew to a staff of six—two secretaries, a CFO, a deputy director, a loan packager, and me—and outgrew that office. We needed space for our growing staff and space for meetings with the decision makers to whom we now had access. Charlie was there again. He found us a larger space in the Philadelphia Building at 1315 Walnut Street, with offices and a conference room. The Urban Coalition paid our lease there as well.

Charlie provided a lot more than office space, too. He helped guide us away from the bank-branch model of lending. The SMA's clients were small-store owners, mom-and-pop bodegas, and often very poor record keepers. The sloppy accounting may have been caused in part by a lack of expertise, but perhaps more by a desire to avoid paying taxes on their income, which made securing a business loan nearly impossible. It also didn't help that the neighborhoods in which they lived and owned their businesses were "redlined" and would have been seen as high risk by any bank. (Redlining was the practice of denying services, including banking, or offering them at disadvantageous terms because of the racial makeup of the neighborhood.). The only loans that these bodega owners could get were loans against the value of their property, such as a mortgage. Charlie told us to move away from that practice, away from PNB, and away from the PNB Bank branch. We needed to work with an institution that, in awarding business loans, took into consideration such things as cash flow and working capital and calibrated adjustments according to whether the businesses made a profit. My predecessor as executive director had based the SMA in Kensington because he had a good relationship with the PNB branch there, but a model based on mortgages and deposits does not work for business and economic development. Putting up a business property as collateral was risky, especially in Kensington. Doing business and getting loans in a neighborhood that was synonymous with redlining was the sort of risk that the SMA was founded to address. The sooner we could outgrow practices that kept us disadvantaged the better.

We changed how we did things because of Charlie, and few changes were more critical to the SMA's success than the change of our loan officer. Charlie introduced us to Bob Price at Girard Bank, and Bob became our loan officer. During my time at the SMA, we applied for $4 million in loans, and Bob never turned us down. We in turn never defaulted on any of them. More than just approving loans, Bob helped the SMA's client businesses take critical steps toward being recognized as viable businesses. He worked with us on developing a customer base and taught the bodega owners some basic bookkeeping.

The other monumental shift was moving to Center City. We were now around a lot of big decision makers and had greater access to organizations that could help us. I was invited to join boards of important civic organizations, such as The Partnership, a nonprofit group created by the business community and led by business leaders to provide assistance to groups just like mine. I also sat on the board of the Greater Philadelphia First Corporation, led by CEOs of the major businesses in Philadelphia. These business relationships were like the keys to the city for an organization like SMA. And I forged relationships with people who would help me throughout my career.

Charlie's guidance was never wrong. Everything he told us to do was the right thing, and everything he offered was helpful. Because of him and his advice, we were more capable and better prepared to offer support to the small businesses we were there to assist.

Once we were settled in Center City, I could get back to our big initiative: getting our members licensed as milk distributors with the Pennsylvania Milk Marketing Board. This deal would allow the SMA to set up a cooperative license to buy dairy products at wholesale prices. Many store owners had deals with their distributors, but these deals occupied a hazy, semi-legal area of business dealings that involved kickbacks. Of the approximately 250 bodegas in the city at the time, 60 were in our co-op. When Bob Price and I began helping these businesses with merchandising, marketing, and basic record-keeping, we found the current arrangement to be a bit shady and a lot less advantageous than it could be. A licensing agreement would present an effective means of increasing business and lowering costs for our members. They would pay into a security that insured prompt payment to dairy producers and distributors, provided the store owners with reliable delivery at a desirable price point, and even offered a dividend based on their participation. It was clear to me that we could do better for our merchants.

The Milk Marketing Board began in the 1930s as the Pennsylvania Milk Control Commission to help control costs and ensure security for producers and distributors in an industry that was beset with chaos and underhanded business practices.[3] They were happy to help, and we began to work out a deal with Johanna Farms.

Just about everyone needs milk. So just about everyone goes to the store to buy it. We were using one of the oldest retail tricks there was to turn that necessity into an opportunity. The agreement we worked out kept the merchants' prices low, and with a little basic marketing guidance, merchants could turn milk into a loss leader. If you've ever wondered why the milk cases are almost always in the corner of the store farthest from the entrance, you should know that they are there so you have to walk past all of the other products for sale on your way to get that gallon of 2 percent. The low prices the merchants pay are passed on to the customers, and to get to the low-priced milk, the customers see just about everything else in the store. That's how a loss leader works.

We employed a truck driver and a collections person, and one Sunday night a month I'd meet with the store owners—their bodegas were often open 24 hours a day, every day—and distribute a dividend to each member of the cooperative that was based on how much they had purchased. They still called it a kickback, but now it was all legal and aboveboard. Johanna Farms was one of the largest dairies in the state, and this arrangement gave them exclusive distributorship to our member store owners. Their law firm was happy to develop the licensing agreement.

It was not all smooth sailing, but once again, thanks to the guidance of Charlie Bowser, we came out of it all right. We hired a truck driver, who made daily deliveries of milk, juice, some ice cream, and even a little yogurt. He collected payments from the store owners and gave the daily receipts to our collections guy, who would deposit them in the bank every night. I don't remember the name of our collections guy, only that he was a welfare-to-work hire and that discrepancies soon appeared. What we were paying for the milk didn't match what was coming back. The accounting was odd, and something smelled rotten. It turns out that

---

3. See *Pennsylvania Milk Marketing Board Fiscal Year Report, 2003–2004*, available at http://www.mmb.pa.gov/Migration/Documents/2003-2004%20Annual%20 Report.pdf.

the man doing the night drops and our accountant were working together to skim a little off the top.

I didn't know what to do. How was I to stop getting ripped off and be made whole again while making sure that the people responsible were dealt with? I had no experience with embezzlement within our own operation, so I sought out Charlie's advice. Charlie told me to go to the district attorney, who at the time was F. Emmett Fitzpatrick. Fitzpatrick brought in our collections guy, who immediately gave himself up. He had taken the money and bought a little used car dealership in North Philadelphia. Fitzpatrick told me this on a Saturday morning, and I immediately went to Judge Bill Lederer, whom I found at the gym, to sign an emergency injunction to assume control of the dealership.

Our collections guy got five years' probation and had to turn over the dinky little car dealership—a lot with maybe eight clunkers and almost no value. That lot is still there today, and when I drive past it, I remember the little embezzler whose name I can't recall. As for our accountant, he disappeared like a puff of smoke from a pile of burning money. He likely fled the country and went back home to Honduras.

Now the problem was how to make up the money. The dealership was worthless, and we sold it off for almost nothing. I decided to put my house up for sale, but Charlie was there again to help. He said that the Urban Coalition would put up half the money, and that I should ask Johanna Farms for the other half. So I did, and they agreed. They had a sweet deal with us, and if helping us out kept intact the exclusive agreement with 60 merchants in Philadelphia, they would be happy to help.

In the four years I spent as executive director, much of my focus for the SMA was on bringing our client business owners up to legitimacy and helping them be more professional. Better business practices and record keeping meant that they had to pay taxes, which they didn't want to do, but it also meant that they could develop their businesses and get loans that didn't involve high-interest rates or putting their property up as collateral. Running a bodega was not easy. Store owners stayed open around the clock and they often lived above their stores; they were tethered to their businesses, eating their meals there, and with little time off, few weekends and even fewer vacations. But the SMA helped many of its member merchants go from just making it to doing well. Many of those store owners were able to retire to Puerto Rico, and a few of the more ambitious ones would manage to buy a supermarket, called Pupo, up on the 2900 block of North Fifth Street, on the Bloque de Oro.

The Bloque de Oro was another project of mine during my time at the SMA. The push for it began in 1974, when I was still in my first year as executive director. I was serving on my second six-month contract, working hard to deliver some tangible results that would satisfy the OMBE and keep our funding coming. For four years I served as executive director one six-month contract after another until I left to go to Washington in 1978, at which point the OMBE felt confident enough in me to offer a two-year contract—which I turned over to the next director.

When Puerto Ricans started migrating to Philadelphia in significant numbers in the 1950s, they had moved to the Spring Garden area in North Philadelphia, and over the decades they had worked their way up the 5th Street corridor. By the 1970s that corridor was in need of some support and economic development.

Ever since I had stopped Mayor Rizzo the year before from punching Father Craven, he had seemed to trust me. On the rare occasion that I would see him, we would exchange a few polite words. One of his aides once told me that he had advised Rizzo that I was someone to keep in mind, someone who was smart and reliable. And so, in 1974, Mayor Rizzo appointed me to the board of the Philadelphia Regional Office of the Economic Development Administration (EDA). The EDA is a federal agency established in the mid-1960s to provide support and economic development for areas of economic distress, to create jobs and growth through investment.

In 1975 I was on the board of the Philadelphia Regional Office along with Rev. Leon Sullivan of Zion Baptist Church—the civil rights titan and developer of the Sullivan Principles for companies operating in apartheid-era South Africa—and 11 white men. Two of those white men, Joe Egan and Walt D'Alessio, became great allies of mine. Both worked for the city, and because of the way they worked together, I always thought of them as Frick and Frack. They were like brothers when, as director of the SMA, I met them in 1974, and they were inseparable till the day Egan passed away in 2009. At the time, the board was hard at work on the upcoming 1976 Bicentennial Celebration in Philadelphia. The idea was to make Philadelphia the focal point of the nation's 200th birthday and to bring attention and tourism dollars through an array of events and programs. The Regional Office wanted to make sure everyone on the board supported the Bicentennial, because the EDA was ready to fund it. A lot of money was available, and Rizzo wanted to be certain the board was unanimous in its support in order to ensure that the city got as much of that money as it could. It was a big project, and an enormous economic opportunity. If Philadelphia could use some development funds for other programs, it would grease the skids for unanimous support of the Bicentennial. So, Egan and D'Alessio came to Leon and me, asking whether we had any thoughts about economic development in our communities.

Yes, we had thoughts.

Leon wanted a new training center for his organization, the Opportunities Industrialization Center, in North Philadelphia. He had founded the center in the mid-1960s in an abandoned jail in North Philadelphia, and he wanted something better, something built to be a training center. That building stands today and still offers training, job placement assistance, and other services to a disadvantaged and insecure population. It was approved, constructed, and opened in 1976 on North Broad Street. It stands next to Progress Plaza, which, it should be noted, Leon Sullivan also brought into existence. As for me, I wanted to revitalize that 5th Street business corridor.

The crown jewel of that corridor would be the Bloque de Oro, a three-block stretch running north on 5th Street from Lehigh to Indiana, in the Fairhill section. Before the Puerto Rican migration up 5th Street, it had been a Jewish section, and the businesses were Jewish owned. When the Puerto Ricans came in, they opened many more businesses, often converting row houses to storefronts.

The area was in need of revitalization. The buildings all needed face-lifts, and some would need to be converted from houses to storefronts. The street was in bad repair, and the whole area seemed to be falling apart, not improving. Egan and D'Alessio told me that we had the city's support—and the EDA's funding—and the first thing to do was to work with a business consultant. And the first thing the consultant and I did was come up with a list of needs.

Phase one of our plan was to make simple improvements to the 5th Street corridor. The stores would be updated and improved with better signage, and some would get help inside as well. The street itself would be repaired and repaved. The sidewalks would be redone, with some designs and color added to the pavement, along with some fanciful touches, such as fake palm trees. All to make 5th Street look more welcoming and more dynamic and to make it easier to get around. Some of the results of that project can still be seen today.

Phase two was to develop a mall on the 2900 block—the northern-

At the groundbreaking of the Bloque de Oro in 1974.
Gathered around the tree (from left to right) with groundbreaking shovels in
hand are (to my left) T. K. Stephenson, director of the Office of Minority
Business Enterprises, and Allan Brown, Girard Bank loan officer, and (to my
right) Carlos Ricardo, owner of the mall; an unidentified city official;
Bob Price, Girard Bank vice president for small business;
and Jim Wade, secretary to the Commonwealth.

most block—of the Bloque de Oro. We would build a two-story structure to house a restaurant and a shoe store, eight businesses in all. But
the thing that might have made our proposal the most attractive when
we submitted it to our loan officer, Bob Price, was our second-floor tenant. No business would want to be on the second floor of our mall, with
no windows for potential customers to walk by and gaze into and no
simple access from the street. But Catholic Social Services was happy to
have it, and they would occupy the entire second-story space. Father
Craven, whom I saw slinging Puerto Rican food to his parishioners at
their little place on 7th and Jefferson Streets, was looking for a bigger
space and one that was farther north, moving as his constituency moved.
Catholic Social Services was a triple-A, gold-plated tenant, and our ar-

rangement was that we would build the second story to their specs, and they would sign a 10-year lease on it. They called it Casa del Carmen.

Tom Craven was a special man. A few years after we installed Catholic Services at Casa del Carmen, I flew to Rome to teach for a semester at Temple's Rome campus. As soon as I got into my lodgings, he called me. I remember it was 11 o'clock in the morning, local time, and I was jet lagged. He told me that I had an audience with the pope in three hours. I was shocked, and even excited through all the fatigue, but all I wanted to do was rest. Get cleaned up! he told me. Get moving! The pope will be waiting.

Father Craven was a man of great dedication and loyalty to his flock, doing whatever he could to help and support them. He was Father then, but he would become a monsignor, even though the Philadelphia Archdiocese's Cardinal Krol didn't care for him much. Cardinal Krol was very conservative and saw Craven as too much of a firebrand and too much an advocate for Latinos. Eventually Krol would ship him out of Casa del Carmen and install him in the very white St. Hugh's Parish on Tioga Street in Kensington. It didn't stay a white parish for very long, though, because many of Father Craven's Puerto Rican former parishioners followed him there. Later he would be transferred again, to West Chester, where, until his death, he served a population that included many Mexican migrant workers.

In all, we assisted about 60 businesses along the 5th Street corridor. And out of this revitalization, the 5th Street Merchants Association was born, which, independent of the Spanish Merchants Association, worked to improve opportunities for the merchants in the area.

In October 1975, someone threw a Molotov cocktail through the window of a house in the Feltonville section of the city. It was a tragic episode in the city's checkered history of racial intolerance. A Puerto Rican family—the Santiagos—had moved into the house on an all-white block. The fire burned down the house and killed five people, who were trapped inside; four of them were children.

As strange as it is to say, racially motivated firebombings and other acts of domestic terrorism were not uncommon at the time. In 1974, I had moved my family out of Camden and into a new housing development built on half of a soybean farm in the little New Jersey town of Easthampton, near Mt. Holly. It was a quiet place for the most part, and like much of suburban New Jersey it was very, very white. The school was good, and we lived on a quiet cul-de-sac and pretty much kept to ourselves, as did our neighbors. It was very different from city living, but it was nice in its way, too. The biggest problem I thought we faced was field mice, which seemed to dispatch in battalions from the farm and invade the house when the weather turned cooler, looking for warmth or food or what I did not know.

Very quiet, very white. We were the only Latinos there, and as I said, we all kept to ourselves. Our kids had a big backyard, but they usually played out front on the street. We had family over for a cookout every once in a while in nice weather. I remember one summer evening, Vilma called me to the kitchen. She pointed out the window, which looked out over the back lawn. There, over the split-rail fence that separated the housing development from the still-working farm, in the middle of the soybean field, blazed a huge burning cross. I had never seen a cross-burning before. It was aimed right at us, the only minorities for I don't know how far. It was quietly terrifying. There was nothing to do but lie low that night. We weren't going to go out and tell the fire department, which was across the main road at the other end of the development. I would stop by the following morning to let them know, and the cross was still smoldering when they went by to spray it down, hissing when the hoses hit it. But that night we went to bed while it still burned. I could almost feel the heat from it, just a hundred yards or so from my house, a bright, angry message from the way things were, trying to scare the way things were going to be.

If we could have afforded it, we would have moved that night and never even bothered to tell the fire department about it. But we could do nothing but stay and live with the memory. It was no use asking around to find out who did it. It was never spoken of or acknowledged by anyone in the neighborhood, as if none of them had seen it out their windows, even though you could have seen it from the highway.

I had a speaking engagement near Mt. Holly in 2016, and I decided to drive by that old house, to see whether it was still there. It was. The whole farm is now tract housing, and the neighborhood still looks very white, but Mt. Holly itself has changed. There are far more African Americans there now. The future is coming, and it doesn't care whether you burn a cross or worse. Hate doesn't stop progress.

Around the time an anonymously placed cross was lighting up a summer night in suburban New Jersey, the Santiagos and their new neighbors were not getting along. Feltonville was a predominantly white North Philadelphia neighborhood that did not welcome Puerto Ricans.

For a year, things had been tense, and then the month before the fire-bombing, someone broke the window of the Santiago family station wagon, poured in a little gasoline, and set it afire. No one was charged or even arrested for that incident. Later, in the aftermath of the five deaths, the white neighbors all insisted that the friction was not related to race; rather, they said, there was friction because the Santiago kids had been allowed to play in the street.

But Radames Santiago, the father of the family had not started posting someone on the porch to keep an eye out for trouble after the car was torched because of a disagreement about child rearing. On the night of the firebombing, the lookout was a young teenage boy. He saw someone approach the house at about 3:00 in the morning and throw a bomb through the front window. The fire spread so fast that only Radames escaped. Mrs. Santiago, the three Santiago children, and a child who was staying with them were unable to escape. The house was destroyed, and two neighboring houses were badly damaged. The police quickly arrested a mentally disabled man named Reds Wilkinson and took him in for questioning. Within a day, he'd signed his confession.

The judge threw out that confession during pretrial proceedings. Wilkinson had been tested with a relative third-grade IQ and reading level. During his time in interrogation (which had lasted 20 nightmarish hours) he had been intimidated, threatened, slapped, stomped on, beaten on the knuckles with a blackjack, and made to sign a confession he was not even able to read. The judge ruled that Wilkinson could not have understood a warning, in the unlikely event one had been given, that what he said or signed could be used against him.

Even without Wilkinson's confession, however, the police had the eyewitness statement of the teenage lookout. Something about the case had smelled wrong to many of us long before the trial started. The Puerto Rican community was split over the issue. Some thought that it was better just to let it be: someone was going to be punished for the deaths of five Latinos, and that was something in Philadelphia. Others of us thought that the police had arrested someone who was convenient, just to close the case. We felt that the wrong guy stood accused. Those of us who felt this way started raising money for an independent investigation. I was the spokesman for the Coalition for Justice, a group of community organizations interested in seeing justice done. I tried to keep pressure up on the case, and I met again with Fitzpatrick, the Philadelphia district attorney, who had promised to keep me abreast of any developments. He assured me that he would welcome any additional evidence our investigation could provide.

The case, as it turned out, was open-and-shut. Reds Wilkinson was quickly convicted and sent to prison in 1976. A short while later, his lawyer, Bob Matthews, came to see me at the SMA office. Matthews had seen me in my capacity as spokesman for the Coalition for Justice, and we knew each other a bit. But as he stood in the doorway and looked me over, he wasn't looking at me as a friend or even an acquaintance. He was considering me, I suppose, or performing a quick evaluation. Then he said "Nelson, God has told me that you can help me with this case." I had never had a better recommendation, so I thought I better listen.

Matthews went over the whole case. He, too, felt an overall sense of wrongness about the night of the firebombing and about the arrest, the confession, the eyewitness report, and the trial. But there were some surprising developments that no one outside of the case knew about. Besides Wilkinson, Matthews told me, a man named McGinnis had also confessed, and, like Wilkinson's confession, his too had been thrown out. In this instance, however, the physical recording of the confession had been thrown into a trashcan. McGinnis had been arrested and charged with a crime, but the charge was for setting fire to the Santiago station wagon. The police had destroyed the evidence. Why? We didn't know. Matthews said that even though the kid who had been posted as lookout had identified Wilkinson, other witnesses had said someone else had thrown the bottle through the window of the house. I said I'd see what I could do.

I went to see Richard Sprague, a big player in the Philadelphia legal community, and asked him to look into the case and to review the files. Sprague had worked as chief counsel for a select committee tasked by the House of Representatives to investigate the murders of John F. Kennedy and Martin Luther King Jr. He agreed to take a look, but when I went back to Fitzpatrick to ask him to provide the files, he gave me a flat no. District attorneys never want to re-examine their convictions, and he said what they usually say: that the trial was over, that a man was paying his debt, and that justice had been served. Besides that, he said, there was no way that he would allow Sprague to have access to the files, nor would he let Sprague talk to anyone involved with the case: not the police, not anyone in jail, just nobody. It seemed like a lot of bluster from Fitzpatrick, as though he was trying to scare me off or divert my attention, talking as if the issue were grandstanding attorneys swooping in and making a big splash in the papers and making his life difficult. But I was growing more confident that Matthews was right, that we who, from the beginning, had suspected that something was off about this case had been right, and that this was an egregious railroading, even by the standards of 1975 Philadelphia law enforcement.

David Marston was the U.S. attorney for the Eastern District of Pennsylvania at the time, and a good man even if he was a Republican from Tennessee. I knew him well enough to speak with him about the case, but I wrote him a formal civil rights complaint in a letter, on behalf of the Latino community, requesting that he look into the case. He agreed to do so, and Fitzpatrick had no way to prevent it. A few months later he called me. He had reviewed the evidence and, he said, the biggest inconsistency lay in the statements and testimony of the lookout kid, whose name was, incidentally, Nelson. Marston suggested that I go talk with him. I asked Juan Ramos, head of the Young Lords, to go with me to the kid's house. He lived on a Puerto Rican block in North Philadelphia, and by this time, many of those in the Puerto Rican community who had just wanted someone, anyone, to pay for the Santiagos' deaths, were not happy that I was re-examining the case. They were upset with me, because what I was doing was risky. At least someone had been held responsible. As I picked away at that conviction, I risked vacating it, and what if Wilkinson was set free and no one was ever made to answer for it? Ramos drove me up to see the boy and stayed with me throughout the visit.

It was clear to me that the young man was nervous the moment I sat down with him. Nelson Garcia, all of 14 years old, was itchy. He could hardly sit still. I tried to put him at ease, telling him that my name was Nelson, too, and that I was not there to get him in trouble. I said I'd look out for him, but I had to ask him some questions. I told him that several people had reviewed the case, and when we looked at his testimony and reviewed what he had said to the police, we couldn't see how it was possible that he could have seen who threw the firebomb. I waited for him to answer.

He burst into tears. Yes, not only was something clearly wrong; it was critically important that we make everything official. He had something to say, and I wanted to be sure it would be admissible, so I called Marston and asked him to call Richard Furia, a classmate of mine from Temple, and assign him as the kid's lawyer and to send a court reporter out to the Garcia house right away. We needed to get Nelson's statement that afternoon. Rick was a good lawyer and he arrived first. While we waited for the stenographer, Rick, who was having back trouble at the time, lay on the floor, and from there secured immunity for Nelson. The stenographer took down his statement.

Nelson told us that while the house was still smoldering, the police started applying pressure on him, telling him that Reds Wilkinson had been in the area and hadn't he seen Reds Wilkinson? They called him Reds because of his red hair. Hadn't the kid seen a flash of red hair, caught in the streetlight or the match light, just before the firebomb hit the window? So wasn't the person who threw the firebomb through the window Reds Wilkinson? It was Reds wasn't it? Wasn't it, kid?

The Philadelphia police in 1975 rarely seemed more interested in doing detective work than in just leaning on and threatening witnesses, and then beating confessions out of whatever poor sap was convenient. Young Nelson was the witness, and Wilkinson had been the sap. The boy's statement was the thread that unraveled the whole case. Bob Matthews was right, and so was David Marston. As the conviction fell apart, it was hard to believe all of the things we found out. Not only had McGinnis confessed but other witnesses had implicated him, and all of that evidence had been disregarded because McGinnis was connected to a Democratic ward leader in the neighborhood. Those connections could buy you a lot in those days, but perhaps never as much as in this instance, when small-time political expediency and cronyism outweighed the innocent lives of four children and a mother. It was a stunning miscarriage of justice, even for Philadelphia.

Wilkinson had been railroaded to protect McGinnis. It was as plain as could be. He was released from prison, but only after 15 months. Matthews sued the city for violating Wilkinson's civil rights and won damages. Six Philadelphia homicide detectives were indicted by a federal grand jury for their actions in the case, which went all the way to the Supreme Court. All were convicted and sentenced to 15 months in federal prison.

Justice was served, but racial violence continued in the city. Perhaps as a reprisal for the firebombing, or perhaps only because the poor kid found himself on the wrong block at the wrong time, not long after the Santiago fire-bombing case was wrapped up, a white teenager named Daly was beaten to death by a group of Puerto Rican boys wielding baseball bats. I knew that if no one did anything about it, more violence would come. It would probably come anyway, but I felt that someone had to speak up and ask everyone to stop and think for a moment.

Back in the 1970s, local radio affiliates would provide air time for a short editorial by someone in the community. So, between the news and late-night programming, I presented my plea for peace. Violence begat violence, retaliation only led to further retaliation and escalation, and the cycle would not end. After presenting, I got some blowback from the Puerto Rican community, who thought that I was taking up for the white kid. Well, of course I was. What had happened to him was terrible. He'd been beaten to death. I tried to explain that I didn't want anyone to be killed, white, black, or brown. I asked the white community directly for peace, to not in turn kill one of ours. The whole thing had to end.

My editorial wouldn't solve racial issues in Philadelphia, but I knew I had a responsibility to lend my voice and my abilities to the struggle whenever I could. And I would look for opportunities to learn and grow wherever I could. My best-laid plans kept being scuttled, so I might as well do the next right thing and not plan too far ahead. I wasn't going to be an accountant. I wasn't going back to New York, and even if I did, my family wouldn't be there. After three years of law school, I wasn't even a practicing attorney anymore.

So in 1975 when I came across a brochure about the White House Fellowship program, I thought, "Let's see." I applied for it. Like just about every other Latino in the United States, I had been aware of the young Mexican American Henry Cisneros and his work with the Nixon administration and his time as a White House Fellow. He'd used his experience in the White House as a launching pad to go on to bigger and better things. Not many Mexican Americans had been a White House Fellow, but no Puerto Rican had, so why not see how far I could go?

To my surprise, I was selected as a regional finalist. But then I didn't make the cut. I was disappointed, but I was busy. I had more than enough to keep me occupied in the coming year. I had joined the board of the Puerto Rican Legal Defense and Education Fund. I was filing lawsuits, too, one against the election board for bilingual election materials, and one against the school district for bilingual education—an issue very dear to me. I had continuing work on the 5th Street business corridor and the Bloque de Oro and dealings with the Archdiocese of Philadelphia. The Bicentennial was coming, and the SMA was opening a new restaurant, called Meson Don Quijote, in Society Hill near Jimmy Tayoun's Middle East restaurant. Like Middle East, which had belly dancers, Meson Don Quijote offered professional flamenco—I don't remember the guitar player's name, but he played while Julia Lopez danced. We were helping member merchants open Pupo Supermarkets, the first Latino-owned supermarket in the city. The other big project—still in the pipeline when I left the SMA—included plans for a cash-and-carry warehouse. And on top of it all, I had ongoing community advocacy responsibilities and a bilingual column in the *Sunday* and *Evening Bulletin*.

So, I was satisfied that I had applied for the White House Fellowship and that, though I'd made it far in the process, it was not for me. But then I ran into the great Judge Clifford Scott Green, who had chaired the Philadelphia panel of the White House Fellowship selection committee. We were on the Temple campus for a board meeting of Temple-LEAP, the legal education program for middle and high school students that teaches the law through discussions of democracy and citizenship. He told me that he'd been disappointed that I hadn't gone through. He said that one of the members of the selection committee had, on her own, shot down my chances. Ethel Allen was a member of the Philadelphia City Council and a colorful character. She referred to herself as a "B.F.R." which stood for "black female Republican." She had been a practicing osteopath who liked to tell stories about her "house calls in the ghetto." In one story, she was lured to a house under false pretenses and found herself surrounded by four men aiming to take the drugs they hoped she had in her bag. All she had that they'd get was her gun, which she took out and waved around. She would go on in 1976 to give a speech at the Republican National Convention in support of Gerald Ford, but in 1975, she still wielded enough influence to take me out of the running. According to Judge Green, she referred to me as "too ethnic."

I couldn't believe it, but Allen was a strange one. In 1979 she would join Governor Dick Thornburgh's cabinet in Harrisburg as his secretary of the Commonwealth. And, not even a year later, she would be fired for missing more than 20 workdays in a single 40-day period, and for taking honorariums for speeches that other state employees had written. The governor asked her to resign and she refused, so he fired her.

But back in 1976, I was furious. Judge Green urged me to reapply for the following year in the hope of getting a fairer shot, and I said I would, but my plan was to reapply and then bring a lawsuit that would change the way applications for the White House Fellowship were reviewed. The fact that I could be turned down because of something as blatantly racist as being "too ethnic" was a travesty, and I was eager to take it on.

But I was never able to, because on my 30th birthday, I was interviewed and selected as a White House Fellow.

7

WHITE HOUSE FELLOWSHIP, RUNNING FOR JUDGE

The White House

I HAD SOMEHOW MANAGED to throw a monkey wrench into things again. After reapplying for the White House Fellowship and expecting to be passed over again, I'd been selected as a finalist. I was invited to spend the weekend in Washington interviewing with the Fellowship commissioners. The program got started on a Friday morning. All the finalists were to get on the bus at the Civil Service Commission's parking lot in downtown Washington for a trip to Airlie House, an extravagant conference center in the northern Virginia countryside.

We were still living in New Jersey then and I rose early, before the sun, to drive down for a long weekend of grilling by government types. The interviews would be a whole new experience in a different arena than what I was used to. I wasn't sure what a politician or lifelong civil servant would be looking for in a candidate, or what types of answers they'd best respond to. I had to keep reminding myself that I didn't even want to be selected: I wanted to go through the process and be turned down so I could sue them.

I was in a hurry that morning. Even though I'd risen early, I still felt as though I was late. Two portentous things happened on my trip to D.C. from New Jersey, a good omen and a bad one. First, I was pulled over and ticketed for speeding. Sitting on the side of the highway, waiting for the trooper to write me up, I worried I'd miss the bus. I'd been speeding, which might end up making me late. It didn't seem like a good sign. Why did I always seem to get in my own way? But then I got back on the road and, crossing the Maryland border, I saw a rainbow appear over the highway. It looked as though I would drive right under it on my way to the interview, as if the hidden gateway to the Promised Land had revealed itself. I didn't know what to make of it all or what I wanted or, really, what good luck or bad luck might be in this strange situation.

The bus was still there when I pulled into the parking lot. I parked and ran to board as it sat idling, the last person to get on. Landis Jones, the director of the Fellowship program, was standing by the door waiting, and I took the first open seat I saw, next to Martha Darling. She sat quietly and didn't say a thing, just drank her Diet Coke. The bus pulled out almost as soon as I sat down, taking 30 finalists for their weekend of high-level, high-stakes interrogation. The place had a pool and some lovely grounds you could walk. It even had skeet shooting. I'd never seen anything like it. I got to my room and met my roommate, a double-amputee banker from Dallas and veteran of the Vietnam War. We got along well, and I helped him out in a room and a place that wasn't very easy to get around in if you were in a wheelchair. He was an impressive guy, and I remember watching him swim in the pool with confidence and ease.

The interviews started soon after we arrived and ran all through the weekend. The 30 commissioners, all appointed by the president, would pair up and interview each of us individually. The interviews were intense but not unfriendly. During down time, the candidates would swim or go skeet shooting. I did neither. I sat by the pool sometimes or went to my room. I never shot at the clay pigeons. Having a loaded gun in my hands, shooting at a moving target flying across the sky, and among a highly competitive group of men also handling loaded weapons and for whom I was a rival, seemed like more potential danger than I needed to invite into the weekend.

The interviews were a blur. There were 15 in all. I met a few commissioners who would become great allies during my year in Washington and beyond: Ada Deer from Wisconsin, who had helped restore her Menominee tribe to official federal recognition; Vicente Ximenez, founder of GI Forum and the first Latino undersecretary of state during the Lyndon Johnson administration; and Julia Taft, who worked in the State Department and whose husband was a nephew of President William Howard Taft's. The one interview I remember most distinctly was the one I missed. I had been up late the night before helping my roommate and had fallen asleep during a break the following morning. I missed meeting with two commissioners, and one of them was John Gardner, the former chairman of the Carnegie Corporation, who had approached President Johnson in the 1960s with the very idea of the President's Commission for White House Fellows and who now chaired it. I couldn't have made a worse impression with a more important person. I assumed that I had ruined my chances for consideration, but apparently I did not. Rather than chalk me up as a no-show who lacked the drive or the organizational skills to keep to a simple schedule, they asked me to meet them over lunch.

Monday was my birthday. It was May 23, 1977, and we were all bussed back to Washington, where we filed into a big auditorium at the offices of the Civil Service Commission, which is now called the Office of Personnel Management. We didn't know how many of us would be selected, but I assumed about half of us would make it through. All 30 of us were given envelopes, thanked for our time, and excused. We left the auditorium and dispersed to find a little corner of the building where we could open our envelopes in private, where our glee wouldn't make us any enemies, and our disappointment could be nursed alone. I found a vacant stretch of hallway and opened mine. To my great surprise, I had been accepted.

I didn't know how to feel. I hadn't expected to be chosen, nor had I intended to be. I couldn't even say that I'd hoped to be. I had gone through the motions with the intention of getting a sense of the process, so that I could use it as ammunition for a lawsuit in which I would force them to change their selection process. I called Vilma and told her that the good news was I had been given a great honor and had been selected as a White House Fellow. The bad news was the lawsuit was a nonstarter and it was time to start packing.

We needed to make preparations for another abrupt turn in my life. The Spanish Merchants Association (SMA) would need a new executive director. I hoped to leave the association to the competent and professional Bill Salas. Bill knew what needed to be done and everyone knew that he could do it. But he didn't think he was cut out to lead, because he hated the politics and the glad-handing. He was an earnest man and he was deeply uncomfortable about all the diplomacy he thought the job would entail. He felt he lacked whatever one needed—the stomach, perhaps—for all the backslapping and flattery and posing for photos.

Instead, Bill would start a shoe business with his wife and the SMA would turn the reins over to Guadalberto Medina, also known as Gil, the hot-tempered Temple Law grad whom I had helped get out of trouble for firebombing a bank. Gil was very smart, but he didn't have the same commitment to the SMA that Bill had, or that I and the other board members had, and he made some missteps that would bring the SMA to an end.

But no one suspected that then. At the time all I did was relinquish my directorship and turn my attention to moving to D.C. just as I was growing accustomed to Philadelphia as my home. I planned to return after a year in the capital, equipped with the knowledge I had gained and a broadened perspective that a national point of view would provide me. There were many ways to honor the lasting advice Peter Liacouras had given me after I graduated law school: "Finish what you started." My friend Bob Garcia, a New York state senator, would also advise me that my experience would best be put to use in my own backyard.

I had known Bob since I was a teenager in West Harlem and he was an assemblyman from the Bronx. His sister Aimee Cortes was a prominent preacher with a trio of daughters who sang at her service, and she took me to his house in the Bronx to see whether he could give me some guidance. We hit it off immediately and I considered him a mentor ever after. I'd go to his fundraisers, and when we were protesting for changes at Temple, he came down to meet with students, and Peter Liacouras had him address an assembly. More than once when we had seminars for our client owners at the SMA, Bob came to speak.

At 30 years old I would be one of the youngest White House Fellows, a fact that figured prominently in my preparations. Just as when I met Charlie Bowser at the protest for Julio Osorio, I was young and, more to the point, still foolish. I had demands that I felt needed to be met. The best assignments to get in the Fellowship program were the ones that could best advance a career. Those positions were found in the agencies, such as the Department of Treasury or the Department of Justice. One could make good connections in an agency and go on to a lucrative future among the movers and shakers. But, young and bull-headed, I had other ideas. Reporters who came to interview me were simply looking for a little enthusiasm and a quick quotation to round out their "Local Boy Makes Good" pieces that were due later in the afternoon. But they got a brash and naïve youngish man and his conditions. I told the press that if I wasn't assigned to the vice president, I wasn't even going to accept the Fellowship. Unbeknownst to me, I would not know what my assignment would be till late August, after all the White House Fellows had spent a week interviewing in the areas where we had asked—not demanded, mind you—to be placed.

By the time I would learn what my assignment was, I would already have resigned my position at the SMA, rented out my house in Mt. Holly, signed a lease on a five-bedroom apartment in the cushy Virginia suburb of Alexandria, and enrolled my kids—Vilmarie, now eight; Nelson, six; and Delia Lee, five—in schools in Virginia. But I suppose I just liked the sound of my own bravado.

The second round of interviews for assignment was coupled with an orientation program, and the whole dizzying process was off to a bad start when I couldn't find my car at the end of the first day. D.C. is an easy city to get disoriented in, and after walking around well into the evening, I finally called the police to report my car stolen. I found it when an officer drove me along the route I'd taken in that morning. I thanked him sheepishly and drove back to my hotel. But not even the panic of a lost car and the embarrassment upon finding it could change the fact that I was now on staff at the White House, a reality so surprising that I had trouble believing it. During that orientation week I got to meet the man I had demanded to work for, Walter Mondale, and his chief of staff, Dick Moe, his deputy chief of staff, Michael Berman, and Jim Johnson, the administrative attaché who would be at almost every meeting and on almost every trip. These were Mondale's people, the Minnesota Insiders, his most trusted advisers. They knew their roles and they knew what Fritz—as all who knew him came to call him—wanted and what he needed. It was impressive to meet a group that functioned so well as a team, all working to give the vice president and his agenda the best chance of succeeding. During that first interview, I gathered from Mondale himself that he wanted me to learn and to expand my horizons, so that I could go out and do great things in my next position. From his team I came to understand that if I was going to work in the Office of the Vice President, my success would be measured by how well I supported him. But the fact that I was impressed didn't mean I wasn't also a little arrogant—arrogant in my ignorance of how much I would learn that year and how much Mondale had to teach me. In that meeting he asked me some very simple questions about my background, my interest in bilingual education, my law experience. Besides the Office of the Vice President, I can't remember what other departments I requested or how those interviews went, but I remember how close those men seemed. Moe and Johnson had worked with Mondale since his days as attorney general in Minnesota, and they knew him well. Berman used to shine Mondale's shoes and get him books to read. He was kind of a Guy Friday, and as silly as some of it seemed, as demeaning as working in the White House only to shine the vice president's shoes appeared to be, I would come to see that he was indispensable. He understood Mondale, and he knew his needs. I learned how important it was for people in power to have people they could trust. That was how things worked in Washington and probably the world over.

Mondale was an interesting character. He had been a protégé of the elder statesman of Minnesota politics Hubert Humphrey, who had helped create the Minnesota Democratic-Farmer-Labor Party in the 1940s and served as Johnson's vice president. Mondale had been Minnesota's attorney general when Humphrey was one of the state's senators, and he was appointed to Humphrey's vacated seat in 1964, where he served until 1976. Mondale had sponsored the Fair Housing Act and created the Office of Fair Housing and Equal Opportunity in the Department of Housing and Urban Development (HUD), which made him something of a hero to me.

He had turned down George McGovern when asked to join the ticket as vice president, but Mondale was ready when Jimmy Carter invited him aboard. Carter was something of an outsider and needed a well-known and well-respected running mate. The Washington establishment found it easy to dismiss the former governor of Georgia as a bit of a lightweight with his peanut-farmer persona and his easy smile and his accent. I thought Carter was brilliant and always impressively prepared. I remember a cabinet meeting that year during which, rather than ask HUD secretary Patricia Harris about the ins and outs of her department's budget numbers and units, he rattled them off himself from memory.

Loyalty was Mondale's most distinguishing feature, as far as I was concerned. But he wasn't foolish, and he didn't offer his loyalty without its being earned. Before joining the Carter ticket, Mondale had spoken to his mentor, Humphrey, who, like Mondale, had been selected by a southern politician to shore up the northern vote. But Humphrey's experience as vice president had been difficult and lonely. He had not gotten along with Johnson and often had felt frozen out of the proceedings. Humphrey told Mondale to write up a contract, before accepting the

With President Jimmy Carter on the White House lawn during Hispanic Heritage Month, enjoying one of the first public events I attended as a White House Fellow. Vice President Walter Mondale is in the center background.

position, that defined what the vice president's role would be. It was an unprecedented step, but Mondale took Humphrey's advice and went on to fundamentally change the vice presidency. He was the first vice president to have his office in the West Wing of the White House, where all vice presidents have been ever since. Before the Carter administration, the vice president's offices were next door in the Old Executive Office, which is now called the Eisenhower Building. Mondale also instituted a weekly lunch meeting with the president—a tradition that has been carried on—and he was involved in all discussions with the president's chief of staff. Mondale learned well from Humphrey's experience as an isolated figurehead with a big title and almost no responsibility. He transformed the role of vice president from a handshake in a blue suit to an integral part of the administration, a key adviser and protector of the president's agenda and his reputation. And he rewarded President Carter's acceptance of this new role, too, and never tried to upstage him or act like a usurper. When Carter took a vacation, Mondale could have stayed in Washington and effectively been in command, but that's when he'd head back to Minnesota to go ice-fishing or take some other trip.

Despite all of my missteps, I got the assignment I'd hoped for, and in September my family picked up and moved to the nation's capital. A friend, Al Solivan, the only Puerto Rican I ever met with that name, had suggested the big apartment we rented in Alexandria. Al had lived in the complex during his stint in the nation's capital. Though he had a hook for a hand, he was a tremendous cook and would invite the whole apartment complex when he made paella by the swimming pool. The complex was right off of I-395, just over the bridge coming out of D.C., on Van Dorn Street. It was full of transplants, and the schools were full of their kids. School in Virginia was not easy for my three little ones, and they would have a few encounters that reminded us that we were Latinos living south of the Mason-Dixon Line. Reminding ourselves that we would be there for just a year helped. Vilma had left her teaching job in Philadelphia and stayed home to take care of them, and she got them through. For her own support, she joined a group of wives of White House Fellows.

Seventeen of us had been selected to the Fellowship. We were a very young, very white, very male group. Five were Vietnam veterans. I was the only Latino and the first Puerto Rican in the program, even if I was a Nuyorican. I was also in some respects the least experienced and least prepared. I had never worked in politics and had no experience working on the staff of an administration. Many of the other Fellows were much more comfortable in this environment, and on September 1, our first official day, they hit the ground running. They seemed to approach the Fellowship the same way they would approach any professional situation: as a competition and not a cooperative effort in which we would all pull together for the best results. But in some respects my inexperience in this area had brought me to the White House in the first place. John Gardner knew what my background was—he had sacrificed his lunch hour to hear all about my time in public service—and he saw the Fellowship as an opportunity for me to gain a broader perspective. Doing so would require a steep learning curve, but Lyndon Johnson had founded the Fellowship on the belief that "a genuinely free society cannot be a spectator society," and the more that society's leaders know about democracy and how government works, the better. Gardner and the director of the White House Fellowship, Landis Jones, were taking a chance in order to give my advocacy a national perspective.

That first day when I received my assignment to the staff of the vice president, I also received an office, a desk, and an assistant. My assistant would prove to be more than competent, my office would always be small and always right by the copy room, but my desk was a story unto itself. The desk was nothing particularly special, but when I opened the drawer, I saw right there, scratched in the tray, "Richard Nixon." At first, I thought it was someone's idea of a joke, but I learned that it was tradition on Capitol Hill to put your name in your desk, and that I was actually using the desk Nixon had used when he was vice president. It hadn't been even four years since he had resigned, and the shame of Watergate was still a visceral wound in Washington, especially there in the White House, and nobody wanted anything to do with anything Nixon had touched. The desk had likely come over from the Old Executive Building when Mondale brought the vice president's office into the White House. And it fell to me in my little office by the copy room. I spent a year working at the desk that had once held the hopes of a vice president before he became a national disgrace.

I was assigned to cover charities and urban, Latino, veterans, homelessness, and Native American issues. I was tasked with answering all correspondence, preparing talking points, memos, and speeches, and staffing all meetings in those areas. I was also expected to attend all budget meetings and presentations on urban issues in the Office of Management and Budget and to keep the Office of the Vice President up-to-date on any new developments. Urban affairs was a new area of concern at the federal level. President Carter had formed the Commission on Urban Policy, and I was Mondale's official representative at those meetings. Also, I often met with HUD. Once I shared a presentation on inner city development at an urban policy conference with some representatives from that department, and I gave a presentation on bilingual education at the National Association of Bilingual Educators Conference in Anaheim, California.

The first few months on the job were frustrating, and at times overwhelming. It took me a while to get used to the new environment and to understand how things worked. But even during those first anxious months, I was very aware of the improbability of my good fortune: here I was, a poor kid from the projects in Harlem, getting paid to provide information and guidance to the vice president of the United States. I was working with people at the highest levels of government. I could barely believe it. If representatives from the Red Cross or the March of

*In conversation with Vice President Walter Mondale,
one of the most respectful people I have ever known, who taught me
a great deal about dignity and loyalty.*

Dimes were coming in, I'd prepare talking points for the vice president
and organize the meetings. All my work went through his speechwriter
and the deputy chief of staff.

This was the big time. If the vice president was going to speak at the
Urban League, I would review what Urban League president Vernon
Jordan had to say in his most recent public remarks. I would find out
what the Urban League hoped to hear from the vice president, prepare
something accordingly, and run it up the chain. My work would be there
for Mondale to use, if he wanted. Mondale was an experienced and skillful speaker, so sometimes he'd change things on the fly, using as much
or as little of the prepared text as he deemed necessary. But my draft was
there if he needed it.

When Mondale spoke at a Latino event in California, I was charged
with drafting the talking points. In doing so, I drew on the words of
Father Patricio Flores, a Mexican American priest from San Antonio
whom I had once heard speak. Father Flores, a staunch proponent of the

power of the Latino vote, advocated for bilingual voting information. He would go on to become the first Mexican American bishop in the Catholic Church. Father Flores had only one speech, and he gave it wherever he went. The theme was "Your Voice Is Your Vote," and it was an effective message.

"*El que no habla ni Dios lo oye,*" he'd say, which means if you don't speak, not even God can hear you. So I put those words in Mondale's speech, with a reference to Father Flores, and they worked. They helped connect the vice president to his audience.

At times I was starstruck on the job, but I learned about things I otherwise would never have been aware of (which, I believe, was one of the aspirations of the founders of the Fellowship). I once went to an Office of Management and Budget meeting that I mistakenly thought was on urban policy but that was actually on classified issues, spy satellites and such. Not knowing that those materials were not to leave the room, I took a copy of the budget back to my office, as I always did. Two very serious men came to my door and informed me of the policy and took the copies back. I didn't catch their names or where they were from, but they meant business.

I received a crash course in veterans' issues during that year. I had never served in the military, and I had no idea of the extent of the trauma that had followed soldiers back from Vietnam. So many men my age bore the physical and psychic scars of their time there. Listening to the stories of the veterans I worked with as Fellows and seeing how they comported themselves taught me to feel a great respect for those in the service.

In 1978, Native Americans held a march on Washington. I staffed the event and arranged for a leadership group to meet with Vice President Mondale in the morning. He had many Blackfeet Indian constituents in Minnesota, and he was looking forward to sitting down with them. The time for the meeting came, but the tribal leaders were nowhere to be found. I was mortified by the wait and worried that it reflected poorly on me. I sweated out the hours as morning passed into afternoon. But Mondale never became impatient or upset. The Blackfeet were important constituents, and Mondale knew there was a lot of activity going on during the demonstration. In addition to their being a reliable voting bloc for Mondale, the Blackfeet owned uranium mines and had other commercial dealings. It was worth his time to meet with them. When they did arrive, I was struck by the great respect they showed him. They called him a

"Great White Father" for the support he had given them in Minnesota. And the vice president, as ever, was gracious and kind.

That was his way whenever I was around him. I never saw him raise his voice or dress anyone down. He was always warm and considerate. The people around him felt trusted and that trust inspired deep loyalty. In such a powerful position and with so many responsibilities, Mondale never lost his sense of humanity. He took it as his solemn duty to treat everyone he met with respect.

Mondale was never anything but polite and decent, and he had the kind of grace that made you feel that maybe a little could rub off on you. Sometimes I felt the magic, but at other times I felt nothing but my own human frailty and clumsiness, and no amount of borrowed finesse could keep me from screwing up. I made my share of blunders as a White House Fellow, and I was often shocked by how he handled them. He supported every suggestion I made to him about holding a meeting, no matter the group, including giving me the go-ahead to run a meeting with Hispanic leaders to establish some priorities about the issues we in the Latino community could address. I spent a lot of time working on the attendee list with Vilma Martinez, the president of the Mexican American Legal Defense and Educational Fund, one of the leading civil rights organizations in the Latino community at the time. We pored over the names to make sure the list was comprehensive. Everyone we could think of who deserved a seat at that table had one. The invitations went out and the attendees showed up and the meeting went very well. It felt as though we were at the beginning of a new discussion about education and jobs, as though this could serve as the groundwork for a national Latino agenda. I wanted to reconvene the national Latino leadership group with the vice president himself. He agreed to meet with me and discuss my idea. With our invitation list and our proposed agenda all set, we were scheduled to finalize everything with Mondale, when, on the morning of the meeting, we found out that a Mexican American community leader in Corpus Christi was upset that he hadn't been invited. We hadn't invited him to the first meeting, and he wasn't on the list for the second meeting, either. He was angry enough to yell about his exclusion and the insult of it all and prominent enough to publish his feelings in a Texas newspaper. I caught wind of the editorial and went to Mondale to tell him about it. He listened as I explained my oversight and apologized for the faux pas and offered ideas about how to smooth things over. Nervous and embarrassed, I may have gone on a little long, but he listened and he thanked me for my candor. He then asked me for the invitation list and that was it: no dressing down, no strategizing, nothing but a thank-you and then I was shown out of his office. That was that. As it turned out, Mondale held the follow-up meeting. He attended and listened, and the insulted community leader from Corpus Christi was once again left off the list. I was surprised, but more than that I was deeply moved by what he'd done. He had backed me up in a way that I could not have anticipated. He had subtly and gracefully but firmly shown me his support while delivering a clear message about what you get from the Office of the Vice President when you throw a tantrum.

Another time, I had a discussion with the president of the Labor Council for Latin American Advancement, Hank Lacayo, about the relative scarcity of Latinos working in the federal government. In 1978, the Carter administration had a hundred Latino political appointees, and only a few of them were in senior executive roles in intelligence or defense or any other agencies. After that preliminary discussion I asked the Office of the Vice President for permission to host a full meeting on the issue. Hank and I wanted to see more Latinos admitted to positions in the civil service, and we hoped that Mondale would consider attending our meeting. Latino labor leaders had been trying for a long time to have such a meeting but hadn't yet been able to book it. Mondale was familiar with Hank and he respected his work. He not only agreed to attend the meeting; he set it in the Cabinet Room of the White House, right by the Rose Garden. It was more than we had any reason to expect. After countless failures to secure even a small room to pack into, we had secured a meeting with the vice president in one of the most famous meeting places in the political universe. There we were, sitting and talking as presidents and dignitaries, leaders and diplomats from every corner of the world had sat and talked over the years. Walking into the Cabinet Room and seeing your name at your seat at that table was like joining hands with history itself. That meeting alone established my reputation among Latino labor leaders nationwide.

That year, I took several trips out of the country. In fact, the first time I set foot anywhere off American soil (as well as the second and the third), I did so as a White House Fellow. The first trip was to Mexico for trade negotiations and discussions of gas and oil rights with the administration of Mexican president José Lopez Portillo. The morning we were to leave, I was awakened by two soldiers at my door, rousting me early to get me to *Air Force Two* before the famous blizzard of 1978 dumped three feet of snow on the Eastern Seaboard. The soldiers waited while I dressed and got me to the plane in what was, for me, record time. I joined the vice president as part of his entourage, and along with the commissioner of the Immigration and Naturalization Service, Lionel Castillo, and our security team, we flew out of town just ahead of the storm. We landed in Mexico City, dropped our bags at the hotel, and headed right back out to a beautiful state building, where we sat in an ornate room around a big table to discuss matters of international significance. Castillo and I spent most of the trip together, attending meetings and taking advantage of our down time to visit such places as Garibaldi Plaza, where we had a shot of tequila and paid a mariachi band to play a few songs for us. Castillo also took me for an off-the-record meeting with intellectuals and underground figures in the immigration movement. These were professors and smugglers, community activists and public servants—people who occupied points along a more fluid spectrum of legality than we would ever find at a White House roundtable. Castillo was the head of a federal agency, but he was also a Latino from Houston, and he had enough credibility with these people that they would meet with him to discuss their views on immigration. Castillo was smart, and he thought of immigration as an issue best approached with more tools than simple arrest, detention, and repatriation. To him, immigration was more than a legal issue or a border squabble, and the people were more than their legal status. Because of his openness, he was able to learn what bright people on the Mexican side of the border had to say. The Immigration and Naturalization Service, an agency defined by the last word in its name, has become Immigration and Customs Enforcement, an agency that continues to identify with the last word in its name.

When we got back to the hotel, we each found in our rooms an invitation to a state dinner at Los Pinos, President Lopez Portillo's residence. The dinner was about to begin, and we were going to be late, but we rushed back out and made it in time to avoid insulting our hosts. I'd never experienced anything like that dinner, a table full of luminaries and everyone so well dressed—military leaders with their medals sparkling on their dress uniforms and women in formal gowns, the crystal and silver gleaming on the table, the food, the entertainment, the company, the room itself. Everything that happened that evening was imbued with a sense of grandeur, and I had to keep telling myself that, yes,

I was actually listening to the president of Mexico as he held forth, and, yes, I really was laughing along with the vice president of the United States as he gracefully and aptly responded. How was it that I had come to be a part of this?

Before we headed back to the snows of Washington, D.C., Mondale took us to Chapultepec to tour the 5,000-year-old Mayan ruins. The visit gave me an overwhelming sense of history. I had always thought of Western civilization as being 500 years old, but here was something far older. I walked around these strange and beautiful structures and up the steep steps. I could see the intricate carvings that had survived through millennia and all these signs of a culture that had encompassed more than just beliefs and art; it had been advanced enough to create cities. Visiting the ruins was like stumbling into ancient Egypt or something from a distant time yet disorientingly near, right next door to the United States. The world was growing larger for me, or deeper, and I was beginning to see beyond my own experience on the East Coast in the 20th century. From then on, travel became a kind of compulsion, and I took every opportunity to travel wherever I could to learn about the world, to see every possible part of this planet: the Middle East, the Far East, Europe, and South America. I stopped for only a year, after being arrested in the Soviet Union for meeting with Refuseniks.

I jumped at the chance for another official visit when the White House was organizing a fact-finding trip to Panama as President Carter negotiated to hand over control of the Panama Canal to the country it cut through. Actually, it would turn out to be two visits to learn about the issues facing those in the Canal Zone and the needs and wishes of the Panamanian government and its people. The United States had controlled the canal since finishing construction of it in 1914, but it was expensive to defend and the cost of expanding it would be exorbitant. Ships were growing ever larger and, if it was not widened and deepened, the canal would soon be unusable.

Carter's plan was simple and obvious—just return the area to the Panamanians—but that plan was receiving a lot of criticism in the United States. How could the tiny backward nation of Panama possibly handle a passage so crucial to international trade? Surely Panamanians lacked the intelligence and the sophistication to be left in charge of something so consequential to international trade. Their leader, General Omar Torrijos, was seen as little more than a military strongman, and he was described on the record in Congress as a drug addict. At the heart of the objection, it seemed to me, were an anxiety about losing something valuable and a very familiar strain of racism. I would soon meet with Americans in Panama, who, faced with the loss of their impossibly luxurious lifestyle, seethed with resentment.

On that first trip to Panama I went as a member of the entourage of Abelardo Valdez, or Lalo as he was known, an ambassador in the State Department. (Lalo is a great man and a good friend whom I have loved dearly since he invited me to a fantastic restaurant in D.C. during my first week at the White House. He was the first person in Washington to invite me out to dinner for a meal that I would never have been able to afford on my own. He has been my good friend ever since.) We met with canal operators, with residents of the Canal Zone, and with Lalo's counterpart in the Panamanian government. We brought our findings back for the White House to use in a public information campaign.

I took a second trip to Panama, in which all the White House Fellows and the executive director, Landis Jones, joined State Department officials on a fact-finding mission. That trip was memorable for many reasons, not the least of which was a thrilling helicopter ride through the Canal Zone. We zoomed over that narrow stretch of land that held two oceans apart, and I saw it laid out beneath me in one breathtaking view, delicate and mighty like the fingers of God and Adam touching.

My breath was taken away again when we were invited to the home of an American doctor working in the Canal Zone. He and his family lived in a mansion situated on a private golf course, his kids went to private schools for the children of American expatriates, and his house was cleaned and his grounds maintained by cheap Panamanian labor. His life was one of opulence and beauty, and, boy, was he mad. He invited us in and, after dispensing with the pleasantries, went on a tirade about how stupid the Panamanians were, how ill-equipped to run the canal, feckless, useless, unable to even operate the equipment. I found his shocking mixture of condescension, racial animus, and petulant rage more than I could stomach, and so I walked out of his house. I'd made a scene, and the other Fellows were angry that I'd left them in the awkward aftermath, but it would have been worse had I stayed. And while they blamed me for the situation, I saw it differently. I saw leaving as the most dignified response to such ignorance, regardless of how wealthy the source. They were unhappy with me then, but soon they would be very glad to have me along when our trucks broke down in the middle of nowhere.

Panama is two coastal cities, Colon and Panama City, at either end of the canal, with a lot of country all around and a little in between. We were in two trucks heading from Panama City on the one coast to Colon on the other, on a rough stretch in that little bit of country in the middle. The terrain was rocky. At times it was unclear whether we were on any kind of road at all. Both trucks were getting badly beaten up, bottoming out and bouncing around till both of them broke down. It turned out that their undercarriages had been gashed and their oil pans had ripped open. These trucks weren't taking us anywhere. As the only Spanish speaker in the group, I struck out in search of help. We had passed a farm not too far back, so I headed off on foot. When I reached the farm, the farmer greeted me kindly. I told him what had happened, and he offered me soup for everyone and his truck to take us back to Panama City. It was not a quick negotiation. He wasn't driving any kind of bargain; it was just that things can move slowly in the country. When I finally got back to the broken-down trucks with the soup and the good news, I told them that all I'd had to do was offer B. J. Hawkins, who had been a professor at UCLA and was working on her Ph.D. before accepting her Fellowship, in trade. I don't believe she ever forgave me.

The negotiations for the canal went well, too, and Panama and the United States agreed to a gradual handover, to be completed in 1999. The canal has been a great boon to the Panamanian economy, and none of the predicted disasters occurred, even though brown people have been operating the canal for 40 years.

The most lasting lesson I learned as a White House Fellow gave me a deeper understanding of what leadership and public service look like, and it was Walter Mondale who taught it to me. Sometimes you get applause and glory as a public figure, but many times your role presents you with a choice between easy-but-wrong and right-but-terrible. We were flying to Los Angeles on *Air Force Two*—the vice president, President Carter's chief of staff Hamilton Jordan, and a typical entourage—to plan a birthday celebration for the president. We received news in flight that President Carter had just entered into an agreement with the Saudi Arabian government to sell the country U.S. fighter jets. The political environment we had expected when we took off from the East Coast would no longer be awaiting us when we landed on the West Coast. At the planning meeting, Mondale would be facing several representatives of the Jewish community just as they had learned about a deal between the United States and an avowed antagonist of Israel.

Mondale appeared to have three choices. He could just cancel the event, turn the plane around, and go back home and let President Carter answer what questions would come in about the deal. He could just preside over the planning meeting and try to ward off questions from an angry group of constituents. Or he could cancel the planning meeting and meet the Jewish community to discuss what had happened.

Naturally, Mondale was upset. He'd been blindsided. He had had no idea that the president was negotiating with the Saudis. Carter had given him no warning that anything like this was developing, but Mondale kept cool. He spoke at some length with Jordan—a political wunderkind and a man only a few years older than I was. He could have inferred that Jordan knew more than he had but had withheld the information. I certainly did, but Mondale saw the bigger picture, in which Jordan's loyalty to his president had required him to keep quiet. Mondale made the honorable decision that he would stand up in front of an angry constituency as a representative of the Office of the President of the United States and answer their questions. He and Jordan spent the rest of the flight hammering out their talking points. They sent out an announcement that the birthday planning meeting was canceled, and after we landed, we went to a big auditorium, where Mondale stood up and took the brunt of the Jewish community's anger and bemusement. He answered their questions as best he could, but there was nothing he could say to change their minds, which he knew as soon as he heard about the sale of the planes. No one went into that auditorium happy, and no one left happy, either. Mondale, however, was loyal, and he absorbed a lot of punishment for his president with no hope of thanks. Nobody thanks the punching bag for taking a beating, and nobody who might have been unfair apologizes. Mondale was a loyal man, and he served accordingly, knowing that sometimes being yelled at and cursed is exactly what your job is.

Washington in general, and the White House in particular, was a cutthroat environment, but I served in the light of Walter Mondale's beneficence. I counted myself almost singularly lucky. Inside the White House I worked with a decent and honorable vice president, while outside, in D.C., I found the Latino community very welcoming and supportive. I tried to advocate for the issues we all believed were important, and working side by side with good people, I cemented lifelong friendships with people whose help over the years had a profound and lasting effect on me and determined the course of my life.

Henry Cisneros was one of those people. I had admired him from afar long before I got to the White House. He had been a trailblazer in the White House Fellowship program, and his star continued to rise after he left. Henry was still a guiding light for me while I was in the Fellowship program. When I began to feel overwhelmed, as I very quickly did, I picked up the phone and called him down in San Antonio. He was a city councilman then, but he would take the time to speak with me and he always gave me good guidance. We stayed in touch and he continued to be supportive when I got back to Philadelphia, and once he was appointed secretary of HUD, he would offer me a job whenever we spoke.

I became good friends with Hank Lacayo through our work together in the White House. He, too, would serve as a mentor, and he connected me with the big Latino labor leaders. Hank also introduced me to his sister Carmela, a nun who was vice chair of the Democratic National Committee, the first Latina to be named to that post. To this day, Carmela has remained a strong connection and a rock of stability. She was CEO of the National Association for Hispanic Elderly—a position she still holds—and Hank asked me to serve on her board. I am still there. For decades the association has brought jobs to elderly people looking for work in North Philadelphia. Once Carmela got to know me and learned of my interest in bilingual education, she introduced me to a few advocates, including a sharp young man named Federico Peña. Federico was out in Denver, working with the Chicano Education Project to secure the president's support for the reauthorization of bilingual education. We met and he provided me with some language that could be used for the bill. I forwarded it with a letter to Joseph Califano, the secretary of education. Not long after that, President Carter mentioned it in his State of the Union address. That language became part of a bill that soon after passed into law.

Another Latino who came to see me was a man I'd known before—Juan Ramos from the Young Lords. When he didn't show up on time for our arranged meeting in my office in the White House, I thought perhaps he was just late, but after waiting an hour, I went to look for him. I went straight to the security check-in and found him sitting in the waiting room. Security wouldn't clear him to come through, and he wouldn't leave. I raised a fuss until they admitted him, but not without an official escort. Two security guys accompanied us back to my office, and they wouldn't let him out of their sight till I shut the door. They waited there on the other side of the door while Juan and I met inside. At lulls in the conversation I thought I could almost hear them breathing, and when I opened the door again, there they were, ready to escort him out. There must have been a big file on him somewhere. There may still be.

Bob Garcia, now a New York state senator, also re-entered my life during my time in Washington. In November 1977, Ed Koch won the New York City mayoral election, defeating, among others, U.S. Representative Herman Badillo. Koch soon tapped Badillo to be his deputy mayor. Why anyone would give up a seat in the U.S. House of Representatives to become a city's second-in-command was a mystery to many, but I supposed Badillo had a plan. Bob Garcia had been a loyal supporter of Badillo's, and I thought that he should run for the vacated seat. But Bob took some convincing. So did Badillo, it turned out. I called Badillo to ask for his endorsement. Bob, a veteran of the Korean War, had been an electrical engineer at IBM. Trustworthy, honorable, and bright, Bob seemed like a great candidate. And he'd been loyal to Badillo, too, but Badillo was noncommittal. He told me that as a lawyer and accountant, he didn't see anyone in the political landscape smart enough to fill his shoes. So while he wouldn't endorse my friend, it seemed that he wasn't going to throw his name in with any of the other dummies he saw running.

Bob wasn't sure, but he decided at least to look into running for the vacated House seat. It was a crowded field, especially on the Democratic side. Bob was strong on prisons but had little knowledge of such issues as housing or economic development, so I set up briefings for him with HUD to get him up to speed. He was thinking about the position, but he wasn't getting any support. I told him he had to declare that he was running before anyone would bother endorsing him. So he did. And people came out for him. Bob was well-liked in his district, in part because everyone knew he was fair. He treated everyone the same and he was a representative to all in his district. We started holding fundraisers. Representative Charlie Rangel was one of the first big names to endorse him, and eventually Badillo followed.

On Valentine's Day 1978, Bob Garcia, running as a Republican against six Democrats, was elected to the U.S. House of Representatives. He was accepted by the Democratic Caucus, though, and a week later was sworn in as a Democrat. He moved into my big apartment in Virginia that month and lived with us for the rest of our time there. He

At the annual conference of the U.S. Hispanic Leadership Institute (USHLI) in Chicago. From left to right: To my left are Rey Gonzalez, vice chair of USHLI; Jack Otero, AFL-CIO board member; Luis Nuñez, the first national director of Aspira; Mary Gonzalez-Koenig, Chicago community leader; Dolores Huerta, Farm Workers Union co-founder; my longtime friend Henry Cisneros; Carlos Cantu, former chairman and president of ServiceMaster; Juan Andrade, founder and CEO of USHLI; and my good friend Hank Lacayo, United Automobile Workers political director, and to my right is Luis Alvarez, director of the National Urban Fellows program.

and Hank Lacayo stayed with me through the decades to follow, and together they helped shape the Hispanic Caucus into a force in national politics.

The friends I made in Washington were some of the most loyal people I've ever encountered. Federico Peña worked with me on immigration issues and other political concerns, supporting me whenever I ran for office. And when there was another candidate I asked him to support, he'd get behind that person too. Henry Cisneros helped to develop an important Latino agency I was working with in North Philadelphia. Hank and Carmela Lacayo have supported me in innumerable ways. Carmela has probably prayed for me more than anyone besides my mother, and she has served the community right beside me. Hank helped fund my campaign for judge.

I was even honored a couple of times in Washington when one Latino group or another had a reception for me. I have never forgotten their kindness, but as my year in D.C. was winding down, I was concerned that if I didn't put some kind of a plan in place, I would be not only one of the first Puerto Rican White House Fellows but also one of the last. Just as I would have been unsatisfied with my time at Temple Law if I had graduated and moved on without instituting a process that insured access to more Latino students, I wanted to leave the White House knowing that Latino issues would still have their advocates. I shared my concerns with Judge Jose Cabranes, former ambassador Gabriel Guerra Mondragon, Miriam Cruz, Juan Manuel Pasalaqua, Rick Hernandez, and others. Rick, a Mexican American who hailed from New Mexico, was a political appointee who had a good relationship with President Carter's team in the White House. Rick and I worked with the White House to install a liaison to advocate for Latino issues at the administration. Rick recommended Esteban Torres, who had been an assistant to President Carter before his appointment as ambassador to UNESCO. Torres had been involved in labor and community development before coming to Washington, and under Carter he had acted as a consultant to Congress. He was well respected and welcomed to the position by both the White House and the Latino leadership. He brought in two aides, Gilbert Colon, a Puerto Rican, and Raul Tapia, a Mexican American. They arrived with staffs of their own and would advocate for Latino issues and have input on personnel decisions.

With these people in place, I was confident that Latino issues would have strong advocacy. I myself became a commissioner of the White House Fellows and actively recruited Latino candidates. Latino issues needed advocacy at the national level, and now I could leave Washington unworried about whether my time there would turn out to be just a brief flash of Latino visibility followed by a return to obscurity and inconsequence. The White House Fellowship's 2014 class was also its 50th, and I am proud to know that it had the largest number of Latino participants in the history of the White House Fellowship program.

I left the White House a changed man. My perspective had expanded. I saw how big the country was, and how much possibility there was. I made some connections that would last me the rest of my life. But more than anything else, I learned what it takes to be a successful person. Here I had been in the presence of a man who had made it to the position of second in command in the United States, a man who had transformed the position into what it is today. And he hadn't done it by being self-centered or by searching for fights to prove himself. Fritz Mondale reached his position by being decent and loyal. He did it not by defeating those he faced but by trying to find a way for everyone to win. He brought in the rising tide to lift all the boats.

He showed me that the old adage is true, that politics is the art of compromise. It's a simple lesson, but so few of us learn it. He worked to keep everyone on the same side, because he felt that everyone was. He knew that no one goes into a negotiation thinking that he or she is the bad guy or the adversary. Everyone is the hero of his or her own story, and everyone needs allies. Meet everyone as your ally and not your enemy, and you can go far. Ironically, I had set foot in the White House only because I had hoped not to be chosen, so that I could sue. I wanted to sue first and then try to work it out later. It was the approach of the adversary and the outsider, which was what I had been and how I had felt. But I left the White House understanding that often you can get further by working out differences, by seeing the other party's needs and trying to help attain them. Filing suit is a last resort. If I was going to change my approach, I would have to change my perception of myself from that of an outsider and an opponent to that of an ally.

I would stick with Fritz Mondale from then on. When the Carter-Mondale ticket ran for re-election in 1980, I opened an office in Philadelphia and was proud to be a delegate at the Democratic National Convention. I welcomed First Lady Rosalyn Carter to Philadelphia and accompanied her on a tour of a Philadelphia public school. I walked with Ted Mondale, Fritz's son, in the Philadelphia Puerto Rican Day Parade. My support of Mondale had to be limited during his presidential campaign in 1984 because of my position on the bench, but still I attended the convention. I was not the first judge to attend a political convention, but nonetheless, I found myself in some hot water with my colleagues.

The Campaign

On September 1, 1978, my tenure as a White House Fellow came to an end, and I packed up my family and moved back to Philadelphia. I received offers to stay in Washington to fill positions in disparate fields. Father Geno Barrone, for instance, assistant secretary at HUD, with whom I had worked on urban policy, offered to make me his deputy assistant secretary. He and his large inner circle of bright people from Baltimore working at HUD were doing some great work, such as developing the dollar-a-house program, which seemed very promising. But I was focused on getting back to my life at home. I had always thought I was given this opportunity at the White House so that I could bring my experience back to Philadelphia and put it to use there.

The job with the SMA I'd hoped to return to was no longer a possibility. Soon after I left, Gil Medina had merged the association with Leevy Redcross, a black accounting firm that took the contract with the Office of Minority Business Enterprise (OMBE). Leevy Redcross tried to offer the same services the SMA had offered, but it was in the business of accounting, not economic development. That was the last contract that OMBE offered Leevy Redcross, and just a year after I'd left it, there was no SMA to return to.

After earning his CPA, Gil went off to Camden City Council and then joined New Jersey governor Christie Todd Whitman's administration as, of all things, the secretary of economic development. Gil was one of the smartest people I ever met, and all he did was erase the SMA and become a conservative Republican in New Jersey. I could not have been more disappointed in him.

As my year in the White House was winding down, I'd accepted an offer from Ragan Henry. Henry was an African American attorney with numerous media holdings. I had taken a two-credit course with him at Temple and we'd kept in touch. We would talk occasionally when I was a White House Fellow, and he would float the idea of my joining his law firm, Wolf Block Schorr and Solis-Cohen. Wolf Block was a major law firm in Philadelphia, representing a largely Jewish client list, and Henry did a lot of work in the buying and selling of broadcasting licenses. Selling to minorities was a big deal then, because of the tax breaks the Federal Communications Commission was granting.

I decided to join Wolf Block because of all I stood to learn about the basics of law and the specifics of contracts. Bernard Borish, a senior partner at the firm who ran the litigation department, took me in hand and showed me the ropes of filing, answering pleadings, and contract negotiations. He named me to the Committee for Services to the Spanish-Speaking Community and, moreover, he made me feel welcome. He would discuss with me ways in which Wolf Block could reach out to a more diverse clientele. It was known as the Jewish law firm back then, and it was looking for ways to grow beyond that reputation.

I worked with some great legal minds and some very adept attorneys at Wolf Block. Skip Minisi, for instance, another partner at the firm, gave me a terrific education during the three years I was there. Skip was a college football referee on weekends in the fall; he had been a great player at the University of Pennsylvania in the 1940s. He even went professional for a year but then quit to study the law. He headed the Committee of 70.

But Howard Gittis was probably the most important influence on me then and thereafter. What a great man he was. He had stood before the Supreme Court and argued—and won!—the case for Frank Rizzo when a group in Philadelphia was trying to recall him after his re-election. He represented the Speaker of the Pennsylvania State House Herbert Fineman when he was tried in a corruption case. But beyond his legal acumen and his prominence, he was as fine a mentor as any man has been to me. I learned so much from Howard. I loved him and respected him, and he was always very good to me.

Though I stayed at Wolf Block for only three years, my time there was a very important point in my life. It got me back into the law, and it provided me with some great connections. I worked on some prominent cases, too, including the divorce between Kenny Gamble and his wife, Dee Dee Sharp. I represented After Six and worked on contracts for the purchase, manufacture, and delivery of tuxedoes. I met Ralph Roberts and worked with his accountant on deals for Comcast in the Meadowlands and in Michigan, and I won them an urban development action grant there.

At that point in my life and my career, three years was a lifetime. Law school lasted three years, my stint at the SMA lasted a staggering four, and for one year I'd been a White House Fellow. I had been thinking about what to do next, and Ed Rendell, district attorney for Philadelphia at the time, had been putting thoughts in my head about running for the bench. It was 1980, and the governor of Pennsylvania, Dick Thornburgh, had been making some noises about appointing the first Hispanic judge to the bench.

Judgeships were very often conferred to friends and family of the powerful and connected. It's a function of being close to the right people, especially in a city like Philadelphia. Whom you know determines your access to power, and I didn't feel the relationships I had with powerful people would help me. Sure, some powerful figures in city government and in civic circles knew me, but was I someone they'd stick their neck out for? I didn't think so. I was young, too, and at 33, I'd be the youngest judge ever voted to the bench. And there had never been a Latino judge appointed in Pennsylvania. I was an outsider and a long shot, and my plans had never really included being a judge. So, of course, I ran.

My team was small. I appointed Vilma my campaign manager and made Stephen Levin, a good friend from Wolf Block, my treasurer. I started soliciting support wherever I could. In retrospect, I did have a lot of people rooting for me and supporting me. They were widespread, but, boy, were they dedicated. Hank Lacayo and his connections in the Latino labor movement helped raise funds for me. I had support from associates and friends at Wolf Block, and within the Philadelphia Latino community. That didn't mean that I wasn't a long shot, for surely I was, but I did have help. Not many people besides my own mother thought it would be enough.

I entered the Democratic primary. I visited each of Philadelphia's 66 wards and campaigned. I spoke to ward leaders and contributed money to their wards to cover the expenses associated with setting up a polling station, printing and distributing campaign materials, and so on. As slim as my chances were, I seemed to be doing pretty well in the month leading up to the election. The odds were never anything other than very long. Philadelphia mayor Bill Green had promised me support, and Governor Thornburgh was giving me some attention as well, but these were just promises, and from politicians no less. I was still being left off of ballots and there were precincts where I was openly reviled, places like Kensington, where I'd confronted systemic racism in white neighborhoods resistant to demographic change.

The second weekend in May 1981, just a couple of days before the primary, I was fussing around the house, unable to do much of anything. I was thinking about my chances and about my life, but more than anything my thoughts kept coming back to my grandfather. He had died early that spring in Puerto Rico, and the demands of the campaign had kept me from going to his funeral. Big, powerful Pedro Cancel, who rode his beautiful horse back and forth across the island, who had sired perhaps dozens of illegitimate children whom he would not provide for, who had frightened my mother so badly that she left home at nine years old, had passed away a saved man. After a life of disregard, profligacy, and violence, he had converted at age 80 and lived another 17 years comforted by his belief.

And who had ministered to him in his old age? Who was also a comfort to him? My mother, who with Miserain had moved back to Puerto Rico in 1973, the year after I finished law school. She had helped her father find his way to God. She helped him learn to read, too, and by the time he died, he had memorized the Book of Psalms. After living a life full of sin, the brawler was now going to saunter through the Pearly Gates. I had always been conflicted about my grandfather and his larger-than-life presence, his charisma, and both his repellent and his attractive qualities, which were equally easy to see. He had been saved, but his good fortune did not seem earned. He was just lucky that his daughter, whom he had once frightened off, had decades later returned and saved his soul. His luck was her miracle. Maria's faith had its own gravity, and other bodies floating aimlessly in the void were gently but inescapably drawn to it. And while I may have resented Pedro and his clean escape from this world, Maria had no such compunction. She was the embodiment of faith and love. She had saved her son and had surely saved others, too. Now she had saved her father.

I was thinking about all of this on the Sunday before the primary. There was little else to do at that point. I had done everything I'd been asked to do, everything I could think of, but my chances still looked slim. In fact, as I thought about it, I couldn't see how I could win. Going into the primary, the things in my favor were few, some friends with connections, the vague promises of a mayor and a governor, and a surprising endorsement by the *Philadelphia Inquirer.* Against me were the basic facts of who I was: too young, too unconnected, and, frankly, probably too Latino. No 33-year-old had ever been elected to the bench. I think about it today, and I wonder how I could possibly look at a 33-year-old lawyer—a baby!—and see the gravitas necessary to be a judge.

I was left off many of the official ballots that were circulating; I was fighting against a perception of myself as more of a perpetual outsider, an agitator, or a gadfly. Rather than cultivating allies among the powerful, I more often challenged and alienated them. The Feltonville fire-bombing case of a few years earlier had garnered me some attention, for better and worse, which directly affected my run for the bench. On the positive side, political heavyweights such as district attorney Ed Rendell, who would go on to be mayor of Philadelphia, governor of Pennsylvania, and chairman of the Democratic National Committee, noticed and had encouraged me to run. On the negative side, some ward leaders and people in North Philadelphia and the river wards did not care for me. I had made the police and the ward leaders look bad, and I had helped their friends and neighbors off to prison. Add these feelings to a large and established anti-black, anti-Hispanic contingent that didn't like me or what I stood for. Most of the ballots I was being left off of were in the river wards, over which ward leaders had a lot of authority. Attitudes about me in those neighborhoods at the time could best be summed up by the vandalism done to my house in Kensington during the campaign. I had bought the house in partnership with Dorothy Moore, my old friend from the Temple Black Law Student Association, on a Friday, and the following day we took Ernie Jones to see it. Later that same day, someone went through the empty house and gutted it, smashing windows and tearing up the floors and walls, so it would be uninhabitable.

And finally, while no one had told me they wouldn't include me on their ballot or endorse me because I was Latino, the long and Latino-free history of jurisprudence in the Commonwealth was not on my side.

I sat and I stewed about my terrible chances. I cringed as a scene I'd made in Anna Verna's office came back to torment me. Verna was to be president of Philadelphia City Council. A few weeks earlier, with my friend Oscar Rosario, who worked in Mayor Rizzo's administration, I had stopped in at Verna's polling office at Front and Chestnut Streets. I had no specific plan. It was just a perfunctory visit so I could say hello, shake a few hands, kiss a convenient baby, and say a few hopeful words about democracy and how much I'd appreciate the support of anyone within earshot. But when I got there, Verna's husband was handing out his own "good judges" ballot. My name wasn't on it. I wouldn't have been surprised to see this up in Kensington, but not in a district as cosmopolitan as this one.

I was hurt. I was indignant. I grabbed the ballots right out of his hand and started ripping them up in the middle of her office. I made a real scene, yelling at everyone there and at no one in particular—maybe just raging against the system itself—about how easy it was to mistreat and ignore a good candidate, an endorsed candidate, just because he didn't belong to the right clubs. I don't actually remember what I said, but I said it with great fervor and at high volume, and it wasn't very nice. A candidate with any idea what he was doing would have handled the situation with more tact and grace. I risked not only forever ruining my chances in Verna's ward and with Verna herself but also being chased into the street and beaten. Things like that happened regularly in Philadelphia politics, which can be a contact sport, and not in a metaphorical sense. But no one did anything. They just stood around stunned as I ranted, which, as I recalled it, made me cringe all the more.

All that Sunday I added up what I had and subtracted what I didn't have. I thought about my grandfather, who had lived a sinner and died

a saint. I prayed. I made a promise to God. I said that if he would inter-
cede on my behalf and I won one of the available bench seats, I would
dedicate more than three-quarters of my time to the poor and the disadvantaged.

Tuesday was the primary. I spent the day campaigning and pressing
the flesh. I remember the day as one long blur of getting into and out of
the car, from before sunrise till well after sundown. The polls opened
and the polls closed. In the wee hours of Wednesday morning, I found
myself driving up Broad Street, heading home behind E. Steven Collins,
who was reporting for radio station WDAS at the time and driving the
car in front of me. E. Steven was a big presence in the black community
in Philadelphia and a good friend of mine. I was listening to the news
reports on KYW, and at a stoplight I heard the newsman say my name
as he read off the winners. It was hard to comprehend.

I had won.

I had won! There was still a general election come fall, but winning
the Democratic primary was tantamount to winning the general.

E. Steven must have been listening, too, because when I jumped out
of my car, he jumped out of his, and we started jumping around together, hugging in the middle of North Broad Street like Mummers on
New Year's Day. The radio announced that my friend Augusta Clark
had also won. Her house wasn't far, and all the lights were off when we
got there, but we were not deterred. We banged on her door until we
woke her up to tell her the good news.

I had actually won! Against very long odds, I'd won. I had received
more than 90 percent of the black vote and just enough of the vote in
the Northeast and a little in South Philadelphia. And in Anna Verna's
ward, after throwing a tantrum like a spoiled child, I was the top vote-
getter. I knew I had made an impression, but I never imagined it would
have helped me. Another miracle.

8

JUDICIAL TENURE (PART I), TEMPLE UNIVERSITY HOSPITAL'S BOARD OF GOVERNORS, TEACHING AT TEMPLE UNIVERSITY LAW SCHOOL, TRAVELS

I WAS READY TO GET TO WORK. Being a lawyer at a big-time law firm had been a great experience, but I never anticipated how much it would seem like a sales job. And campaigning had felt like one long advertisement for myself, peddling my dynamism and responsibility and my capacity at 33 years old to transform into a wise and even-tempered arbiter of the law.

Now came the actual work. After I won the primary, Governor Dick Thornburgh appointed me to the bench, where I could serve as a judge until the general election in the fall. After the election would come the confirmation, but in all regards save the ceremonial, I was a judge. I appeared for a brief, perfunctory hearing before the Pennsylvania State Senate with another new judge, Victor DiNubile. My senator, the liberal Republican Phil Price, introduced me. I knew him from his time as the executive director of a community economic development organization called the Allegheny Foundation and considered him a friend. The hearing was as brief as a mugshot, or an introduction at a cocktail party: barely more thoroughgoing than name, rank, and serial number.

On July 20, 1981, I had a swearing-in ceremony in a room in City Hall with no air conditioning and almost no air. It was a jubilant occasion for me in Room 653, bringing together friends old and new, including Carl Singley and Howard Gittis, other mentors, family, the mayor, the district attorney, and the Philadelphia Bar chancellor. Ragan Henry,

My swearing in on July 20, 1981, when—at age 34—I became the first Latino judge in the state of Pennsylvania. My wife, Vilma, with the corsage, is on the left; Mom and Pop are behind her. To my right is the court officer, and beyond him is Mayor Bill Green. Partly obscured by the clapping hands of Bob Garcia is my mentor (in glasses) Howard Gittis.

who had recruited me to Wolf Block and taught me at Temple Law School, was the master of ceremonies. My mother was so proud of me. A photograph of my youngest child, Delia Lee, sleeping through the whole thing appeared in the next day's *Daily News*.

Like most new judges, I would begin my time on the bench hearing cases in the waiver program, in which a felony criminal defendant waives a jury trial and goes before a judge who will determine the facts and evidence of the case, render a verdict, and administer sentencing. The waiver program is a necessary expedient; it keeps the court system from getting bogged down. If every case, criminal and civil, went before a jury, the justice system would screech to a halt. A speedy trial would be a constitutional figment, one of our most basic civil rights would be trampled, and the wait for a court date would stretch into decades. A judge must keep one eye on the scales of justice and the other on the clock and the calendar. Administrative speed must be a component of the administration of justice.

The waiver program also gives new judges a chance to learn the ropes. My first year was spent mostly presiding over drug and alcohol cases, along with some theft, burglary, and robbery cases. The key traits I cultivated in that capacity were a high standard for reasonable doubt and fairness in sentencing. No judge in the waiver program could be considered a hanging judge, because there would be no enticement to forgo the time-consuming process of going through a jury trial. No defense attorney would seek a speedier path to a tougher sentence.

I worked hard as a judge, and my staff worked hard, too. A waiver program judge could hear half a dozen cases in a day. I was young and I was driven and in that first year I probably heard a thousand felony cases. My court started promptly at 9:00 A.M., and I did not continue cases to the following day. I worked until the trials I had on the day's docket were heard and adjudicated, which made for some late nights. I remember a Wednesday evening before Thanksgiving when Carl Singley was waiting outside the courtroom for me so we could go to a preholiday dinner that had started an hour earlier. It was 8:00 and the lawyer from the public defender's office was imploring me for a hearing for his client who had been in jail for six months for throwing a bottle at a police officer.

His client had a master's degree from the University of Pennsylvania in city planning and no prior record, but he did have a history of mental illness and had been off his medication. Sitting in jail for six months seemed like a lot, or at least enough. I suggested that his lawyer advise him to capitulate to the facts, and I found him guilty and released him with time served as long as he came back to my court the day after Thanksgiving with proof that he was on his medication regimen. He did so, and I never saw him again. In hindsight I regret finding him guilty, because in dispatching the case quickly, I gave him a criminal record. But he never would have gotten out of jail for the holiday otherwise.

After hearing another drug offense, I found a man guilty and gave him two years' probation with a mandatory weekly drug screening and appearance in my court every Friday. He showed up every Friday for two years but stayed clean for only a year and 51 weeks, failing his very last Friday test. He stood before me and we talked about his sentence. Did he remember what I'd told him would happen if he failed? He did. He was facing two and a half to five years, and he got it. Off he went to state prison.

I often chose to be lenient up front. I would give the defendant who stood before me the benefit of the doubt, but if my word or my reputation was going to mean anything, I had to be firm. A judge who is irresolute, who would fudge a sentencing to be nice, is a judge whose decisions don't mean anything. He or she is a judge that people will try to walk all over. That judge erodes the purpose and the power of the judicial system and is capitulating to the forces of lawlessness. Justice wears a blindfold to stay impartial, not naïve.

I did waiver trials for two years, and then it was time to move on. The new judges would take over the waiver hearings, and I went to the major jury program. I presided over robberies and other crimes, excluding homicide, which had its own program in the courts. A lot of sex crimes came through my courtroom, and those cases were the most difficult. Crimes of rape and sexual assault are particularly egregious, and though I sat behind the bench in a black robe, I was a human being with my own experience—including an assault in the tenement hallway when I was a boy of five. These cases have always been difficult to try and were even more so then. Issues of identification and evidence make convictions more onerous to achieve, the question often boiling down to whom you believe, the accuser or the accused. I heard so many cases in which boyfriends of the mothers of raped children stood trial. I wanted to throw all the adults in jail, the rapist boyfriends and their girlfriends who knew about the assault and may have even negotiated it.

The world can be a merciless and gruesome place, and I was exposed to a lot of it. The burden of all I saw wore on me and seemed to grow heavier with each successive trial. I remember one case in particular in which a teenage girl claimed she had been raped by her landlord, who had come in through her window at night and attacked her. The evidence presented for identification was a set of bite marks, which a dental expert claimed tied the landlord to the crime. The jury didn't believe strongly enough in the connection and found the defendant not guilty. As a judge, I could guide the case, rule on evidence, and give the jury instructions, but the jury determined the facts and administered a verdict. I often presided over cases in which the verdict seemed wrong, and in this case, I believe that the system failed that particular young woman. Justice is a tough business, and the jury system is neither foolproof nor flawless. Many people came before me asking for justice and left empty-handed.

Furthermore, I seemed to be getting more than my fair share of these types of cases. The assistant district attorney who handled sexual assault and abuse cases at that time was Patrice Tucker, who would go on to become the first African American woman appointed to the U.S. District Court for the Eastern District of Pennsylvania and its first female chief judge. She wanted to have as many of those cases tried in front of me as possible because I was fair to the accusers. While she did not have the authority to select the judge who would hear her cases, a certain amount of finagling and politicking always went on behind the scenes, both by the District Attorney's Office and by defense attorneys. But I had come to feel that after two years in the major jury program I'd had enough.

I didn't want the facts of my own life—my young children and my history of sexual abuse—to weigh on how I presided. I worried that the time might come when I would lose my perspective. I didn't want to be a judge with compromised judgment. It got to the point where whenever President Judge Ed Bradley saw me coming, he would flinch, waiting for me to ask to be reassigned. Finally I sat down with him and told him I didn't think I could do the job anymore. Could I be placed on the civil side? I had four years of experience, which was not a lot of seniority, but he said he'd consider my request.

Civil cases are easier. Money is at stake, not someone's life or someone's freedom. I was known as an efficient and industrious jurist who kept his criminal cases moving. My commitment to getting cases heard and determined would serve well on the civil side of the Philadelphia court system, which was beset with a seemingly intractable seven-year backlog. But the criminal side didn't want to lose me either. The U.S. Constitution guarantees the rights of the accused, including the right to a speedy trial and freedom from cruel and unusual punishment. Those guarantees are embedded in our definition of ourselves as a nation, and I was an asset on the criminal bench. But Judge Bradley moved me over to the civil side in the hope that I could help address that enormous backlog. And my life, as a result, got better.

At the beginning of the year, each judge received a list of the 200 or so major cases slated for trial in his or her courtroom. The majority of civil cases settle out of court, and I wanted to see to it that the parties in these cases had every opportunity to come to a decision between themselves without taking up the court's time. Immediately I would publish a list of the cases and set a date for trial to begin. Over the course of two days I would hold a conference in my chambers for every case and meet with every attorney. This conference would in most instances be the first time the opposing lawyers had spoken with each other face-to-face. If by being put in a room together they could work things out without me, all the better. Every year, my annual docket would go from 200 cases to about 100 in those two days. The two sides would come to some kind of settlement right there in the waiting area, or the cases would just go away.

Some of the cases I sat for were an honor to witness. I oversaw back-to-back defamation trials in which the plaintiff was represented by the prominent personal injury lawyer Jim Beasley. Both plaintiffs were suing the *Philadelphia Inquirer* for defamation, and in both instances the newspaper was represented by Bill Lytton. Richard Sprague was suing in the first trial, one of many times he went after the *Inquirer*. Sometimes he won, but not always. Beasley and Lytton spent six weeks in front of me, and the days were long. I'd come in about 8:00 A.M. and do preliminary motions for a 9:00 A.M. start, and we'd usually go in front of the jury until about 5:00 P.M., and then go over objections and other housekeeping matters until 8:00 P.M. It was remarkable to watch the two lawyers litigate in front of me. And after six weeks, the jury came back in favor of the defendant.

The next week, there Lytton and Beasley were again. This time Beasley was representing F. Emmett Fitzpatrick, the former Philadelphia district attorney. It was another long case, another six weeks of long days, and again, the jury found for the defendant: another stunning defeat for Beasley, a big name in personal injury circles, who rarely lost.

Coincidentally, I had first met both plaintiffs, Sprague and Fitzpatrick, in the aftermath of the Santiago firebombing back in 1975. Sprague had agreed to review the case if he could look at the files, and Fitzpatrick, as district attorney, had said he could review them over his dead body.

But it was the attorneys in the two trials who were most memorable. Lytton was thorough and indefatigable, and Beasley would never stop trying new angles on old case law. More than once I had to call a recess to review some assertion he had brought up out of left field. I felt like a referee in the heavyweight championship and its rematch and was privileged to be a disinterested witness. I had a deep appreciation of good lawyers litigating tough cases. Beasley did lose both times, but defamation is hard to prove, especially when the plaintiff is a public figure.

After three months arguing in front of me over the span of the two cases, Lytton seemed to have submitted his two weeks' notice along with his billable hours and left the law firm. He took a corporate job somewhere as general counsel. Beasley filed an ethical complaint against him, which I don't believe went anywhere. Beasley wasn't used to losing, especially not twice in a row, and he did not take it well.

Even the court reporter, Lance Brusilow, had his life changed by the two trials. Court reporters take notes in shorthand or on a stenograph, which then need to be converted into a transcript that a layperson can read. The process of transcription can take a few days, but court reporters can at their discretion and for a fee provide the notes earlier. The days were long, and both sides wanted daily copies the following day. Brusilow worked every day, all day, and then left to—I could only imagine—spend all night on the transcription. I remember asking whether he wanted someone to take over for him after lunch. He never did, and the money he made charging by the page was quite a windfall. He took that money and started his own business providing court-reporting services. It's in operation to this day.

In my six years as a civil trial judge, I oversaw several big cases and made decisions on others, including a potential class-action copyright infringement case that a group sought to bring against Kodak. I had to deny the plaintiff's request for class action, ruling that a previous class-action suit in Chicago had granted plaintiffs adequate representation. The two cases that figured most prominently in my time on the civil court bench, however, were *AFSCME v. City of Philadelphia* in 1987, and *Drummond v. University of Pennsylvania* in 1993.

The AFSCME (American Federation of State, County and Municipal Employees) case stemmed from a restraining order sought by the labor union to keep work from being done in Fairmount Park with non-union labor. I oversaw the case without a jury.

AFSCME argued that using non-union employees violated an iron-clad contract with the city, and employees in the AFSCME union would lose money. The city, on behalf of the Fairmount Park Commission, argued that they had been given charitable donations earmarked for much-needed improvements in the park, and that since the money was not part of the city's budget, the contract did not apply.

The city further argued that nothing had been done in the park for 22 years, no work of any sort, because there was no budget for it. And here was a big pot of donations that the Fairmount Park Commission wanted to use for a volunteer program. The union wanted those charitable funds to be applied to work for their employees.

I looked back to an old decision by U.S. Supreme Court justice Benjamin Cardozo on charitable contributions, in which he continued the common law idea that consideration of the law be tempered by equity. In the old days of British law, a starving man who steals a loaf of bread was, in purely legal terms, a thief and only that. But because of his condition, or his situation, he could fall upon the mercy of the king. That idea has developed into the idea of equity. Cardozo took that idea and established a public interest exception when there is just cause to apply a charitable gift to a circumstance in which there is a need.

The city's contract said in no ambiguous terms that all work done on city property had to be done by city employees. But there was work that needed to be done and that wasn't being done, and the charitable monies donated were sitting there unused, and the park was suffering. I decided against the plaintiffs, and while I made some enemies in the labor unions, the appellate court affirmed my decision, which thereafter changed the way organizations set themselves up in Philadelphia. The Art Museum and the Free Library adopted the same approach as the Fairmount Park Commission, creating a charitable arm to use donations to get work done through volunteer programs. The exceptions my decision carved out helped many public institutions put their charitable contributions to good use without all the red tape.

The University of Pennsylvania case involved the Mayor's Scholarships. It was brought by 13 minors represented by their parents or a friend and 14 organizational plaintiffs, which included labor unions and community organizations. They were suing the University of Pennsylvania, the City of Philadelphia, and the mayor of Philadelphia, Ed Rendell. The Mayor's Scholarships had been instituted in 1882, when the city conveyed land to the University of Pennsylvania. In partial exchange for the land grant, the university would maintain a number of full scholarships for graduates of the city's secondary school system. Originally there were to be 50 scholarships amounting to $150 each, which was the cost of tuition at the time. Over the years, the number of scholarships increased (as did tuition) until, in 1977, it was determined to be 125 four-year full-tuition scholarships awarded to graduates from all city schools. But the university stopped giving full scholarships, offering instead a need-based package of a $500 grant and other financial aid, including work-study and loans. And for the city's part, the mayor had awarded scholarships to non-Philadelphia high school graduates. Both practices were in direct violation of the 1977 ordinance and all others that had gone before it.

I noted these clear violations, but the case had an underlying problem. The plaintiffs who brought the case were already at Penn. Neither the university's practices nor the mayor's widening of the recipient pool beyond city limits had affected those students' ability to attend the University of Pennsylvania. They were there now, they had not applied for the Mayor's Scholarship, and they would not be direct beneficiaries of a change to the administration of the Mayor's Scholarship; therefore, they had no standing. A direct beneficiary would be a high school student or high school graduate who had been accepted to Penn and was seeking aid.

My decision to dismiss the case for lack of standing went directly counter to what I wanted college education to be: accessible, fair, and inclusive. The city, the mayor, and the university had all violated the terms of the ordinance, but the case could go forward only if pursued by someone who would be harmed by the violations. My heart had no standing in my determination, either. It couldn't. I agreed with much of what Michael Churchill of the Public Interest Law Center of Philadelphia argued, in principle, but the law bound me to rule against my preferences and my desire for justice. So I wrote my decision, noting what I saw as clear violations of the ordinance, and denied the petition for relief. I hoped that the case would continue and the next judge, on appeal, would look into it. Eventually the case settled.

When I was still fairly new to the bench, Mayor Bill Green assigned me to a task force charged with addressing the need for more black and Latino cops on the police force. The idea was, in order to facilitate investigations as well as good community relations, to hire cops who looked like people in the neighborhoods they patrolled. With about 9,000 officers on duty, only 600 were African American, but that was far better than the mere 35 who were Puerto Rican. I joined the task force, chaired by former justice Bruce Kauffman. He was then managing partner at Dilworth Paxson, and we used my courtroom to hear testimony from witnesses, including the Guardian Civic League, which represented African American officers, and the Spanish American Law Enforcement Association (SALEA), which represented Latinos.

The Guardian Civic League had won a civil rights suit, arguing discrimination, to increase their numbers, and SALEA was following their lead. As the lawsuit wore on, and Mayor Green's term was coming to an end, Green approached me with his concerns and asked me to talk

Addressing a group of high school students in the nonjury trial room.
Especially as a judge, I took my responsibility as a role model very seriously.

to his city solicitor, Alan Davis. Green wanted to see the numbers of minority representation on the force improve and said he hoped we could come to some resolution. Davis was a friend with whom I had worked at Wolf Block, where he'd been a partner. Davis and I feared that with a new mayor coming in, we risked having to start from square one, which meant SALEA could lose the lawsuit and we would set ourselves back years. I asked him whether he would consider settling.

During our hearings, our task force had hit upon the idea of selective certification. It means that an officer who passes the certification test and takes an additional test in a specific skill, such as Spanish-language facility, can be selected for a specific need, such as patrolling a predominantly Spanish-speaking neighborhood. If we could settle out of court and agree on instituting some measures, we could get more Spanish-speaking officers out there in communities where they were needed. Davis agreed. And now on a police force of about 6,000, more than 800 officers are Latino.

I had not forgotten my deal with God. Back before the election I had promised him that if I won, I would devote most of my time to helping the poor and the needy. He had held up his end of the bargain. The agreement was plain: I had to do my part.

Even though the Spanish Merchant's Association (SMA) no longer existed, the businesses the association had supported did, and I kept an eye on them. I was proud of how well they had done, and I was gratified that not a single business that had received a loan had defaulted. So I was upset when Bob Price, my loan officer from Girard Bank and a trusted friend, told me that the mall on the 2900 block of 5th Street—the mall with the businesses on the first floor and Catholic Services on the second floor, the crown jewel of the Bloque de Oro—had run into some financial trouble and Carlos Ricardo, its owner, was in danger of defaulting on the loan. As tenants turned over, Ricardo had replaced tenant-owned businesses with businesses of his own. He had seen other businesses make money there, and he thought he could double his profits by running his own businesses, including a shoe store and a restaurant, in the mall's storefronts. But of course what he had done was to double his risk and double his exposure, and now his businesses were failing. He was in deep financial trouble. But, Bob said, there was some good news. I could take over the mall.

I couldn't do it by myself, and certainly not personally, but I saw a way. In 1978, when I was executive director of the SMA, I had incorporated a nonprofit drug rehabilitation program that had been run by Asuncion Muñoz, whom everyone called Mike and who was now my judicial aide. The service had since closed down, but the organization still existed as a nonprofit entity. So I restructured it as a community economic development corporation, recruited a group of top-flight community leaders who would voluntarily staff it, and ran it out of my chambers. The board included Bill Salas; Carlos Esparza, director of the Philadelphia Regional Office of Personnel Management, whom I had met when I was a White House Fellow; Angel Franqui, a real estate attorney; Rafael Porrata-Doria, a Temple University Law School professor; Bonnie Camarda, an administrator at my church who later became the development director of the Salvation Army (I talked the Salvation Army into developing its headquarters with the Latino community in mind, and today it still sits across the street from this new group's headquarters at Front Street and Allegheny Avenue in the Kensington neighborhood); and Judge Eduardo Robreno, an Operation Peter Pan kid from Cuba who had come to the United States as a teenager through the Catholic Church's program and had been fostered by a white family in Massachusetts. Robreno came under my mentorship after he graduated from Rutgers Law School. He was the first Cuban American federal judge in the United States and is now senior judge in the U.S. District Court for the Eastern District of Pennsylvania.

We founded the Hispanic Association of Contractors and Enterprises (HACE) for the express reason of taking over the mall in the Bloque de Oro. We inherited the loan, too, and worked to get things back on track. In the end we saved the mall and paid back the loan, keeping the record of the SMA's disposal and repayment perfect. After a year of all-volunteer work by this small group of devoted people, I asked Bill Salas for the second time to take the helm of an economic development corporation. Since he had declined when I asked him to run the SMA, I knew he'd be reluctant to take on the leadership of HACE for the same reasons, but the other members and I kept at him. HACE was getting things back on track for the mall, but there was much more work to do, and in the vacuum created by the absence of the SMA, we were the only ones left to do it.

Bill was never comfortable doing the political part of the job, and because it was community work, we couldn't pay him a king's ransom. What we could offer, with funding I had secured from the business community, was a three-year contract that would provide him a salary—something he hadn't had since his shoe store had closed. It wouldn't be a lot, but it would be something. To make the decision easier, I hired his wife as my assistant. That meant another income and, more important, health benefits for both of them. Bill still resisted the idea. Once again, it seemed that everyone besides Bill knew that he'd be perfect for the job. He didn't think he would be able to do it, or maybe be able to stand doing it, but after much encouragement from the people around him he agreed to take the job. (Who knows? Maybe he'd learned his lesson from the fate of the SMA.)

Bill eventually moved into an office at the mall and slowly began to put together a staff. After taking over, HACE had contracted with Herman Idler's real estate office, in Kensington, to collect rents and find tenants, but now we took that back in-house. Bill held the position of executive director for 25 years and did a fantastic job, revitalizing the area around Front Street and Allegheny Avenue and bringing support and life to the Latino business community. I don't know when, if ever, he came around to thinking he was the right man for the job, but he clearly was. The street they renamed for him in North Philadelphia stands as testament.

HACE would later move to Front and Allegheny Streets, where it remains, and its director is now Maria Gonzalez. Rafael Porrata-Doria remains on the board, the one original member. He was the first Latino to get tenure at Temple Law School, even though my friend Carl Singley, who was the dean of the law school at the time, originally denied it. I asked Peter Liacouras, then university president, to override Carl's decision and grant Rafael a presidential appointment. Which he did. That may have started the rift between Peter and Carl that ended with Carl's firing.

Peter Liacouras had remained a friend. In 1973, he'd asked Ernie Jones and me, newly minted graduates of the law school, to start a legal aid program at Temple. I had started at the SMA by then, but we went ahead and did it. The Temple Legal Aid program operated under an exception in the law that allowed law students to represent indigent clients at court. Ernie was there full time as the program's director, and I worked Wednesdays and Saturdays so night students could also participate.

Ernie hired a young Latina, Nancy Delgado (now Nancy Wright), as his secretary. Smart as a whip, Nancy had graduated from high school at age 16. She wanted to work with Aspira, the Latino youth organization where I was chairman, but I persuaded her to work with Ernie, in the hope that she would go to college at Temple. She didn't go to Temple. She earned her degree elsewhere and later moved to Washington, D.C., where in the 1990s we would meet again and she would be my secretary when I was general counsel at Housing and Urban Development. She retired years later as a fair housing investigator. The legal aid program still exists and gives some participating students credits for their work.

In 1975, while I was still at the SMA, university president Marvin Wachman asked me to serve on the Board of Governors for Temple University Hospital. The hospital had recently gone bankrupt, and the state had purchased the hospital's land and was leasing it back to the hospital for next to nothing as a way to provide some financial assistance. One of the conditions of the arrangement was that the board would have members from the community, not just trustees and university leadership. As a result, five of us were added to the six incumbent trustees and others, including the dean of the medical school and the head physician.

I was appointed chair of the Professional Affairs Committee, which provided final approval to doctors seeking admitting privileges. June Brown, a doctor, served on the committee, too. Her husband, Bill, had chaired the Equal Employment Opportunity Commission (EEOC) under President Richard Nixon and was now a partner at the prestigious Schnader law firm. The process to grant admitting privileges had several tiers, beginning with the university and continuing with the hospital. The Professional Affairs Committee was the final hoop to jump through. As we looked into the admitting process and went through the statistics, I was surprised and disappointed to learn that Temple University Hospital, sitting in the middle of North Philadelphia, a predominantly black area in which many black doctors lived and worked, had not granted admitting privileges to a single one of them. There could simply be no good reason for the lack of black doctors. June and I knew that we had enough members on the committee concerned about this issue to take a stand. At the next board meeting, I announced that the Professional Affairs Committee would grant no further admitting privileges until we saw some black doctors included.

The board, and the hospital itself, were shocked. Surely we couldn't, we wouldn't, simply stop granting privileges because we wanted to change the process. It was a surprising move and a very activist stand to take. But we held firm. Several governors were furious and yelled about it, but Milton Rock, who disagreed as well, took me to breakfast.

At the time I was young and still learning my way around. I had no idea what a giant Milton Rock was. He had founded and was running the worldwide consulting firm Hay Associates and had quite literally written the book on employee and executive compensation. He was as wealthy as he was gracious, and his main tool with me seemed to be taking me to breakfast near his Rittenhouse Square home and gently trying to convince me to change my mind. I told him I couldn't, that adding some qualified African American doctors was not a difficult thing to do. Rather, it seemed difficult not to do it, and it was important to do it. Furthermore, it would be good to have doctors from the community with privileges at the community's hospital. Milton never insisted, but, man, he persisted.

To prove my point, June and Bill Brown hosted a reception at their home for several African American doctors who had admitting privileges at the Hospital of the University of Pennsylvania and elsewhere. The point was, See? It can be done.

It seemed we made our point. John Haas, another board governor, secured a grant from the William Penn Foundation to fund a hospital study on the infant mortality rate in North Philadelphia. Infant mortality was a crisis in the neighborhood, with numbers comparable to those of nations in Africa. To oversee the study, the hospital hired an African American gynecologist from Harvard. He headed up the Obstetrics-Gynecology Department and his hiring opened the gates to other African American doctors. It took six months to change how the hospital did things.

I made some lifelong friends during my time on the board, where I served until 1993, when I went back to Washington to work at the Department of Housing and Urban Development. Among them were John Haas; Leon Malmud; Milton Rock, whom I vacationed with and visited with in his house in Dorado, Puerto Rico; and Dan Polett, owner of Wilkie Buick, who sold his dealership's land to Temple so it could build the Liacouras Center on the site. Dan Pollett and Leon Malmud are the last living board members from that time, and Pollett was an important source of support when he chaired the Board of Trustees and I introduced my agenda for diversity. Though all these people would be lifelong friends, they never gave me another committee to chair after that.

My involvement at Temple was ongoing, and I received requests to serve in many different capacities, mostly through my friendship with Peter Liacouras. By the time I had graduated from Temple Law School, worked at Temple Legal Aid, and served on the board of Temple University Hospital and in other venues, including on the board of a legal education program for high school students called LEAP, I had developed the habit of responding to requests and suggestions from Temple University by reflexively saying yes. So in 1983 when Carl Singley—for whom I had put in a good word with Peter when he was up for dean of the Law School—asked me to teach trial advocacy to third-year law students, I agreed.

Now I was a lecturer. It was the first teaching job I'd had since teaching Sunday school to a bunch of kids I'd herded together and walked to church in West Harlem. I don't want to downplay my teaching Sunday school or my time mentoring middle school students—both activities taught me a lot about knowing what you were talking about and keeping the attention of young people—but teaching at the law school where I had learned the law myself was a big deal to me.

Being an instructor there did play to some of my strengths, too. I had background materials and the curriculum was set, so all I had to do was use what was going to be taught (what I myself was going to teach!) and prepare. I can prepare. I am a first-class preparer. And the style of the class was Socratic, with a lot of give and take, so I could get the students involved in a conversation.

It was a great experience for me. My time behind the bench had exposed me to the near-mythical Philadelphia lawyer. I had seen great litigators and poor ones. I knew what good litigators looked like and what skills they exhibited. Law schools teach students concepts in the law but have a terrible record of preparing students to be lawyers. It's odd, really. It seems that law schools have long held the belief that preparing someone for a career in the law would reduce them to being a trade school. But in my class I wanted students to learn how to be effective in the courtroom, and that included my teaching things that are not typically taught in law school, such as:

How to comport yourself in the courtroom—everything from how you dress to how you behave, the way you take control of the room, and how you speak to everyone in there (the judge, the jury, the witness, the other attorneys) will have an impact on how effective you'll be in the court for your client.

How to look at the facts of the case and build a compelling argument, and how to predict what the other side will build from these same facts.

How to do direct examination and cross examination—what the difference is between walking your witness through direct and leading a witness through cross, and how to prepare a witness for both direct and cross examination.

How to introduce exhibits into evidence at trial—the process is specific; you can't just throw everything you want entered into evidence into a bin, and how you handle it is an important part of building a case.

How to work with eyewitnesses—and how to impeach them.

How to work with expert witnesses—and how to impeach them.

How to build a record if the judge's rulings are problematic and you may want to appeal, and how to keep cool when you feel as though your case is being presided over by an incompetent.

The goal of the course was to introduce students to a trial setting, to help them lose their fear of the courtroom. The final was a mock trial held in City Hall in an honest-to-goodness courtroom, with two-student teams that would face off, four at a time. I saw some very good lawyers go through the program, and I could tell at the time that they'd be good.

Wilson Goode's daughter, Muriel, was in my class. She's now the chief of staff for the New York City Corporation Council. I knew she would be successful, just as I knew that Charlie Bowser's daughter, Leslie Bowser Hope, would be. She worked with her father and then worked in the City Solicitor's Office until she passed away, far too young, in the spring of 2017.

I hired many of my law clerks from the top of that class and I always promised that, after graduating, they could join me for a year, and I'd keep them on until they found another position. It was a great job for law graduates transitioning from law school to the real world. They got to see justice in action and they could take part, drafting opinions, learning the ropes, meeting people in the legal community, and doing the basic and essential work of a bureaucracy.

I was a Temple Law School lecturer from 1983 to 1992, when I left for Washington, D.C., again.

I worked hard to accomplish as much as I could when I was behind the bench, doing a volume business in litigation. But the schedule of a judge allows for a lot of down time, and between leave and vacation, I began to realize that I could do something with my time off if I used it all at once. After spending a year as a White House Fellow, I wanted to travel more, to see the world and learn about it through experience and immersion. And so, almost immediately after I returned to Philadelphia, while I was at Wolf Block, I went on some trips.

In my time as one of the only gentile litigators at the Jewish law firm, I benefited from tremendous support and mentorship. I became the judge I was in part because of what I learned at Wolf Block. I learned everything from how to research a case to how to avoid straying too far from common sense. I was very grateful for the mentorship and for what I learned about the history of the Jews. I began to see common cause between the Latino and Jewish communities. As a student of the civil rights movement in the 1960s, I knew how important Jewish support had been to its success. Jewish civil rights activists and donors established the NAACP Legal Defense Fund, and Jews had marched in places like Selma and had supported Dr. Martin Luther King Jr. And those three civil rights workers who were murdered in Philadelphia, Mississippi, included two Jews, Andrew Goodman and Mickey Schwerner, along with the local African American activist James Chaney.

In the 1970s, when Latinos were still a fairly small majority, I thought that if we could align ourselves with the Jewish community, we could learn a lot from them. Bob Fox, a leader at the American Jewish Committee (AJC) and a prominent real estate developer in Philadelphia, invited me to travel to Israel on an AJC-sponsored trip with a group of civic leaders from Philadelphia, and I jumped at the chance. I had much to learn about Jewish history and the issues facing Israel, and the group was full of well-respected and industrious people. It included Ernesta Ballard, a renowned horticulturist and feminist; Richard Gilmore, a Girard Bank executive; John Anderson, a city councilman (who was then involved with revitalizing the Barristers, an African American lawyers' group); John White Jr., an African American political leader; Elmer Young, a banker and Zion Baptist Church trustee; Robert Landis, a Philadelphia Bar Association chancellor; and Fox.

I had come to admire the AJC for its support of Jews around the world and its work in Philadelphia. Puerto Ricans had much to learn from how Israel operated. The United States provides tremendous support to Israel, and Israel would be in trouble without it, yet the State of Israel does not behave like a dependent. Jews have a totally different mindset from the colonized one that is still so rife among Puerto Ricans.

In early 1979 I got on a plane with the illustrious group of civically minded people and flew to Israel. What a beautiful and complex place it was. We toured through desert and city, through a place in which the past felt simultaneous with the present. From the heat on top of Masada you could see the Dead Sea below you, and in the distance, snow-capped mountains that you could ski on. It has always been a place of great importance and often of great strife. The signs of conflict were everywhere, as were the soldiers, on duty at the airport and on the roadside and off duty in the taverns with their submachine guns still slung around their shoulders. In Jerusalem we stayed at the King David Hotel. The building had been bombed by a pro-Israel paramilitary group in 1946 when Israel was Palestine and the hotel housed the British administrative headquarters. I saw the bullet holes from Jordanian sniper fire on the rear wall of the building. And beyond the conflict, in a way that was difficult for an American to fathom, Israel is steeped in ancient history. I had felt like this the previous year, when I had walked across 5,000 years of history in the Mayan ruins of Chapultepec.

We stopped at the Church of the Ten Lepers, or the Church of St. George, where it says in the Gospels that Jesus healed lepers. It was breathing with history, and stone on ancient stone seemed to hold a memory that went back millennia. I'll never forget hearing John White Jr. sing "I Believe" in the chapel. His voice reverberated through 2,000 years of history. I had my Dictaphone with me, and I recorded him. As he sang about hope and faith, I experienced as powerful a moment as any I can remember.

And when we traveled to the mountain where the Gospels say Jesus delivered it, Elmer Young, a deacon at Leon Sullivan's church in Philadelphia, read the Sermon on the Mount.

We met with the mayors of Bethlehem and Jerusalem, the prime minister, and the Knesset, the Israeli legislature. We spoke to Jews; we spoke to Arabs; we even went out into the desert and spoke with Bedouins. A group of Palestinian children gave John White and John Anderson a little bag of figs and talked to them, saying that the land they saw all around them had once all belonged to the Palestinians. When the two men reported the incident to the leaders of the Israeli group we were meeting with, they were told to accept no gifts from Arabs. John White felt insulted, but the Israelis were very careful about such things.

I remember a moment in the northern mountains, on the Israel-Lebanon border, at a place called the Good Fence. There, through the fence, we could see some Lebanese soldiers at their checkpoint. They were yelling "Stevie! Stevie!" and smiling and laughing. We came closer and we could hear their little boom box playing Stevie Wonder. They pointed to the radio and to the African American members of our group. It was a moment of innocent connection and great significance during a trip that altered my perspective.

It was a remarkable trip, and one that deepened my understanding of the history of the Jews and the importance of Israel. Jews have been spread out across the globe, kicked out of countries, and targeted for annihilation. I felt how important it was that the Jews have a homeland.

In 1984, I was again invited on a trip by the AJC, this time to the Soviet Union. This was back during the premierships of Yuri Andropov and Konstantin Chernenko, when Russia was run by the Communist Party and sat behind the Iron Curtain. The Philadelphia AJC originated and organized these trips in part because no place in the world was more generous in its contributions to the cause of Russian Jewry than Philadelphia. Funding was not an issue, but sometimes the organizers couldn't find enough Jews to go, or couldn't secure enough visas from the Soviet government for Jewish travelers. When that happened, they invited crazy people like me.

Between November 1982, when Leonid Brezhnev's long tenure ended, and March 1985, the Soviet Union experienced a lot of turmoil as the leadership passed from Brezhnev to Andropov to Chernenko to Gorbachev. Andropov's short reign gave particular cause for concern. Russia had for much of its history hovered at the oppressive end of the spectrum for its Jewish citizens, and under Andropov, things were bad. When the Communists were in power, Jews lived under an atheistic regime, and they were treated poorly. At the time of our trip, prominent figures were dropping out of sight.

With conditions what they were, many Jews in Russia would attempt to get to the West—to Israel, to the United States, to almost anywhere. But most were refused the right to emigrate, and the reason most often given was their exposure to Soviet state secrets. These Jews trapped in the Soviet Union were known as the Refuseniks. And not only were they stuck there; their conditions, always tenuous anyway, would often worsen. Many Refuseniks were moved to crowded apartment buildings and assigned jobs that were not in their area of study or expertise and were often menial. Any street sweeper in Moscow at the time could have been a Jewish doctor or administrator who had requested permission to leave the country. That's how it was in the old Soviet Union: you lived where they told you to live and worked where you were assigned.

This was not going to be a sunny and inspirational trip like the one to Israel. This was a trip to bring aid, to expose the plight of Soviet Jews to the wider world, and to try to locate a prominent professor who had seemingly disappeared. Alexander Lerner had been the head of the Academy of Sciences under Nikita Khrushchev. He was a cyberneticist and a prominent scientific figure, but no one had heard anything from him or about him for a few years.

While I was working at Wolf Block, Murray Friedman, who headed up the AJC at the time, invited me on the trip. I would join Richard Berkman, an AJC board member, and Dan Segal, chair of the Philadelphia Soviet Jewry Council. We had all agreed on our three main goals:

to meet with as many Soviet Refuseniks as we could, to bring aid and expose their plight to the world, and to try to find Professor Lerner. Hundreds of thousands, perhaps even millions of Jews had been trying to leave Russia but had been prohibited. As Segal and Friedman briefed me on the situation we were heading into, they told me to pack as many pairs of blue jeans and as many telephones as I could fit in my suitcases so that we could pass them out to those we visited with. They would fetch a lot of money. A family could live for six months on the proceeds of one pair of jeans sold on the gray market. We also packed religious materials to aid the Jews in performing services and educating their children in the religious traditions of their faith or teach them Hebrew.

Going through customs in Moscow was frightening. We were all questioned. In a Kodak box I had hidden tapes on the Jewish faith recorded in Hebrew, disguised as film containers. I put my suitcases on a table as directed and waited for the customs agent to open them and confiscate all the jeans and phones and religious materials. She kept asking me questions in Russian. I knew that I was supposed to declare the value of what I had. She pointed to my gold wedding band as if that were necessary to declare. I knew she wanted me to open my suitcases, but I acted as though I couldn't understand what she meant. She signaled to her supervisor, but he was busy overseeing a full-body search of Murray Friedman. Friedman was a Jewish historian, and his books had given him away. The agent couldn't get her boss's attention, and she was tired of me and my playing dumb, so she shoved my suitcases off the table onto the floor and gave me instructions I would have understood in any language: get lost. I had made it. I was behind the Iron Curtain, in Communist Russia, with bags full of contraband, and I had done it all by playing dumb. My Harlem upbringing had served me well.

Moscow in May was cool and overcast, and if people can be overcast, the Russian citizens were too. They all wore dark colors and their faces looked like masks depicting seriousness or despair. There was little to go around, and what there was seemed steeped in misery. The shops never had much merchandise, and what they did have was all a single generic brand. Even if I had wanted anything, I wouldn't have been able to buy it, because foreigners were not permitted to shop. The one time I went to a restaurant, I was served chicken that was mostly bones and a bowl of fatty borscht. I remember the lines. You waited in line for everything. One day I wanted ice cream badly enough to stand in line for it. It came wrapped in cardboard, and while it tasted fine, the whole experience of it was cheerless. The Soviet Union had succeeded in making ice cream sad.

On our first day in Moscow, Segal, Berkman, Friedman, and I went to the home of a married couple for Seder. The couple were leaders among the Jewish Refuseniks, and the woman, I remember, was expecting twins soon. I followed along as best I could when Segal spoke in Hebrew with them. After the dinner, they asked more about their guests, and Segal told them that I was not Jewish. They asked him why then I had come to dinner, or to Russia at all. He told them that, like many Americans, I was concerned about human rights and religious freedom. We left them with some items to sell on the gray market and went on our way. Eventually that couple and their children made it out of the Soviet Union and went to Israel. Later they came to the United States and, during a visit to Philadelphia, they stopped by City Hall looking for me so that they could express their gratitude for my visit all those years earlier.

Everywhere we went we asked about Professor Lerner, and on the morning of the Sabbath, we walked to Moscow's only active synagogue. Many Russian Jews would meet outside of the temple, but few went inside. They suspected that the rabbi worked for the KGB. Out on the sidewalk we met with another leader of the Refuseniks, who put us in contact with many others. Between Moscow and Leningrad, Dan Segal and I visited more than 80 Jewish households and left behind jeans, phones, Hebrew instructional tapes, and whatever else we could to help.

I took a side trip to Leningrad with Dan Segal, and on May Day I took a walk around the city. Soon I was lost, and I asked a woman for directions to my hotel. I had a matchbook from the hotel with its picture and address on it that I hoped would overcome the language barrier. As I tried to communicate with her, a man stepped up and in perfect English asked me what I wanted. I was surprised, having so far come across almost no English speakers in the Soviet Union. I asked him why he spoke so well, and he told me that he had been an Olympian and had learned English as part of his training. He was, in fact, a government agent and had been watching me during my entire time in his country. We were being tailed, and we had to be careful for our own sakes and for the sakes of the people we interacted with, even this woman from whom I was asking directions. We couldn't be too friendly; we couldn't invite any Russians back to our hotel, and we had to be careful with our gifts. Dan saw my little replica Liberty Bells that I'd packed as trinkets to give to dignitaries, and he told me that I shouldn't give them out. They were too easily identifiable as a symbol of America, democracy, or capitalism and would be trouble for anyone too polite not to refuse my naïve token of friendship.

During that side trip to Leningrad I met Rachel. Much of what happened has been forgotten over the years—names I heard and spoke, faces I came across and spent time with, places I went and occurrences that at the time felt as though they were of great moment. That was well over 30 years ago, after all, but I still remember Rachel. I went by myself to meet a young Refusenik couple. I could go alone because they spoke some English. The husband had been an engineer but was now working some menial job as punishment for the crime of seeking to emigrate while Jewish. They were struggling with two young children to support, so I was bringing gifts. I don't even remember their names, but they were sweet, and they were very grateful. Rachel was their seven-year-old daughter. After seeing that I had brought them gifts, Rachel went into the kitchen and returned with a candy bar. It was hers, and it was special. The candy bar was a treasure and Rachel probably hadn't seen many in her seven years and wasn't likely to see another one for quite some time. But she offered it to me. I didn't want to take it, but she told me I had to. I don't believe I've ever witnessed an act of greater generosity than that.

Back in Moscow, and after nine days in the USSR, the members of our traveling group began splitting up. Berkman and Friedman were heading back to the United States, and Segal and I were going to Vilnius in Lithuania. Before we left, we stopped at a rabbi's house, and while we were there someone came to the apartment door and warned us that the police were waiting for us out front. I asked where the back door was, so we could escape. Everyone laughed: these buildings had no back doors. So we were greeted by the police, who asked us a few questions and sent us on our way. Our seats on the flight to Vilnius were close to the front of the old plane, facing backwards. I wasn't sure why, but it seemed like a punishment.

Vilnius was a much more cheerful place than Moscow, and the people seemed much less gloomy or perhaps less oppressed. Even the weather was nicer. But it was still the Soviet Union. Our hotel was fine, like a jolly dormitory. We unpacked and with time left in the day, Dan suggested we go to see one of our Refusenik friends, Raiz. We got on a bus, but the bus got detoured. And then it stopped and everyone got off. So we set off on foot to get to Raiz's apartment. When we arrived at the building, two cars were parked at the entrance. It may have been a foreign land, but my West Harlem instincts told me it was police. Dan agreed, so we waited for a bit to see whether they would leave. Then it began to rain. The cars weren't going anywhere, and we decided not to stand outside getting wet. As we entered the building, we met the two men in black suits, who had been waiting for us. They grabbed us and hustled us right back out. They wanted to know who we were. What were we doing there? Who had given us this address? As we were getting pushed around and interrogated, I heard a voice call down "Shalom!" from a second-story window.

"Shut up!" I called back. "They already got us."

Shalom is a flexible word: it means hello, good-bye, and peace. And sometimes it means all three.

The police shoved us into a car and took us back to the hotel. They had more questions. Then they took us to our rooms and guarded us there. We couldn't leave without their permission, and we were escorted wherever we went. They told us that as tourists, we were not to visit with anyone. We could sightsee, and we could attend events. We were escorted to the orchestra by two women and we were taken to tour a concentration camp from the war. We saw some sights and then were deposited back in our rooms under house arrest. We were there for five days, over Mother's Day weekend. For the first time in my travels, I began to get scared. I began to wonder whether I would ever see my mother again. I started considering what life would be like if I never got back to the United States. I made out a will in case I died in a Russian gulag.

The police took us to the airport on the day we were scheduled to fly back to Moscow, and off we went. I was very happy to see that grumpy gray town after being locked up in Lithuania. We went straight to the U.S. embassy to check in and make copies of our passports. I remember they were serving hamburgers that day. I had never tasted one so good. While we were there, we ran into a foreign correspondent for the *Philadelphia Inquirer* and started talking with him. It turned out that he knew where Professor Lerner was. Sure, he could tell us where. He lived right there in Moscow. After days of questions and dead-ends, and no one knowing anything, here it was, the answer we'd been seeking.

People had been worried about him. Was he sick? Was he under arrest? Or was he maybe dead? No one knew. Professor Lerner had been a high-ranking official in the Communist Party, and his apartment reflected that. We knocked on his door, and he answered. He had nowhere to go. The walls were hung with his own artwork. He'd taken up painting now that he no longer worked at the Academy of Sciences. It turns out that the party had let his wife and daughter leave, and they had gone to Israel. His son and he had been made to stay behind, but they'd been told that if he kept quiet, soon enough they'd both be able to leave too.

We visited. We admired his art and he served us ice cream. This was good stuff served in a dish, not a piece of cardboard. He said that he was keeping a low profile in the hope that his family would one day be reunited. He dreamed of going to Israel and founding an institute and creating an artificial heart to help turn the country into a hub of technology and cybernetic development. His family would eventually be reunited, but not until after the Berlin Wall came down, taking the Communist Party with it. But by then Professor Lerner was nearly 80 years old, and it was too late for his artificial heart and his institute.

At the embassy I had been tipped off that Dan and I were getting some more attention and that we should just stay in our hotel rooms until it was time to fly back to the United States. So we did.

At the Moscow airport, our bags were searched, and all of the film I'd used, all the pictures I'd taken, were taken out and exposed to the light. I returned from the Soviet Union with nothing but my clothes and my memories. But considering I got back at all, it was enough. What I have written here is just about a full cataloging of it.

During a layover in Poland, I looked out my window to see the Polish Army surround the plane while a few passengers boarded. I felt as though I was just holding my breath until we were out from behind the Iron Curtain. When we landed at JFK Airport, I felt I could finally relax. As I came into the Immigration Center, I saw the official portrait of Ronald Reagan hanging on the wall with that grandfatherly smile and the flag behind him, and I saluted it. I have rarely been happier to be an American citizen, and if I was going to be a dissident, I was glad I got to do it here.

That trip really rattled me. I had never felt such vulnerability before, had never felt so exposed, realizing how easy it would have been for some Soviet agent to just remove me from society simply for giving gifts and exchanging ideas with the wrong people. I didn't want to travel for a while after that. I decided I'd just stay close to home. That feeling lasted a year, until I was asked to go back to Israel and take a Latino group with me. My friend Hank Lacayo had taken a trip to Israel with Latino and Jewish labor leaders, and on his return had worked with Project Interchange to put together a trip for others. About 10 of us took this trip, including Lionel Estrada, the chief demographer of the 1980 Census (and the person who replaced "Spanish-speaking" with the term "Hispanic" on the question of ethnicity); Guarione Díaz, CEO of the National Cuban American Association; Gloria Rodriguez, a prominent marketer; Raul Yzaguirre, long-time president and CEO of the National Council of La Raza; Sonia Melero from the Mexican American Legal Defense and Educational Fund; and Samuel Betances, a professor at Northeastern and a close friend whom I'd met at an Aspira conference in Cleveland.

We toured many of the most significant spots. We went to the Wailing Wall in Jerusalem, the last standing remnant of Solomon's Temple. In keeping with tradition, I wrote a prayer on a business card and left it in a crack in the wall. We walked down Via Dolorosa, where Christ carried his cross to his crucifixion. On that street I bought a Star of David that I still wear today. We visited an Argentine kibbutz that had developed a drip irrigation system for their crops. We climbed Masada in 110-degree heat and then went down to the Dead Sea and floated for a while. After that we took mud baths. We also met with members of the Knesset to speak about common cause between Latinos and Jews. As we spoke, one member of our group referred to Yzaguirre as the leader of Latinos in the United States. I was surprised to hear that.

"Oh?" I said. "I never asked him to speak for me."

I sometimes gave my opinions a public airing in the moment, saying things I might in retrospect have kept to myself. But I said what I thought.

From the Knesset we went to Yad Vesham, the Holocaust history museum that cuts through a mountain near Jerusalem. It was overwhelming to see the gas chambers, the portraits, the artifacts—to see the sheer number of the innocent killed and to walk through halls lined with books that hold their names. It was a somber and disturbing experience, and we were all upset. On the bus on the ride back from the museum, we started fighting. Yzaguirre started in on me, asking why I needed to say in front of the Knesset that I didn't support him. We argued, and our exchange got heated, but others quickly intervened and calmed us down. We remembered what we were there for, to learn about the history of Israel and the Jews and to find areas of connection, but Yzaguirre and I never really reconciled.

Later we went to the Jordan River, and in my excitement I jumped in with all my clothes on. It was a relief to let the river wash the tension away, but it was a soggy ride back to the hotel. Despite the occasional tension, I think we all agreed that our trip to Israel was personally significant, and I think we all recognized how important it is that Israel exist.

These trips to Israel planted a seed in my mind that germinated for a long time. I wanted to start a Latino-Jewish coalition, but it took until 2007, 30 years after my first trip, to get it off the ground. What it took was meeting Dina Siegel Vann, a Mexican Jew who worked for the national arm of the AJC. Once when I was down in Washington, Dina walked up to me and said someone had told her that I could put her in touch with some important Latinos. She referred to herself as a "professional Jew." She was funny and energetic and clearly knew how to get things done. So I introduced her to Henry Cisneros and others. Together we started the Latino-Jewish Coalition. And today she is the director of the AJC's Arthur and Rochelle Belfer Institute for Latino and Latin American Affairs. We recently celebrated the organization's 10-year anniversary in Mexico. I also started the Philadelphia Latino-Jewish Coalition, under the auspices of the AJC.

Gloria Rodriguez, Guarione Díaz, Lionel Estrada, and I have remained close ever since we traveled to Israel together. In the intervening years, we've gotten together several times—on a rented boat out of Miami, at Guarione's house in Florida, and in Washington—to reminisce about our trip and catch up with each other.

Other trips followed. I had been bitten by the travel bug and there didn't seem to be any way to get rid of it. As a judge, I traveled to Japan in 1987 (and then again in 1996) and to Peru in 1990. These trips were very illuminating.

In the late 1980s, Japan was the rising economic power in the world. It was exporting more than it imported. It seemed to have cornered the electronics market and was well on its way to dominating the automobile industry. Prime Minister Yasuhiro Nakasone made remarks in 1989, linking Japan's success to the country's racial homogeneity and asserting that the diversity of the United States held it back. He specifically blamed blacks, Puerto Ricans, and Hispanics. Many Americans took offense. It was certainly a statement antithetical to everything I believed. The United States has gained strength from its diversity. It is the melting pot. It is the true land of opportunity. We come from so many places and bring our different ideas and approaches, and isn't that what makes America great? But, as sometimes happens, the racist statements of one group brought out a racist response in the other. Rather than taking the high road, many in the United States took the opportunity to air anti-Japanese sentiments, old beliefs that had led to some shameful moments in our history, such as when the U.S. government put its Japanese American citizens in internment camps during World War II.

To address this controversy, the United States–Japan Foundation started a leadership program to help foster an exchange of ideas. I was selected as one of 10 civic leaders to spend two months observing the Japanese legal system. I had no idea what I was going to find there, but I planned to spend part of the time observing a district court and part of the time with a private law firm.

Japan was a foreign land on the other side of the world, more alien than any place I had been, and I felt more disoriented and out of place there than I had anywhere else, including the Soviet Union. I didn't realize how such an experience would affect me. I couldn't have known what a creature of habit I was until I had those habits taken from me. During the first month I couldn't sleep, and I was lonely. I didn't speak the language, but more important, I didn't understand the cultural reserve or how politeness can be an obstacle. In essence, I didn't know what I didn't know and I didn't know what to ask for, and more than anything else, I was clearly making a mess of how to ask for it. And it would have been considered rude for anyone to volunteer information, such as, say, "Hey, Judge Díaz, that tea you're drinking down all day and night because it's offered is full of caffeine, and that may be the cause of your insomnia." Between the 12-hour time zone change and the caffeination, I spent my nights reading junk novels and tuning in to the American Armed Forces radio station for football games. Everything was different. I missed eating cereal for breakfast, with fruit such as plantains, or potatoes or oatmeal or farina. Breakfast at the International House where I stayed never changed: two eggs, two slices of toast, and coffee. Same thing every morning. That was the hotel's version of an American breakfast, and it made me more homesick than almost anything else. But after a month of insomnia and agitation, I figured out a few things and began to sleep better. Sleeping helped everything. Finally, I felt as though I could function. I studied, read, ate the noodles at the noodle houses, and even enjoyed taking the subways. The trains were crowded during rush hour, but everything was orderly and safe, and the trains kept to a very precise schedule.

Everything seemed to be secondary to punctuality, including in the Tokyo District Court. In the United States, we schedule sessions to start at 9:00 A.M., but court really begins only when the judge decides to get there. In Japan, court was in session at 9:00 A.M. on the dot and ran till noon. After a recess for lunch, court was back in session at 1:00 and ran till 5:00, when it ended. I remember one day in the courthouse cafeteria when the lines were particularly long, we all got our lunches late. At a few minutes before 1, everyone got up, many leaving their food unfinished, and returned to court. No self-respecting judge in Philadelphia would let a good lunch go to waste.

The Japanese court system does not use juries. Cases are heard by a panel of three judges of varying experience, and the administration of justice is entrusted to professionals. The panels are composed generationally. The senior judge usually has 20 years or more of experience, another judge has 10 years' experience, and the third is a newcomer. As judges retire, everyone moves up a slot.

Trials are heard piecemeal. Different parts of a case are heard at different times, and several cases are heard concurrently. Judges keep thorough notes and review regularly. Things moved slowly there, and though a new constitution was written after World War II, based on the New York State Constitution, the courts' procedures never changed very much.

I was the first U.S. judge to serve on the Japanese court. I heard a case brought by educators over their concern that they were not able to teach the Nanking Massacre—a national shame—in their history classes. I did my best, but questions I asked to clarify my understanding were rarely answered; they just seemed to fall into a wide cultural divide between the vulgar curiosity of a loud Westerner and the reserve of Eastern decorum.

Seeing how things were done in Japan gave me a new awareness and an appreciation for the way we do things in the United States. There is a Western quality of messiness and an accompanying ability to cope with it. The melting pot is messy. The United States is in some ways a big, beautiful, messy space. There is trouble and strife and noise, and while we're not great at everything, and we don't deal particularly well with our own history, we have a public space in which to discuss our problems. Japan wasn't Russia, mind you. There wasn't a governmental injunction against questioning the state, but there was that reserve, and I saw it play out in this court case.

Japan's history, like that of almost every nation that's gone to war, has its blemishes. It has its share of dark moments, and perhaps none is darker than the Nanking Massacre. In the winter of 1937 and 1938, over a period of a month and a half, the Japanese army raped and killed an untold number of civilians in Nanking, China, burning and pillaging the city. No one knows how many died because the army destroyed the records after Japan surrendered to the Allies in 1945. But they didn't destroy everything; numerous records survived, along with eyewitness accounts and the unavoidable fact that the people who were killed were no more. The number, which falls in the range of 50,000 to 300,000 civilians and unarmed combatants killed, remains a source of controversy. Though few people in Japan still flatly deny that the massacre occurred, the case I heard was a suit to have it officially included in the history textbooks. The case had dragged on for years, and the opposition was demanding proof, evidence that had been destroyed out of shame. I was puzzled by the argument over what the rest of the world accepted as settled fact, but my questions were mostly shrugged off or dropped into that wide cultural divide.

I observed a criminal case in which the son of a rich man had killed his roommate. He had confessed his crime and his family had given the victim's family money, and he had received a light sentence. It was common, apparently, to view the willing confession and payment as acts of contrition, and part of the defendant's active participation in his or her own rehabilitation. At a family court trial in Kyoto, however, I witnessed a truant punished severely. Education and an orderly society were highly valued and their violations were dealt with harshly.

Kyoto was the site of the preserved Imperial Palace, and the grounds there were beautifully, obsessively kept. It was early fall, but I hardly ever encountered a single fallen leaf. To keep the mess to a minimum and avoid leaf-related accidents, groundskeepers would remove leaves from the trees if they thought they would fall. During my time in Kyoto, I took a side trip to Nagasaki, unaware that it was the anniversary of the U.S. atomic bombing. Survivors of the war had quietly gathered at the memorial. Their number was not overwhelming, but their sparseness and their quiet, sad reflection stood as a firm rebuke to that wanton destruction. Any nation that has engaged in war has a tarnished history. We all have something to answer for.

The Japanese legal system was different from ours, and while I have always admired the American belief in the dignity of the citizen, I brought back with me a greater sense of pride and respect for it. I also had a new appreciation for the importance of the speedy trial. Timeliness is a key component of a functional justice system. On my return, I wrote an article about the Japanese legal system, and in 1988 I attended the U.S.–Japan Conference of Mayors, organized by U.S. attorney general Ed Meese. In 1996 I returned to Japan with the United States–Japan Foundation as part of a U.S. contingent for a conference on trade issues, involving Russia, Japan, China, South Korea, and the United States.

Though my trip to Japan had been marked by disorientation as I tried to figure out what the rules were, I had no problem recognizing that there were rules. Anyone could easily see that there was a governing order, and that there were ironclad rules; the challenge lay in determining what they were. My trip to Peru was something else entirely. Visiting Peru was a descent into chaos.

In 1990, I was given a Fulbright Scholarship to engage in an exchange on our respective judicial systems with lawyers and judges in Peru. But seemingly all of Peru's systems, not merely the judicial, were a shambles. When I arrived, Alberto Fujimori, to almost everyone's surprise, had just been elected president. He had run on an economic and anticorruption platform and had referred to the courts as the "Injustice System." He ran for the Senate and the presidency at the same time and was swept in on the votes of the poor and indigent. He inherited a mess. Things were, in a word, terrible. Inflation was at 400 percent. The leftist guerrilla terrorist group Shining Path had control of much of the Peruvian countryside and was bombing buildings and assassinating public figures. Strikes were seemingly everywhere. The schools were shut down, as were the courts, and the judges I was there to teach were on strike.

After settling myself in the hotel in Lima, I went out to buy bottled water and personal items, but the shelves in all the stores were empty. Peruvian currency was essentially without value, and only the U.S. dollar could buy you anything, but you had to be able to find something to buy. The director of the Fulbright program suggested I do some sightseeing or take a trip somewhere.

I took the opportunity to visit my cousin Maggie, a nun working in Iquitos, where the Amazon River begins, in the jungle. Margarita Cancel was one of my uncle Diego's 10 children. I would stay in their nursery when I visited Puerto Rico as a child, and Maggie was the only girl and the second oldest. I hadn't seen her in many years. I remember her doing the washing and ironing for her brothers when she was younger. I spent a few days in Iquitos. That first night in the jungle region, I took Maggie and her nun friends to dinner at a restaurant that served monkey brains. I told them that I didn't want monkey brains and I didn't drink water but that I enjoyed a beer with dinner. So did they, and we all had a beer with our meal.

The next day I set off with Maggie to see the mission in the little town of Nauta, thinking that I'd head back to the hotel at the end of the day. But Maggie told me we were going on a boat ride—on a steamboat the locals called a *peche-peche* because of the sound it made. She gave me a hammock to string up. I thought it was a good idea to have a place to rest, not knowing that our little trip up the Amazon would take 27 hours. I boarded with chickens, goats, and pigs, and off we went. I felt I knew how Noah felt. The weather was uncharacteristically cold, which was good luck, because it kept the insects down. Nauta was little more than jungle and a building that had once housed rubber plantation workers and was now the mission.

The locals were Indian, and they spoke a Spanish that was syntactically different from mine, ending their sentences with the verb rather than beginning with it, but we understood one another. I remember they held Mass in a church that had a painting of the Last Supper in which the meal was centered on a pig, a jarring image to me because Jews didn't eat pork, but each culture adds something of its own customs to its religion. They called my cousin "Madre" and the children loved her and the two nuns who lived there, but the conditions the locals lived in were awful. The roads were nearly impassable, and the bridges were unsafe. The old plantation building had a generator behind it, but it didn't work. They did have electricity though, generated by a small hydroelectric dam. Many of the kids were too thin, with sunken eyes, and some with swollen bellies. My cousin told me that they lost children every year to disease in the rainy season and to starvation.

They lived at the mercy of the river, what little mercy it offered, rising and falling and taking houses and land with it when it did. I don't know how they managed, living in such deprivation. I spent a few hum-

Listening to a member of the Quechua Indian tribe in the Amazon, where I learned a great deal about the indigenous people of South America.

bling days watching Maggie working to educate the children in the jungle and seeing her fully a member of their community. This was her life, and I admired her for it. When it was time to go, I bought a box of plantains from one of the locals and headed back up the river. I flew back to Lima and thought of my cousin often. I worried about her, but she did all right. She is still in Peru working with the Indians. Only once did she leave, returning to Puerto Rico to take care of her mother when she was dying of cancer and to spend time with her nine brothers. The box of plantains lasted me the entire trip.

I took other side trips, and in a church in Arequipa, I got robbed, though the thieves eventually returned my passport. The police tried to help. They drove me around to see whether I recognized anyone, but I had to admit I could not pick out my assailants from the crowd.

As for the legal system, such as it was, Peru had a three-level court structure that was based on the Roman system of civil codes, as opposed to common law. Two percent of the national budget was constitutionally assigned to the operation of the court system, but in reality it did not receive more than one one-hundredth of 1 percent. Judges were underpaid, courthouses often had no paper, and trials could be postponed because incarcerated defendants could not pay for their own transportation. Bribery was common and fairly out in the open, and it seemed as though everyone was on the take. This made for a system no one trusted. There was a well-founded assumption of corruption, and judges who made unpopular rulings were sometimes brought to mob justice. I read of one instance in which a judge who had found against squatters in a real estate dispute was stoned to death by a mob.

Procedurally, too, there was a great deal of confusion and duplication of effort. Lower court judges would lead the investigation of criminal cases, and the attorney general and the police would keep interfering in each other's work. Through my work in the Fulbright program, I presented some suggestions to the Peruvian Congress and Vice President Maximo San Roman about how they might reform the system, echoing other suggestions made by outsiders to separate areas of responsibility in criminal cases.

After a couple of weeks of travel, I returned to Lima and began teaching. The public universities were still on strike, as were the courts, and the only place I could teach was the Catholic university, Pontifica Universidad del Peru. So I taught administration of justice to middle-class students. I enjoyed their company, and I would have them to my hotel frequently for dinners and discussion. Finally, the courts ended their strike and I was able to fulfill my assignment and hold discussions with the legal community about the administration of justice.

I made other trips—to Albania to teach democracy and the justice system, to Honduras and back to Panama to help monitor elections, and to Korea and China to discuss commerce and education.

Back in Philadelphia, I was taking on new responsibilities as a judge, and I wasn't finished hopping from one career track to another.

9

ADMINISTRATIVE JUDGE, GENERAL COUNSEL AT HOUSING AND URBAN DEVELOPMENT, PHILADELPHIA CITY SOLICITOR

Administrative Judge

PHILADELPHIA WAS IN TROUBLE. The Wilson Goode administration had left the city near bankruptcy. It had been a grim decade defined by municipal deterioration and punctuated by one of the great urban disasters of our lifetime. Until Mayor Goode gave the word during the MOVE standoff in Cobbs Creek, no one had ever intentionally dropped an aerial bomb on a structure within the continental United States. The "unconscionable" decision killed 11 adults and children and burned a city block to the ground.[1] The new mayor, Ed Rendell, took office in 1990, overseeing a city faced with costly and inadequate facilities for the courts, loss of control over its fate as the state began initiating measures to keep it afloat, and federal court orders to build a prison and a criminal courthouse it could not afford. The Pennsylvania Intergovernmental Cooperation Authority had been assembled in Harrisburg to coordinate the process of financing bonds for Philadelphia and monitoring the budget on the city's behalf, because the city couldn't get financing on its own.

Lincoln Steffens had referred to Philadelphia as "corrupt and contented" almost a century earlier, and in many ways his words still held true. Back in 1984 I had served on a committee to reorganize the courts

---

1. See Philadelphia Special Investigation Commission (MOVE) Records, Temple University Libraries, https://library.temple.edu/scrc/philadelphia-special-1.

and the rules under which they operate and had watched as the recommendations were ignored and things only got worse. The courts were inefficient and bogged down with patronage, malfeasance, and mismanagement. Four people were assigned to do the job of one, budgets were ignored, nonexistent money was freely spent, and all for little result. Everyone complained, nothing changed, and woe betide anyone who dared attempt reform.

Outside of Philadelphia, patience was growing thin. State elections had ushered in a new Supreme Court, which increased the court's western weighting. With the election of Ralph Cappy, the 4–3 Pittsburgh-to-Philadelphia ratio was now 5–2 in Pittsburgh's favor. Off-year elections always favored Republicans and the western part of the state, because Philadelphia simply does not turn out for them. Chief Justice Robert N. C. Nix Jr. was from Philadelphia, but the only other Philadelphia justice was James McDermott. The five Pittsburgh judges—Cappy, Stephen Zappalla, and Nicholas Papadakos (known as "Cappy, Zappy, and Pappy") and Rolf Larsen and John Flaherty—created a collegial court and essentially took control as a voting bloc.

They had taken different routes to the bench. The key to Flaherty's election was likely his good name. Name recognition for a judge in an off-year election when voters aren't paying close attention is a real advantage, and Flahertys had been mayors of Pittsburgh and had run for governor and served in the Carter administration's Justice Department. It didn't even matter that John Flaherty wasn't related to any of them. Larsen was an erratic character, and the longest-serving judge on the Supreme Court bench save Nix. Nix, therefore, rather than Larsen, became chief justice, and Larsen, in an effort to get Nix defeated in the next election, threatened to publicize the fact that he was black.[2] Larsen would later be impeached and removed from the bench for buying prescription drugs through his secretary.[3] Cappy, the new arrival, was well-known and well-liked in Pittsburgh and he now joined his good friend the savvy Zappalla. Papadakos had been on the bench since 1984 and had gained notoriety for going on *Nightline* with Ted Koppel and promising to put a stay on mortgage foreclosures in Pennsylvania, a very popular stand to take during a recession.

---

2. David Lauter, "Pa. High Court in Turmoil: Justices Sidestep Misconduct Probe; Impeachment Rumors Abound," *National Law Journal,* June 27, 1983.

3. Associated Press, "Justice Charged in a Drug Scheme," *New York Times,* October 29, 1993.

Philadelphia's civil courts were mired in a seven-year backlog, and the perception of corruption had been confirmed by a Roofers Union bribery and extortion scandal in which 16 judges had been suspended and a few sent to jail. The Supreme Court wanted to perform a complete overhaul of the system, and in 1990 the justices convened to definitively address these issues they had been battling since 1984. The problem wasn't fact-finding; the facts were everywhere and agreed on. Resolutions had been made and measures recommended, but Edward Blake, in his role as president judge in the Court of Common Pleas, had not implemented them. The Supreme Court called an end-around, creating new powers for the administrative judge and transferring to him or her the authority that had been vested in the president judge. The justices wanted someone to take the post who would enact changes and operate free of the customary political backscratching. Unbeknownst to me, my name was being discussed. Justice Nix had known me when I was a law student and a member of the Black Law Student Association, and we had kept in contact. I considered him a valuable adviser and a mentor. I didn't know Justice Papadakos, but he knew of me through our mutual friend Peter Liacouras. He had family in Philadelphia, and, with a relative of his, he had sat in my court unnoticed and watched me at work. He and I would become good friends and socialize when he was in town. The Supreme Court knew I'd been involved in the early attempt at reforms and they made inquiries. Apparently, no one had anything bad to say about me. I was acceptable to Philadelphia power players such as state senator Vincent Fumo and Democratic chairman Bob Brady. I wasn't their first choice, but the thought of me in the new role of administrative judge didn't fill them with horror, either.

There was dirty work to be done, and I was a good candidate to do it. I was young, I was not afraid to rub people the wrong way, and I worked hard. I think my idealism and my naïveté might have been selling points, too. Anyone willing to take on something so intractable as an entrenched Philadelphia bureaucracy with the intention of actually changing something was painting a target on his back. And on his front.

The list of viable candidates was not long. Judge Blake had proved to be one of the staunchest defenders of the problem, aware of the obstacles and presented with possible solutions but unwilling to change anything. Judges Albert Sheppard and Bernard Avellino were involved in the new Judicial Accountability Committee that had been under way since earlier in 1990, but the Supreme Court was wary of them as well. Judge Sheppard chaired the Judicial Accountability Committee. He was the brother-in-law and protégé of Judge Avellino, who, though a very bright jurist, had gained national attention when he lectured a rape defendant, telling him that what he had done was stupid because he was a good-looking man and the woman he had sexually assaulted was unattractive. When asked in the press whether he really felt that the man's crime was aiming too low, he'd dug a deeper hole, saying the victim was the "ugliest girl I have ever seen in my entire life" and repeatedly calling her "coyote ugly." When those comments were published, he made a mealy-mouthed apology and complained that he'd only been quoting a female member of his staff. He asked to be taken off sexual assault cases and was taken off criminal cases altogether.

Judge Avellino, however, was very innovative in his approach to the discovery motion court and efficient in his decisions. Rather than ruling on discovery as things came up at trial or on motions filed daily, he set aside one day a week to rule on all issues of discovery for the entire Civil Division. It was a smart idea that he'd borrowed from the Pittsburgh court system. It saved a lot of time and set a predictable discovery decision time that lawyers could count on. But he felt entitled to take the resulting extra time to go golfing. The Supreme Court didn't look kindly on Avellino's behavior or his reputation. The justices were unimpressed with his brother-in-law, too, perhaps only by association, but they didn't want either of them or any of the old guard to take the new position.

What they needed was someone with the willingness, the wherewithal, and the requisite recklessness to take on an inflexible and ungovernable system that would resent every attempt to improve it. They decided on me without my knowledge and without ever speaking to me about it. I remember walking back to my chambers on the fourth floor late one evening in December and passing Judge Mark Bernstein as he came out of the hallway phone booth. He said he'd been talking to Harrisburg and I'd just been selected for the new position of administrative judge. I brushed him off. I thought he was making a joke, but the next morning I got the official call from the Supreme Court offering me the job. I would need to clean up the waste and budgetary abuses and deliver savings that would allow the Criminal Justice Center to be built, but they were going to give me control of the budget, the authority to hire and fire, and the power to assign any judge anywhere in the Court of Common Pleas I felt necessary.

The Court of Common Pleas in Philadelphia is the First Judicial District, and it encompassed the Trial Division (including the Arbitration Center), Family Court, and Orphans Court. In all there were about 120 judges, 90 of whom were in the trial division. Common Pleas excluded Traffic Court and Municipal Court, which was where most misdemeanors, small claims, landlord/tenant cases, and preliminary hearings are tried.

They wanted me to implement the necessary changes, and they expected me to look for innovative approaches to do what needed doing. There was certainly much work to be done. I accepted, and in December of 1990 I assumed the new position.

The task was overwhelming when viewed as a whole. It included everything in the Court of Common Pleas. There were problems in every corner of my purview, and I knew I needed help. The courts had a huge, bloated budget and were riddled with inefficiency. I went to local business leaders for guidance and support. CoreStates Bank lent me the services of one of its top executives for a year, free of charge. I placed him on my administrative staff and he was involved in most of my early decisions, setting the path for my entire tenure as administrative judge.

I began by focusing on the problems in civil court. Of the main causes of the seven-year backlog, one in particular stood out: the number of complex cases that were gumming up the works. Until we took these on, the amount of change we could bring about would be limited and only for show, like responding to the approaching iceberg by rearranging the deck chairs. With my powers of reassignment, I created the Complex Litigation Center and staffed it with all the civil court senior judges, whom I placed in the Wanamaker Building, across from City Hall. I put Judge Sandra Moss in charge. She was a well-respected judge in the city (and another Temple Law School graduate), gifted in her understanding of these types of complex cases and in her ability to come to a resolution when all hope seemed lost. I set her loose coordinating a docket of nightmare litigations—complex medical malpractice cases and asbestos and other product liability cases—and developing new procedures in the handling of mass tort litigation that would bring her national recognition.

Judge Moss was one of 14 judges who formed the administrative team I assigned to run the various areas of the court. They had volunteered from all over. Some had good relationships with major players in the city, such as Fumo or Mayor Rendell, or with the Supreme Court justices. Others had areas of expertise or interest or specialization. Abraham Gafni was well-liked by the civil bar and was thought of as an intellectual. He took responsibility for the civil trial calendar. Russell Nigro took over arbitration appeals. I assigned him a mandate to have all trials within 60 days. Legrome Davis took over the criminal division's docket. Richard Klein, a Republican—proof I was willing to work with anybody—was tech savvy in a court system that still relied on the typewriter. He had also come forward to overhaul the jury selection system. His jury selection idea involved removing judges as much as possible from the process, as was done in federal court. He said he could make the change in six months. I told him I'd give him six weeks, because I didn't know whether I had six months left in the position. He delivered. His questionnaire and the educational video he threw in to show to jury pools save almost a thousand hours of judges' time every year.

The weekly 7:30 A.M. meeting in my chambers could make for an especially long day, but these committee members were dedicated. They were the ones who identified what needed to be done and who put in the work to make it happen. And there was so much work to do.

I held the position of administrative judge for only 18 months, but I worked fast. Six months into the process I felt that we understood what we had to do, and we spent the rest of our time implementing our programs and monitoring our progress. The complex litigation program headed by Judge Moss was made possible because of the senior judges who served past retirement age and the judge pro tem program that filled in the civil court vacancies.

The judge pro tem program came about because, even before moving judges to the Complex Litigation Center, the civil court backlog needed more bodies. I wanted 50 new judges on the bench to hear more cases. I asked two prominent attorneys, Francis Devine, representing the defense bar, and Allan Gordon, representing the plaintiffs' bar, to work with the Philadelphia Bar Association to agree on a list of 60 lawyers who they believed could serve as judges. They made a list of the best among them. Those 60 lawyers were sworn in as judges pro tem, they worked without compensation, and they immediately made an impact on the backlog. In their first six months they reduced the caseload by 1,300.

In the civil courts, we adopted Judge Avellino's approach to the discovery program in motion court, and Judge Edward Maier oversaw a semi-annual rotation of judges to avoid burning anyone out on the streamlining program. The Complex Litigation Center removed a huge obstacle to the day-to-day proceedings in civil court. The pro tem judges were a further help in loosening up the backlog, and we instituted other programs to keep things moving in civil court. We gave judges more control over their calendars, so if they found themselves available earlier to hear a new case, they could adjust the schedule.

We instituted a case-forward/case-backward approach. I have always believed that in civil cases, nine times out of 10 a willing judge moving ahead with proceedings will lead to a settlement. To keep things moving, we created two teams of judges, one to attack the new cases and the other to address the old cases in the backlog. Our priority was to get the parties to trial or to get them to settle. In the meantime, Judge Nigro's arbitration team was sticking to the commitment of hearing all cases within 60 days.

Judge Gafni and I handled all post-trial motions and opinions, and, to maintain the flow, I oversaw the motion court myself. I had my law clerk oversee a team of four other law clerks, who produced a lot of the writing. Gafni and I would read the opinions of the judges pro tem, review them, edit them, and file them. I also took on the 450 zoning cases and scheduled them myself. The first thing I did was schedule a week during which I'd have a preliminary hearing for every case. If anyone didn't show up, I dismissed the case. In most of those I did hear I'd find for the Zoning Board, because a zoning appeal was often just a stalling tactic by developers. It had been a solid strategy in Philadelphia, where nothing got done in the courts. No one involved in the process knew what to do in the new reality where they had to show up on time and be prepared. Tobey Oxholm, who was with the deputy city solicitor, thanked me for clearing up the zoning backlog but told me I was hard to keep up with.

On the criminal side, major felony trials were divided into four sections, each with four judges presiding, rather than having everything emanate from Calendar Courtroom 625, a dismal place that every day was overflowing with people with nowhere to sit and nowhere to be assigned. Every major felony case had been assigned from there, and the system was unworkable for everyone. Splitting the cases into four areas allowed for far greater efficiency, and because the courts finally had computers (thanks to Judge Klein and changes to our procurement practices), those case assignments were all assembled on a centralized server that tracked everything. We had implemented the felony waiver program, which became the expedited case management program when it grew to include the major felony program. The intent was to divert cases likely to result in guilty pleas early in the process, and the new process was a big success. Under Judge Legrome Davis's supervision of criminal judges, the Rocket Docket, as the process came to be called, made things far more efficient.

We worked hard to eliminate continuances as much as possible in both civil and criminal courts. We warned all litigants and attorneys to be ready to go to trial from the start and no longer to expect continuances, to utter the word "continuance," or even to hold the word in mind. That word was to be stricken from the court's vocabulary. Things moved much more quickly. A court that keeps things moving, one that will not wait until attorneys take their time dotting every *i* and crossing every *t*, is a court in which lawsuits are more likely to settle, and each settlement was a victory over the backlog.

Behind the problems in the civil and criminal courts and other messes within the system lurked the specter of impending municipal bankruptcy. Large bureaucracies have a tendency to lose focus on the wider world. Partly that's by design: the court system certainly should focus on the administration of justice and not calculate financial considerations or budgetary constraints in that administration. But in the midst of a financial crisis in the city, the court system spent money as it always had, and fiscal profligacy was rampant. And as always, the city was of two minds on the topic. On one hand, you'd hear nothing but complaints about how much money went to waste, employing people who didn't contribute to the court's purpose, keeping bad contracts going, and perpetuating the patronage culture, which placed friendships and family relations over efficiency. On the other hand, that was good money for a lot of people, good contracts for friends of powerful people, and taking those positions and those contracts away would rub a lot of influential groups the wrong way. "Stop spending so much money," the city demanded, "but start looking somewhere else."

The good news lay in the number of places to make a difference. Everywhere I turned, I saw opportunities to reduce costs. Procurement, for instance. The court's supplies, its leases, its equipment, and even some of its contracts were negotiated and paid for through the City Procurement Department. Nothing was cheap. Companies that were still willing to deal with a near-bankrupt municipality faced delays in payment if payment came at all. They weren't offering price cuts for the business. Sweetheart deals had been negotiated to reward friends of the powerful, not to get the best price for the city. I created a fund within the Administrative Office of the Pennsylvania Courts (AOPC), outside Philadelphia's control and not afflicted by its troubles, and turned over the duties of buying supplies and equipment to it. The Philadelphia courts' account was funded by the City of Philadelphia, but AOPC did the purchasing. Prices were lower and delivery was quicker when vendors were assured of timely payment.

Through our new procurement system, in the year 1991 A.D., we finally bought touchtone telephones and even computers that were linked up through the court-system network. These technological advances made things around the courthouse far more efficient and were by far the easiest to make.

Almost without exception, every other budgetary decision and measure taken was difficult and varied from painful to hated. The courts had the new Justice Center to pay for, and no matter how the contracts were negotiated or by whom, it was going to cost a lot. And there was the further constraint of a mandate for the city to build a new prison. Waste had to be cut, and the budget needed to be slashed. Call it payroll reduction or personnel elimination: one of the biggest expenses was the court employees, and people needed to go. Each judge in the trial division had a tipstaff as well as a secretary and a clerk. The clerk could write opinions and the secretary could keep a calendar and take care of administrative tasks, but the tipstaff primarily took care of the judge's personal needs—making deliveries, running errands, and doing other things unrelated to the administration of justice. Ninety judges meant 90 tipstaffs, but even eliminating all 90 of them would not completely address the issue. Almost 2,000 court employees worked for the city, and many of them were redundant. I needed to know who was necessary and whom we could get rid of. Three judges stepped forward to lead the staffing committee. These brave souls—Michael Stiles, Frederica Massiah-Jackson, and Russell Nigro—put together a comprehensive list that rated every court officer from best to worst, from most productive to least. They worked with the heads of every department to figure out which positions could go, and which of those could be eliminated by attrition as longer-service employees retired. That task in itself was difficult. Some judges were less inclined to cooperate, and some, such as Judge Blake, simply refused. Blake, having been stripped of virtually all his power by the newly vested authority of the administrative judge, still managed to be an obstacle. He went to the newspapers and said he would not meet with the committee. I insisted, and reminded him that I had the power to hire and fire. He eventually capitulated, but it was a smart posture for him to take, one that kept him popular with his peers.

The panel learned from various department heads—Blake included—that there were specific areas to consider. The Custodial Department, for instance, employed a 55-person crew. Ronald Rubin, who headed a big real estate firm in the city, funded a study that revealed we needed a staff of only 11. I let the custodial team go and sent out a standard request for proposals, awarding the contract to a private cleaning firm, saving the city more than $1.5 million a year.

I also eliminated the wood shop, which made furniture for the courts. I don't think Justice McDermott, the only Philadelphia justice on the Supreme Court besides Nix, could forgive this decision. McDermott was a hanging judge and legal-system boogieman whose empty courtroom in Philadelphia was used to scare defense attorneys into going with a nonjury trial ("Judge McDermott would be happy to hear your case!"). McDermott would die on Father's Day the following year, 1992, sitting at his desk at home. I was leaving a speaking engagement at Sion Church in North Philadelphia that night when I heard the news. He hadn't liked me much before I became administrative judge, hadn't understood, for instance, why I'd go to Japan to try to learn anything. He was an old-school, America-first, hard-line conservative Republican who still held a grudge for Pearl Harbor. I was a dyed-in-the-wool Democrat and activist. The "woodchuckers," as they were called, had restored his Philadelphia chambers to their original condition. He was proud of his chambers and entering them felt like walking into the past, when City Hall had first been built. Getting rid of the wood shop was for McDermott the last straw. I had declared myself his enemy by doing so.

The Probation Department was overextended but could not hire any new probation officers because of the four layers of management sitting over those officers. We saved a lot of money by getting rid of the management layer cake, and with the personnel budget no longer maxed out, the state gave us funding to staff up on officers.

It was difficult work. Hard as it was for the panel of judges to make their recommendations, I didn't want them to take any unnecessary flak from peers, associates, attention-seeking politicians, the papers, or the public. It was my job as the leader of this effort to delegate my authority but to carry the responsibility. They submitted their ranked list of court officers and recommendations from the departments. Six months in we eliminated 500 positions without reducing services or efficiency. Most of the people we let go had been serving long enough to receive a city pension, but 500 was a huge number and the announcement caused a great deal of controversy. No one had ever seen a layoff this massive in a city institution.

The Teamsters saw it as a labor issue, even though none of the discharged employees was union, and they gave me the full treatment, complete with the giant inflatable rat and the truck endlessly circling City Hall, blaring unflattering messages about me over a loudspeaker and papering the sidewalk with literature that called me a "banana republic dictator."

Firing 500 people is always going to be a wildly unpopular thing to do, but I took the hit. And in 1991, that move by itself saved the city millions.

I learned something unsurprising about being unpopular: people around you will sometimes try to turn your unpopularity to their own advantage. Not everyone is your friend, and President Judge Edward Blake certainly wasn't mine. He had actually refused to speak to me since the Supreme Court had stripped him of his president judge powers and given them to me. I understood why he hadn't done anything. No one wants to make the hard decisions, but someone had to. I also understood why he was working so hard to capitalize on my role as the so-called executioner of the Trial Division. With virtually no administrative authority, Blake met with the Teamsters. He took a poll among the 120 judges in the Court of Common Pleas, asking whether I should be removed, which resulted in only five votes in favor and two abstentions.

Blake had served as administrative and president judge since ousting his friend Judge Bradley, and he was popular among his peers. With my job reductions, I provided a scoundrel against whom he could play the hero. He played it well, talking about my friendship with Supreme Court justice Papadakos. Papadakos was despised in the Philadelphia courts. He was a Pittsburgher and a shouter, and he would shout often about the bloated system in Philadelphia. He was seen in Philadelphia as a cross-state loudmouth bully from a rinky-dink little town who couldn't understand how a big city worked or even how to deliver a proper zinger. When he pronounced that Philadelphia judges should spend more time in court and less time at the beach, anyone with any sense knew that Philadelphia judges didn't go to "the beach," they went down the shore.

To calm things down, I wanted to meet with the Teamsters myself, but the AOPC lawyers said it would be a bad idea. The only union employees the courts had were in the Probation Department, and they were AFSCME. Meeting with the Teamsters might look as though I was considering letting another union into the shop. I didn't meet with them. Judge Blake did and made some political hay by doing so.

As controversial as the layoffs were, only four lawsuits resulted from them. One woman who had been an administrator had called me a "dirty spic" and sued that her job elimination had been retaliatory. I agreed to rehire her in a different department. Another suit was brought by the deputy prothonotary and vice chair of the Republican Party. Two others were brought by Republicans who said the firings were politically motivated. Those suits were dismissed because I hadn't known their party affiliations.

We saved money elsewhere, too. Since the 1970s, the court system had been growing beyond City Hall and had spread to buildings all over Center City, necessitating the construction of the Criminal Justice Center, which now stands at 13th and Juniper Streets. Judge Craig Lord was heading up the newly created Commerce Court, which was similar to Judge Moss's Complex Litigation Center in that it diverted commercial and business issues, but to a team of one judge, Lord himself. I called it the Business Court then and had assigned Lord because he was the smartest judge in the system when it came to matters of real estate. He had come to the bench from a prominent law firm, where he'd chaired the real estate department. He reviewed and ruled on all cases concerning mergers and acquisitions, land sales, and other business transactions. He was the perfect person to lead the renegotiation of all the court's leases and to wade through all the sweetheart deals worked out during the Rizzo administration. He worked with the AOPC, converting leases that charged $22 a square foot into leases for $11 a square foot. The lease he negotiated for the Complex Litigation Center was $6 a square foot.

All the upheaval was alienating to the court system, and I had set myself in opposition to many who preferred the traditional slow and ineffective pace of things. But I had more enemies still to make when I instituted a judge-ranking system.

There were virtually no judges in the civil courts at this time, because almost all had been reassigned and now served in criminal court, hearing cases in the homicide, major jury, and waiver programs. The civil courts were staffed with the 50 pro tem judges, overseen by Judge Gafni and me to make sure things kept moving and stayed on track. Judge John Herron had worked as an attorney on the State Ethics Board, which oversees judges, and he had experience in the Criminal Division. He had ideas for how to calculate the efficacy of a judge's work. Part of the mystique or the gravitas of being a judge is that you are serving justice, not making widgets on an assembly line. My suggesting that judicial productivity be measured ran contrary to the professional image of a judge. Judges see themselves as thinkers, as wise and considered. Judges are expected to be judicious. After all, that's where the word "judicious" comes from. One would expect, then, that among judges a judge-ranking system would be repugnant. But justice delayed is justice denied, and if there was anything that defined the Philadelphia justice system at the time, it was delay. So, Judge Herron came up with criteria for judicial accountability in the three programs in the Criminal Division.

Judges were reviewed for what they did, how long they took to do it, and how important what they were doing was. How long did it take for a major jury trial to get to a verdict? Or a general jury trial? How quickly were nonjury waiver trials disposed of? Herron created formulas that calculated issues such as daily output, factoring in the matters handled, multiplied by an assigned value, and reviewed over the number of work days taken. With six judges from the Criminal and Civil Divisions, Herron tracked the evaluations and ranked all the judges according to their performance. Few judges came out in support of the evaluation system or of any such evaluation, but the peer pressure was interesting to see. At the end of a term, I provided the top performers with the assignment of their choice.

Judges complained because the formula was unfair. They complained that the computers weren't working properly to track their work. One judge complained that the formula didn't factor in his judicial accomplishments in the seven years before the evaluation system was launched. Thirty judges complained to the court's director of data processing when the process began, most referring to it as a "disaster." Judge Klein, my Republican friend and great supporter, who had led the charge for better technology and speedier jury selection, called it "garbage."

But then the ranking system leaked to the press. The *Philadelphia Inquirer* got hold of the evaluations and published the names of the best and worst performers and gave out their evaluation numbers. Reporters followed one of the worst performers to a restaurant and waited outside during his two-hour lunch. When he caught wind of the ambush awaiting him, he tried to escape by diving out the bathroom window but was caught anyway.

There were controversies and near uprisings, but all these measures were working. With all the changes now instituted, by the six-month mark of my time as administrative judge, we were on our way to effectively eliminating the huge backlog on the civil side, we had come into compliance with the American Bar Association's two-year rule for criminal and civil cases, and we saved the city $14 million a year for 20 years. I had the support of the Philadelphia Bar Association, City Council, and the mayor. While my efforts earned me several determined enemies within the court system, they delivered the city its Criminal Justice Center. Later, when I was serving as city solicitor, the court tried to raise the budget. I opposed it. They knew what I knew and backed down.

The summer of 1992 found the Supreme Court planning again, and again without my knowledge. At the end of July and from beyond the grave, Justice McDermott would reach out to have his revenge against the man who fired his beloved woodchuckers. From what I gather, shortly before his death, McDermott proposed that all the administrative judges be reapproved by the Supreme Court, with a unanimous vote needed to retain each position. The only no vote cast by any justice for any administrative judge was the one McDermott cast when my name came up. So, I was out, but they held the announcement until after the summer break, when new administrative judges would be put in place. I learned of my replacement when a story about the new administrative judges ran in the paper on July 21. On August 1, I was back to being just a judge. Alex Bonavitacola took my place. He'd been in Family Court, which had been told to make changes but had made none. He was amiable and well-liked, and he maintained most of the changes I'd instituted, with the exception of the judge evaluations, which he discontinued. The other changes would have been harder to undo. Bonavitacola was probably the perfect judge for the courts after all the upheaval, even if I thought his taking over had happened a little too soon. But he brought peace to the valley.

Ironically, the day after I was replaced as administrative judge, the

Foundation for the Improvement of Justice announced that it was going to recognize me for the work I'd done. Judge Klein, who had been so full of surprises, had one more left. I could not resent him for being a Republican because he'd been a great ally. I could not fault him for publicly trashing the judge-ranking system because he'd done so much to improve the workings of the court. And now I learned that he had been the one to nominate me back in the spring. The Teamsters, still no fans of mine, threatened to protest the foundation if it gave me the award, but it went ahead and did so anyway.

I went back to civil court, overseeing jury trials, and I decided to run for Supreme Court justice. The new Philadelphia mayor, Ed Rendell, said he'd support me. I thought I might have a good chance. The primaries would be in the spring of 1993. That fall, Bill Clinton was elected president. And somewhere among all those elections and inaugurations and changes of season, Rendell had thrown his support behind Russell Nigro. I learned this right before going to Washington to attend a reception for Nydia Velazquez, the first female Puerto Rican U.S. representative in history, out of New York. I was a little deflated, but I had promised to go to the reception with a young man whose grandfather I'd helped open a grocery store back in my days as executive director of the Spanish Merchants Association. At that reception I gave my card to a woman named Sara Manzano. She was looking for a job, and later I would recommend her to Mari Carmen Aponte in the Clinton administration, who was looking for lawyers. Sara had asked whether I would pass along her résumé, and I had. I would forget having promised anything or having spoken to Aponte about it, but Sara would remember.

I withdrew my name from the running in February, before the primary and as a favor to Rendell, paving the way for Nigro to face the Republican candidate in an election he would lose. I began to hear rumors of the possibility that President Clinton was considering me to head the Equal Employment Opportunity Commission. Another right turn in the trajectory of my life. I was ready, so I started filling out the paperwork.

My friend Henry Cisneros, the newly appointed secretary of Housing and Urban Development (HUD), came to Philadelphia in early 1993 for a big HUD conference. U.S. representative Tom Foglietta put me next to him at the head table. I had followed Henry's career, as had many other Latinos of my generation, from his days as the first Latino White House Fellow. I had watched as he moved up the ranks of Texas politics. He had been a mentor to me ever since we worked together on Latino voter registration projects like the one that had helped him to become the mayor of San Antonio. Henry was the new wave of Latino leadership: well-educated, innovative, and dedicated to economic development. He could relate to anybody and was trusted in Texas. As mayor he still lived in the same house with his father, and he never had his own street paved.

It was good to catch up with him. He had been on Clinton's transition team after the election, and then he was appointed to HUD. At the conference, sitting at the head table, he asked me whether I would like to come to Washington again and join him as general counsel. He had been talking to Senator Harris Wofford and Representative Foglietta about it, and they agreed that I was the right person for the job. There was a backlog of litigation at HUD, and if I had a reputation for anything, it was for getting bureaucracies moving. And Henry knew my dedication to the issues of housing and civil rights.

I didn't mind the idea of going back to Washington, but I said no. I didn't want to work for a friend, and I was waiting to hear about the EEOC job. Very well, Henry said, but he wasn't giving up.

As fate would have it, the EEOC job evaporated quickly. Raul Yzaguirre, the man with whom I'd argued on the bus in Israel about who spoke for all U.S. Latinos, was not my enemy. We were friendly, but Yzaguirre's people didn't like me, and they opposed my nomination. Still early in 1993, I was out of consideration. Gilbert Casellas would eventually be tagged as commissioner. In the meantime, Henry saw to it that I got no other nominations for federal jobs. All the while he was calling me regularly to discuss problems with the Philadelphia Housing Authority (PHA), which was in disarray. Properties were in bad shape, crime-riddled and dilapidated, and there was a huge tenant lawsuit filed against the PHA claiming the housing was uninhabitable and that the agency wasn't providing proper maintenance. As had been true with the courts, the agency was in real financial trouble.

Henry offered me the job again, this time when I was in the courtroom. My law clerk answered the phone. I said I'd call him back. It was clear, though, not only that he wanted me to work with him but also that he was very concerned about the PHA and the people it was supposed to serve. Henry was such a good operative in part because he did really care about what he was doing. And while trying to reel me in, he was already acting as though we were working together. I wanted to help. Housing was to me the pre-eminent public issue, and while I knew I was being worked over, the Cisneros treatment was still highly effective. The mouse may know the boa constrictor is preparing to eat it, but there's little it can do but get squeezed.

In April 1993 I took an eighth grader I had been mentoring, Nakia Merriwether, the daughter of Royce Merriwether, on a day trip to Washington to show her around HUD. She met with people in all the various departments, and toward the end of the day, I sat in on her discussion with Henry. At one point, and with no shame, Henry asked her if she thought I would be a good candidate for general counsel at HUD. She said she thought so. Ruthless, he continued, telling her that HUD was facing real challenges, that I was just the man to address them. She agreed. Somewhere in their brief discussion of my fit as general counsel, I gave up. I stopped fighting. It was no use anyway, so I accepted. And into the jaws of the waiting snake I went.

General Counsel at Housing and Urban Development

Henry Cisneros submitted my name to President Clinton for the position of general counsel of HUD. The president then submitted it to Congress for confirmation. I began working on more paperwork for the FBI. The background checks would begin, and if all went well, a few months of thorough investigation and interviews with colleagues, friends, and family would lead to a hearing and then confirmation.

In the meantime, Henry had me working. After years of mismanagement, the PHA was a shambles. The agency's properties were barely habitable, and it was facing lawsuits and financial problems. Henry and I discussed the options and I suggested that HUD should take the drastic step of officially declaring the PHA in default, which it was. When that step was made official, HUD could then take over the PHA and run it from the federal level however it saw fit. Neither one of us wanted the feds to sweep in and start running things. We agreed that HUD should provide support and guidance until the PHA could get clear of its troubles. We could approach, I suggested, offering a partnership. The city would remain involved in every part of the process, and the co-operative leadership group could get the agency back to functional and out of default and then turn it back over to the city. There were internal obstacles though, and cardinal among them was the board.

Before Wilson Goode left the Mayor's Office in January 1992, he appointed himself chair of the PHA board. He had good intentions, but he was not going to support a federal takeover of the city agency, and he wouldn't trust HUD to merely help the PHA get back on its feet. I thought that the board, led by Goode, would either fight us at every step or just check out and be uncooperative. The board was dominated by South Philadelphia business interests and would likely follow Goode's lead. Their response would be the fundamental Philadelphia reflex— this is a mess, yes, but it's ours, we like it, and we don't want anyone telling us how to clean it up. The only help they would accept was the kind that let them keep failing in the exact same way. Their oversight had steered the PHA into its current predicament, and we wanted them all out. We needed new blood, but we didn't want to force the issue. Henry and I wanted the board's leadership to include Mayor Ed Rendell as board chair, and City Council president John Street as his second-in-command. Henry asked the White House to offer Goode a position, and they did, in the Department of Education. He accepted.

The next step was to get Rendell to take the post and to have him and Street oversee the PHA. I did not doubt that Street would join and be an active influence on the board, nor did I think that Rendell would turn down the position, but making sure Rendell stayed interested—not eventually delegating the job to one of his people—would be the trick. If Rendell accepted without a sense of the fight that faced him and the possibilities if he succeeded, I feared he would soon have second thoughts. This project was going to be a lot of work, and he would face a lot of opposition from that bloc of entrenched South Philly business leaders. We needed Rendell in there, active and energetic and fighting. So we'd provide him with an ally, one who would never quit, and one who would make him look bad if he did. I wanted Rendell to know right when he accepted that there would be someone in the vice chair position who would work tirelessly to turn things around, an ally but not a delegate. Street's presence and his approach would help keep Rendell engaged.

In August, Henry and I invited Rendell to sit down to talk about the PHA. Henry did all the talking. He reviewed the situation and asked Rendell to be the PHA's chairman of the board. Rendell was always ready to take on missions like this, and he agreed to all of it, to the conditions of the municipal-federal partnership, to the position itself, and even to having Street as vice chair. We all knew how tough Street was.

He'd been a strong advocate for squatters in North Philadelphia. He would get in and fight without compunction to change the board. Together, he and Rendell could make the PHA work again. Rendell said it sounded good, sure, but John probably wouldn't accept. I knew he would say that, and before he could get up and walk out, I asked for a moment. It was the end of the summer, and Street was on vacation, but I had the phone number where he was staying. I called Street and he answered. I put him on speakerphone. I said that I was sitting down with the secretary of HUD and the mayor, and we were interested in taking the PHA in a new direction. Henry explained his vision for the partnership between PHA and HUD again, and said that the mayor was going to chair the board. Would Street serve as vice chair? Street immediately agreed.

Street was in many ways the key figure on the board. He served there for 16 years, a powerhouse, remaining even when he was mayor himself; for 16 years the PHA set about the business of improving housing for the poor and indigent. Street led the charge to take down the high-rises, and he developed the neighborhood transition initiative. He even found ways to add resources to the effort, creating a neighborhood program that brought more affordable housing to North Philadelphia. Years later, Rendell gave a very magnanimous speech at the ceremony to hang Street's mayoral portrait in City Hall. Now a former mayor of Philadelphia and governor of Pennsylvania, Rendell attributed all of the PHA's successes to the efforts of John Street.

With the board now shaping up, the next move was to get a new executive director. I wanted John White Jr., a high-profile former ward leader, city councilman, state representative, and secretary of Health and Human Services in the administration of Bob Casey. White was a friend of mine, and I went to meet him in his office at the investment firm where he now worked, across the street from City Hall. I told him we needed someone like him to run the PHA, and I assured him that he'd have all the support he needed. White was a leader, and he was dedicated to the city, but he wasn't experienced in anything like running a housing authority. Henry was going to provide him with terrific people, including bringing in the director of the St. Louis Housing Authority to be the PHA's deputy executive director. But why, White asked me, should he give up his cushy, corporate-job salary to run an agency like that? I asked him whether he remembered what he'd said just a month or two earlier when I told him I was considering taking the HUD job.

He had said that he would give his right arm to work with Henry Cisneros. Now was his chance to cut it off and get to work. I wrote up the partnership agreement, and Henry, Rendell, and Street all signed it.

Getting the PHA in order was a good start to my time at HUD, except for the fact that I was not yet working at HUD. The investigation into my background continued, and it wasn't going well. One of the FBI's investigators had sat down with Judge Bill Lederer, who was not an ardent supporter of mine. Lederer had overseen a large staff that conducted mental health hearings and investigations, worked as hearing examiners, and determined whether a person should be committed to a mental institution for being a danger to himself or herself or others. As administrative judge I had taken over Lederer's program and installed senior judges to run those hearings and to make those decisions, eliminating another big expenditure for the court. Lederer resented what I had done and said I had pushed him out of the program. He had gotten worked up talking to the investigator, who had taken him literally and had written up the incident as if I'd physically rousted a colleague and given him the bum's rush out of the courtroom.

That same investigator came to see me, and at some point during our discussion told me that his wife had run off with a black Puerto Rican. He said he didn't like my kind much and seemed to hold me personally responsible for his children's being taken away. His report portrayed me as violent, ruthless, and unable and unwilling to work with anyone. Senator Donald Riegle, chairman of the Committee on Banking, Housing, and Urban Affairs, read the report and asked Henry whether I was the guy he really wanted. Henry told him I was, and that the person he read about in the report was not the man he'd known for years. He said that anyone who took on a bureaucracy as entrenched as the Philadelphia court system—and cleaned it up—had guts and knew how to get things done. I demanded to be re-examined by someone who wasn't predisposed to disliking me, and Henry saw to it that it happened. The second time through the process turned out much better.

I had my Senate confirmation hearing in August, on the last day of the session before Congress went on break. Maryland senator Paul Sarbanes led the hearing. I was touched that Senator Wofford stopped by to greet me. He had all along been interested in getting me to this position. And I was truly honored when Pennsylvania senator Arlen Spector came by just to say hello. He said he had no business being in that hearing room and was not even on the committee, but he wanted to be there in support. He had recently had surgery for brain cancer and his head was still bandaged, but here he was, shaking my hand and wishing me well.

The hearing itself was uneventful. I gave an opening statement, answered some brief and perfunctory questions, and that was that. I took my family out to lunch, and the next day I found out that my daughter Delia Lee was pregnant with our first grandchild. It was an auspicious couple of days.

I left the bench in Philadelphia on August 9 and took the job as general counsel at HUD on August 10. I moved into a little apartment three blocks from the office. My son, Nelson, got an internship at Fannie Mae in Washington before graduating from Drexel, and he moved in with me. Six months later, when he graduated, they made him an honest-to-goodness job offer.

One of my first orders of business was to look at the almost 20 housing desegregation lawsuits filed against HUD and various housing authorities, alleging a broad spectrum of racially discriminatory practices. Plaintiffs claimed that HUD and the public housing authorities systematically segregated racial and ethnic minorities. I had grown up in public housing and I saw my appointment as an opportunity to right some of these wrongs. And there were many, including one in Dallas, Texas, brought by an attorney named Jack Daniels on behalf of tenants who lived in a high-rise that had been built on the site of a smelting factory. In Dallas, in Philadelphia, and in many other cities, HUD was facing lawsuits, crumbling infrastructure, and financially troubled agencies.

And PHA's situation was as dire as that in any other city. As its new partner organization, we began to work on resolving the lawsuits brought against PHA by addressing the issues the tenants were facing. Often that meant getting all parties to agree to put the lawsuit in abeyance and to create actual solutions to problems of habitability. In many cases, the tenants' groups were right. I knew what unlivable conditions were like, and I knew how important housing can be in a person's life. I was there to make it right. I would make that promise to the tenants and their lawyers as I had made it to myself, and as I had sworn to God. I did so with activists like Nelly Reynolds, a tenants' rights activist who headed one group. In almost every instance, what the tenants wanted was a decent place to live, not a cash settlement. I tried to show good faith, and I most often got it in return. In this particular case, we found a fund of $200 million that was just lying fallow and apparently forgotten, and we applied that money to fixing the problems.

Sometimes the issue of trust was a big hurdle. Jack Daniels and his clients living atop a toxic waste site had been fighting HUD for eight years by the time I came along, and the case was now in court. I told him that I wanted to work with him and help his clients. Eight years in, he wasn't buying it from the new D.C. lawyer. The time for making friends had long since passed for Jack; he was there to fight for his clients against an obdurate government entity. I started to gain his trust in court one day. In cases brought against the government, the Justice Department was always first chair, and I as the HUD attorney was second. I can't remember exactly what was happening, but I was growing frustrated, trying to point out to the judge that HUD wanted the same thing the tenants' group did, but he wasn't listening. In exasperation, I threw my pen at him, which got the Justice Department, as first chair, held in contempt of court. The representatives from the Justice Department were not pleased, and when they told Henry about it and asked that I be disciplined, he again stood up for me. He told them flatly that he had brought me on board to be just that type of advocate.

The first big crisis at HUD during my tenure hit Labor Day weekend in 1993 and was centered on Orange County, Texas. A U.S. district judge had ordered the desegregation of public housing projects in 36 Texas counties, and in 1992 the Orange County Housing Authority announced plans to integrate the housing project in the town of Vidor. Before the first nonwhite person could even move in, the Ku Klux Klan started holding protests and demonstrations there. Vidor was a mean place with a long history of racism. With an all-white population of about 11,000, it was known as a "sundown town," where black people were not welcome after dark; the Klan had a storefront on Main Street. Things did not go smoothly when the first black residents since the 1920s moved in.

First was John DecQuir, who arrived in February 1993. The following month William Simpson moved in. In July, Brenda Lanus and Alexis Selders and their families moved in. All of them were confronted immediately with racially motivated hostility and intimidation, and a month after moving in, the women and their families moved out, soon followed by DecQuir. Simpson stayed for a while, afraid to leave his apartment, but in September, he, too, left Vidor. He moved to Beaumont. In a tragic turn, he was shot and killed in a street mugging on his first night there. He had fled a nightmare and immediately met his death. It was a terrible end to a terrible story.

Meanwhile, back in Vidor, the Klan led a "Victory in Vidor" parade.[4] Henry was furious. Not only was this an untenable turn of events that highlighted the failings of public housing; Texas was Henry's home. The murder hit him hard. As for me, it brought back memories of my young family in a quiet New Jersey cul-de-sac. We had moved for better schools, security, a little room, and a chance for the children to run around. We had hoped to find a little piece of the good life America promised until that night I saw through the kitchen window a furious cross burning orange in a field of soybeans. This quiet, nice place was not meant for us. We were not welcome.

A group of us met all weekend to discuss what could be done. There was a lot of anger over what had happened, but I also felt that the HUD lawyers saw no course of action we could take. Henry insisted that there was. To live in public housing, tenants have to agree to a few simple rules, one of which is that they are not to break any laws. The housing authority itself, which was managing properties funded by HUD, had the legal obligation to uphold all federal laws. Housing discrimination is a violation of the 1964 Civil Rights Act. The Civil Rights Act had never been used in this way before, but civil rights infringements are a violation of the law, and the local housing authority had failed. There was something we could do: HUD could assume authority over public housing in Vidor.

It would be a drastic move, and exactly what we had worked to avoid in Philadelphia, but it was necessary. I wrote the opinion that provided a legal basis for taking over the Vidor Public Housing Agency, and the Justice Department concurred. It was a novel use of the act, but it gave us a means by which to remedy a wrong that had been done. Not even two weeks later we were on the ground in Vidor with Webb Hubbell, the associate U.S. attorney general. Henry was still angry. He told the papers, referring to the black residents who had been pushed into leaving: "They were forced to move out. They were harassed and threatened and taunted with racial violence and obscene gestures. Teenagers put on white sheets to scare African-American children. Such behavior is simply unacceptable, and we can do something about it."[5]

Not long after, I was in Texas at a meeting of the county judges for

---

4. Sam Howe Verhovek, "Blacks Moved to Texas Housing Project," *New York Times*, January 14, 1993.

5. Sue Anne Pressley, "Cisneros Moves to Open Up Town in East Texas to Blacks," *Washington Post*, September 15, 1993.

Vidor, making HUD's case for assuming control of the PHA. They concurred, but reluctantly. Assuming administrative receivership of Beaumont and Orange counties' Public Housing Authorities allowed HUD to develop and implement a plan that would move in African American families in enough numbers that they would be able to stay. We also provided for some protection in the early stages of the change. Not only did the number of new families desegregate housing in the area; it desegregated the school system.

At the end of the George H. W. Bush administration, New York representative Bill Green issued a report about the approaching public housing crisis. The entire system was failing. Poverty was not being addressed so much as it was being clustered and institutionalized.

Henry wanted to make some fundamental changes. He wanted to make public housing look more like market-rate housing and give the people who lived there some room to breathe and access to such services as public transportation and education. And he wanted housing authorities to stop acting like rent collectors and become more entrepreneurial. All across the United States, these government slumlords ran tumbledown properties riddled with crime. There was no innovation, no thought given to alternatives, and no effort to address existing problems. Most cities were still employing a decades-old model that had not worked anywhere besides New York City, and there only provisionally. In most major cities at this time, public housing was high-rises. But high-rise buildings were maintenance nightmares, with crime-ridden stairwells and elevators that continually broke down. High-rises had been used in New York because of the density of the population. During Clinton's first administration, we began working with cities that didn't have the same issues as New York—which was, in essence, all of the cities we worked with save New York—to come up with alternatives.

In Vidor, that involved taking over the housing authority and firing those remaining top officials who hadn't had the good sense to resign. We made improvements, building a community center and installing central air in every unit. We instituted van service. It was helpful that Ruth Woods, the mayor of Vidor, believed in what we were doing and was vocal in her support of desegregation. And because of those who did not support our efforts, federal marshals were there when we moved in the first black families in the early morning hours of January 1994. The marshals stayed to ensure that the families were safe and that they felt so. One year after the murder of William Simpson in Beaumont, about 25 black families were living in Vidor, and they were there to stay.

Another situation—my job offered an inexhaustible supply of "situations"—had cropped up in the Bronx, two or three months into my tenure. Tenants were claiming discrimination by the owners of two buildings. One building housed only white tenants, and the other building, in a less desirable neighborhood, housed only blacks and Latinos and other people of color. The assistant general counsel in New York refused to issue a charge because there was no direct discrimination, which goes to intention. That may have been so. The landlords may not have meant to be discriminatory, but that was not the test I wanted to apply. The practice, for whatever its intent may have been, had a discriminatory outcome. The legal shorthand for this is "disparate impact." The assistant general counsel still refused to apply the disparate impact test to the case, so I removed him and reassigned him to Hawaii. He refused the reassignment, too, so I fired him. He sued me, claiming I fired him for being a conservative Republican. I had no idea what his political affiliation was, nor did I care. He simply wouldn't do his job, so he lost it. He lost the case, too.

I am proud that the application of disparate impact has become a lasting part of my legacy. In *Texas Department of Housing and Community Affairs v. The Inclusive Communities Project, Inc.* in 2015, the U.S. Supreme Court "upheld the right to make claims under the Fair Housing Act against unintentionally discriminatory practices that produce unequal outcomes."[6] Justice Anthony Kennedy wrote the opinion in a 5–4 decision.

In 1995, federal judge Norma Shapiro issued an opinion that could have ruined public housing because it was financially impossible. She was handling a case in which tenants in Chester, Pennsylvania, sued the Housing Authority and the city because the buildings they lived in were not habitable. Shapiro in her opinion determined that any vacant public housing unit was considered constructive demolition. If that opinion became an order, every vacant unit in the United States would have to be replaced. There was no budget for that and never would be, and if

6. See "Supreme Court Backs 'Disparate Impact' Claims and Strengthens Fair Housing Act," Public Interest Law Center, accessed June 26, 2018, https://www.pubintlaw.org/cases-and-projects/supreme-court-backs-disparate-impact-claims-and-strengthens-fair-housing-act/.

such an order were issued, the Justice Department would fight it all the way to the Supreme Court. Shapiro and I knew each other from my days as administrative judge. I asked her not to issue an order but to appoint a receiver for the City of Chester Housing Authority. She did so and wound up overseeing it for 20 years, giving it up only when she retired in 2015.

In St. Louis, the housing authority was asking whether it could partner with private developers to build public and market-rate housing in the same development. Every now and again, it seemed, a public housing agency asked whether it could use HUD monies to fund a partnership like this, and the answer always came back no. It couldn't do anything on public housing land besides public housing. HUD always said no because the HUD lawyers kept coming back to the simple fact that no such partnership had ever been authorized. But I did not think like an administrator; I thought like a judge.

A judge, for example, approaches a criminal case by considering what is prohibited, not what is authorized. I considered negatively the question of what was allowed: Did anything forbid a public-private partnership? Thinking about the question positively, my lawyers had concluded that since it hadn't been authorized or appropriated, it wasn't permissible. So I sent them to the law books and told them to research where there was anything in federal or state law prohibiting such an arrangement. We reviewed the 1937 Housing Act, which established HUD's precursor, the Federal Housing Administration, by which public housing received public monies. We also reviewed the laws of all 50 states. We came up with no prohibition.

So I wrote a negative opinion, saying there was nothing in the law that prohibited a partnership between a public housing authority and private developers. Federal funding could be used for development and an operating subsidy. Developers were excited, but they didn't know how to go about doing anything. The housing authorities were saying such a partnership would never work because they couldn't sell the land. That was true, but I pointed out that they could lease it. And in St. Louis, for what came to be known as the "Díaz Opinion" had been written, they got to work. And while they were working, the Office of Management and Budget issued new rules about how to go about this new partnership. And thus a new era in public housing began, in which public financing could fund a combination of public and market-rate housing.

Federal money had been drying up for decades, and this new approach—revitalizing the worst public housing and focusing on mixed-income development—which was formalized in a program known as HOPE VI, became a shot in the arm for public housing. Money worked better and could go farther in this partnership than it had before. Before, with a budget of $200 million, a housing authority could build a high-rise. But in the new reality, with $200 million, a housing authority could go to a developer and offer an opportunity to build 1,000 units, half of which would be public housing and half market-rate housing. We could use that $200 million to get financing, and the developer would create something desirable for everyone: better housing and greater diversity in income, replacing the practice of shunting away the poor folks in their skyscraper poverty crates, far from public transportation and the better houses and schools.

In Baltimore, we got rid of all the high-rises in response to a lawsuit there. In Philadelphia, high-rises were torn down and replaced with hundreds of public and market-rate housing units. The areas where the high-rises had been became more livable, and with Section-8 housing, residents could move to different areas as well. HOPE VI began to receive some funding from Congress, too. Amazing what a little success can do. Through HOPE VI and the approach of public-private partnership, I was able to resolve $9 billion in lawsuits from tenants' groups and housing authorities across the United States.

Just before Christmas 1994, Andrew Cuomo, assistant secretary in the Office of Community Planning and Development (CPD), came to me. Cuomo's office sat within HUD and was responsible for dispersing monies and giving support to communities in need. He was in the early stages of the Empowerment Zone selection process. Clinton had campaigned on investing in infrastructure, but he'd had to curb those ambitions for his higher priority of deficit reduction to have any chance of success. The Empowerment Zone was a compromise, a package of tax benefits and federal financial resources aimed at encouraging new businesses to move into impoverished areas. It was a supply-side approach to stimulating growth through business opportunities. Aid was based on how many employees a business would hire from within the zone, and Empowerment Zones would have staffs on site to offer support.

Cuomo asked me to sign off on his selections, which was part of my job. But no one had seen any of this before, and it seemed he had skipped all the steps that were supposed to lead him to his recommendations. The White House hadn't yet vetted the applicants, nor had Cuomo's own staff yet finished weighting them. The selection process was supposed to be a competition, and CPD staff would assign points to each applicant. I called Henry, who was off for the holiday. He told me to wait until he could look the selections over.

When everyone returned to the office in January, we held a meeting about the possible winners. Cuomo was very apologetic and assured us he'd go through proper channels. Henry had some problems with Cuomo's list of winners, including the fact that there seemed to be enormous areas of need that had gone unaddressed, including in New York and Philadelphia and Camden, New Jersey. How were we to choose? I said I'd draft some rules, and I wrote an opinion requiring that all cities selected had to have been visited by the secretary of HUD and his input considered. Kansas City and Los Angeles had been named, but Henry had other programs to address the very real needs those cities had. Both were given small Empowerment Zones, which offered tax benefits to businesses that would set up shop there and other alternatively funded resources. New York was selected, specifically Spanish Harlem and the Bronx. Camden was, too, as were Philadelphia neighborhoods in North Philadelphia, West Philadelphia, and along North American Street.

Each city installed staffs to woo new businesses and alert corporate interests to the tax benefits and financing opportunities. The Empowerment Zones lasted for 10 years, and businesses that took advantage would get priority in federal funding and programs. Philadelphia got a big boost because of its Empowerment Zone.

At HUD I also found ways to help social programs in Philadelphia, including several homelessness programs. Sister Mary Scullion is a significant figure in the homeless community in Philadelphia. She ran Project HOME, a very effective homelessness support program. Sister Mary would go into any community, impoverished or otherwise, including such well-to-do areas as Rittenhouse Square and Fairmount Park, and put homeless people there. At the time, she was trying to open a homeless shelter near the Fairmount section of the city, but the city was blocking her. I called David L. Cohen, Mayor Rendell's chief of staff, and told him that if he didn't stop, Secretary Cisneros himself would make sure all the HUD money going to Philadelphia dried up. That solved the problem. I also helped APM, a Latino homeless support group with direct grants and support.

In other developments, I found an old urban development action grant from the Carter administration for hotel construction on the Del-

*Standing with Sister Mary Scullion, founder of Project HOME
and a champion of the homeless in Philadelphia, after she was awarded an
honorary doctorate by Temple University.*

aware waterfront. At the time, that area was underdeveloped and Delaware Avenue was lined with crumbling piers and abandoned buildings and warehouses. It was not a promising area for a hotel, and the Hyatt Company had never taken advantage of the grant. But now the time was right, and the Hyatt at Penn's Landing was ready to break ground. Perhaps we could provide assistance by making use of a grant that had been idle for decades. I determined that money committed and not returned to the Treasury could be used for the earmarked project. I didn't want to waste it, because it could be put to great use, but if it were to be returned to the Treasury, it would simply vanish. I decided we could use it and prayed no one would challenge me. No one did, and now a Hilton Hotel stands on the Delaware waterfront. With these things done, I felt I could return to Philadelphia after my time at HUD with my head held high.

And the time had come to do just that. Clinton's first term was coming to an end and Henry and I were moving on. Henry had been hounded by a Justice Department investigation that had begun in the spring of 1995. He was financially supporting a former mistress and had underreported the amount to the FBI on his security clearance forms. He offered his resignation when the investigation began, but Clinton refused it. Publicly, the president vocally supported Henry; privately he asked him to stay on through his first term. So when Clinton was reelected, Henry retendered his resignation. Andrew Cuomo was going to be the incoming HUD secretary, and he asked that I stay on in my role. I turned him down. I had committed long before to go to work at the Philadelphia law firm of Blank Rome. Managing partner David Girard-diCarlo had approached me when I was a judge. I had asked him to wait six months so I could make it to 10 years on the bench. With 10 years in, I would qualify for a judicial pension and lifetime health benefits. But then I was named administrative judge, so six months became two years, which then turned into six years by the time I went to work for Henry at HUD.

My loyalty had always been to Henry and my tenure ended with his. I was there to protect and support my friend, acting as a legal gatekeeper who kept Henry informed of what decisions were under consideration. I had joined him reluctantly, worried what our working together would do to our friendship (and to my admiration of him).

On the last night of Clinton's first term, Henry and I reflected on what was ending and what was next. He was going to Univision as president and chief operating officer, but he didn't feel that he could just leave. I had received some great news earlier that day about the lawsuit brought by the tenants in Dallas who were living on the site of a smelting factory. After 12 years of fighting and scrapping and advocating against the *federales*, Jack Daniels, now a friend of mine, had won. Those feds would fund the construction of 950 alternative housing units in West Dallas and provide transportation. The high-rise would be vacated, demolished, and never spoken or thought of again. And an additional $94 million would go to the City of Dallas for neighborhood equalization. I could think of no better way to end my time at HUD.

But Henry wasn't quite finished. He headed over to the White House one last time and waited at the bottom of the stairs that led to the president's living quarters. When the president came through the Grand Hall to retire for the evening, Henry planned to ask for a moment. He was going to wish him well and thank him for the honor of serving. Henry would point out that he'd served the president well and make a parting request. He would say that he couldn't leave his post until he was assured that the president would hire more Latinos to his cabinet. He would ask Clinton whom he would like to bring in.

The next morning, Henry called me to tell me he had finally successfully resigned, and he gave me the privilege of calling the accomplished Aída Álvarez, a Harvard graduate—as well as an investigative journalist who had won an Associated Press Award for her work on guerrillas in El Salvador, the former head of the New York Hospital Corporation, an investment banker, and director of the Office of Federal Housing Enterprise Oversight—to tell her she would be appointed administrator of the Small Business Association. She would be the first Puerto Rican and the first Latina to serve in a president's cabinet. I was a big admirer and had advocated for her. Henry further told me that Federico Peña, who had also packed his bags to leave the next day after heading up Clinton's Department of Transportation, was going to be secretary of energy. And with those appointments in place, we came to the end of our time at HUD.

Henry is one of the smartest men I ever worked for. If he had been able to stay in that job for eight years, he could have accomplished some amazing things. I think Henry was the best secretary HUD ever had. He understood how to run a city because of his time as mayor. He understood discrimination in the lives of everyone and the bedrock importance of fair housing. He understood the importance of education for urban kids and had developed a program that granted a scholarship to a state university in Texas to any graduate of a San Antonio high school with a B average or better. As a White House Fellow and as a mayor of a major U.S. city, he set a path for other Latinos to follow. He was a trailblazer with a Ph.D. who had taught urban policy at the University of Texas. He brought the full power of his intelligence to bear in every role he occupied.

Henry would have testified under oath about the discriminatory practices in place in the federal government's own policies. He had many times identified the real problem that underlay what we referred to euphemistically as "inner city issues," and he would tell anyone who asked that the problem was race. He walked the walk and would talk the talk.

Smart, well read, and approachable, he can express himself to anyone, from migrant workers to kings and presidents. Henry has brains, but Henry has heart too. He is charismatic, but he has led a humble life. I had always admired him, and our four years together only increased my esteem. He was and remains an exceptional man, and one I am proud to call a friend.

City Solicitor

With some sadness I left my little apartment three blocks from the office. My son, still at Fannie Mae, took over the lease. The son was smarter than his father, though, and he bought the apartment and would later turn a good profit on it. In February 1998 I left him to return to Philadelphia and start work at Blank Rome.

Things felt very different back in Philadelphia. I had left a house full of children to go back to Washington. Now Nelson was in D.C.; Vilmarie was married and living her own life; and Delia Lee had moved to North Philadelphia to start over on her own. After she had had a baby and married the father, he had left her. The place I came back to on JFK Boulevard seemed cavernously empty and at the same time too small for just Vilma and me. With our grown children gone, all that was left was the sense that there was nothing between us.

The long hours I worked at Blank Rome helped keep me out of the house. Vilma was working as a legislative assistant to John Street, who was still City Council president then. We rarely saw each other. I asked Vilma to go to counseling with me, which she did a couple of times, then stopped. I asked the children to go, too. They weren't interested. Vilmarie said it was a waste of time.

I was splitting my time among Blank Rome offices in Philadelphia, New York, and Washington. Sara Manzano, whose résumé I had passed along to Mari Carmen Aponte, had been working in New York as assistant general counsel at HUD. As general counsel I had called her office, but I rarely spoke with her. Still we had been collegial enough that I had gone with other associates from HUD to her mother's funeral in 1996. Now, here she was in 1998 at a New York Hispanic Bar Association gathering on Wall Street while working in the HUD regional office in New York. We hit it off.

She was straightforward but kind. Professionally, she had been very loyal and good at her job. She was smart and honest and it didn't hurt that she was good-looking. Though I knew she was from Harlem, until we got talking, I did not know that she and I had grown up in the same high-rise in New York. We had been just four floors apart, yet had never met. We had both struggled, worked hard, studied the law, and gone on to better things. I knew how difficult that journey had been for me, and I felt a kind of kinship with a fellow striver. Why had we not met? Our families knew each other, but we had lived in different orbits. To her, I had been the kid in the Rice High School jacket she'd see running off to play baseball. Meeting her now at the Hispanic Bar Association event wasn't some kind of one-in-a-million shot, but it felt somehow like the right thing happening at the right time.

At this point I had been seeing that therapist for about six months. I had needed to pay someone to tell me that I was unhappy and that I was probably depressed and needed a change. As I talked with Sara, I remembered that my therapist had said to me more than once that at some point I would have to do something to be happy. I told Sara that I'd like to see her.

In April 1999 I moved out and left the place on JFK Boulevard to Vilma. I asked her for a divorce. I promised to do right by her and I believe I have. I rented an apartment in the Art Museum area close enough to work that I could walk there.

Working at Blank Rome, I felt I'd been given access to a sphere of influence I'd never known existed. I went to the Pennsylvania Society gathering at the Waldorf-Astoria in New York City. I felt I was meeting the people behind the people who were in power. I was learning about how money worked. And at last I felt I was putting together how to actually be a successful lawyer in private practice.

It was a great time for me. I proposed to Sara in August 1999, and on January 11, 2002, we would marry. I write the date here so I'll never forget it. We bought a house in Chestnut Hill, near a nice big park, and moved in. The year 2000 was the best I'd ever had as a lawyer. By November I had billed close to $5 million. That was the month when John Street called me. He had been mayor only since January, but it already looked as though he was going to lose his city solicitor, Ken Trujillo. After serving for under a year, Trujillo was talking about going back to his law firm to see through some cases that were wrapping up. To tell the truth, he didn't like the position. My old friend Carl Singley had been on John's transition team and had worked Trujillo hard to get him to join the new administration. But Trujillo was a golfer, a networker, and a class-action litigator, who happened to have a huge lawsuit settling at the law firm from which he had never divested. Going back would allow him to take the huge fee and make his name as a lawyer. Staying on as city solicitor would, in effect, be giving up $1 million to stay in a job he found boring.

Street asked me to take the position—just when I was getting the hang of working at a law firm and starting to earn a good living. I had been attached to Street ever since I had recruited him to Temple Law School. I had taken pride as I watched his career unfold, beginning with his election to City Council; he had gone on to be elected president of City Council, and now he was mayor. And here he was, not only asking for my help but also offering a very appealing job. The city solicitor represents every city employee, including every member of City Council, the district attorney, the city controller, and the mayor, as well as the police and every functionary in every department in Philadelphia. The city solicitor is a member of the mayor's cabinet and is the final word on the interpretation of the city charter. City solicitor is the only position mandated by the city charter.

But I was making good money!

I went to see Blank Rome's managing partner David Girard-diCarlo, the man who'd patiently waited six years to hire me.

"Nelson," he said. "What are you doing? You're just beginning to figure this out."

I couldn't argue with him, but I was excited by the prospect of the new position. So I sought out my great mentor Howard Gittis to ask him what he thought. Howard knew me well, knew how much I loved public service and how much I loved Street.

"Nelson!" he said. "Why are you hesitating? Take the job!"

He was right. I had to take the job. The day after I accepted, an article came out in the *Legal Intelligencer* saying that Jim Eisenhower and I were competing for the position. I was being considered? No, I had been offered the job, and I had considered it. I wasn't competing with anyone. Eisenhower felt the same way, and he called me, demanding to know what I wanted with his job. I called Street and he said it was a big mix-up. I was the guy he wanted; he had never offered the job to Eisenhower, though his chief of staff had interviewed him. The job was mine. And it was.

Girard-diCarlo threw me a big dinner and gave me a bonus check. He was very good to me and always generous.

Time for another right turn. This time back working for the city.

But the job of city solicitor was like nothing else I'd ever done. One day I would be arguing in front of the Pennsylvania Supreme Court, and the next day I'd be at the Philadelphia International Airport discussing the need for tachometers. I worked with Philadelphia Gas Works, which was operating at a major deficit, attending every board meeting. I sat on the Convention Center board and others as the mayor's designee. I argued cases in court. I negotiated contracts. I interpreted policy. Of course, not every city solicitor approached the job in the same way. Trujillo, for instance, was far less hands-on. I was a contrast to him in just about every respect. He approached the job like a personal injury attorney, seeking out cases that could bring the city money. In this respect he was not successful, and his affirmative litigation department had actually cost the city money. I approached it in the same way I approached any matter of law, as I had in writing the Díaz Opinion: as a judge would. Government was a defensive entity. To treat it as a money-making endeavor was anathema to me. The government's job was to enforce rights, to protect, and I found the idea of affirmative litigation to be a terrible one. Government is not a business any more than its citizens are customers, and this frame of reference leads to all kinds of trouble, from the efforts of the police or the Parking Authority to fulfill a quota of tickets every month to the practice of civil forfeiture.

City solicitor was a job that could make a big impact, and I had more fun as city solicitor than I had had in any other job I ever held. I loved the work and had a good team under me. My deputy city solicitor, Romy Díaz, had worked at the Environmental Protection Agency and was a much needed asset in regulatory issues. After leaving the agency in D.C., he had planned to move to Cherry Hill, New Jersey, to join his partner, take the bar exam, and go into private practice. When he called me for advice, I told him to live in a real city and practice law in a real city. I said I was going to be city solicitor, and I wanted him to come work for me. I didn't know in what capacity or for what salary, but I promised the work would be rewarding. He accepted, and when I was named, one of the first phone calls I received was from Romy, asking when he was joining and what his role was going to be.

I recruited Eva Plaza from D.C. to handle retail issues, code issues, and licenses and inspections. I had worked with her when I was at HUD and she was at Justice. She was a Harvard graduate with a strong civil litigation background, and she had dealt with the intricacies of city governments. She was a great addition.

The first action I took when I started in the new job was to close down Trujillo's affirmative litigation committee. Shelley Smith had run it, and I met with her to tell her what I was doing and why I was doing it and to say that I wanted her to move over and head up the Labor and Employment Unit. It was a good opportunity for her. Negotiations with the police and fire departments' unions were coming up, and these were high-profile negotiations. To my great surprise, she flatly turned me down. I thought she'd be a good fit in the position, but I wasn't going to beg. I told her she could return to the Civil Rights Division to report to her old boss, Carlton Johnson. She left angry. I wasn't very happy either. But soon she was back, with Johnson. She had reconsidered and would be happy to take the job. Johnson was a good boss, and he had apparently explained that this move was good for her career.

Both Romy Díaz and Shelley Smith would go on to serve as city solicitors. Smith served for eight years under Mayor Michael Nutter.

During my time as administrative judge, Family Court had not been under my jurisdiction, and no steps had ever been taken to change how it functioned. Cases still moved slowly, and there remained an enormous backlog. I met with Kevin Dougherty, president judge of Family Court, to see what could be done. Justice Dougherty was a worker, like me, and he was always open to doing things differently if it made things better. As I saw it, the biggest obstacle to getting things moving was the lawyers. Family Court did not operate like a real court. For instance, if they wanted a social worker to testify in a case, they would just ask. And so everyone treated an appearance at family court as optional. There were too many friendly relationships among lawyers and witnesses, and the clients suffered. The court needed to subpoena witnesses and stop issuing continuances. Dougherty agreed. We had all of the lawyers shipped out and moved to other courts, and we brought in 30 young law school graduates, trained them, and set them loose. That change had an immediate effect. Things started moving much more quickly.

Alba Martinez, head of Health and Human Services, was so grateful for the removal of that millstone around her department's neck, that she offered to pay those new lawyers with federal funding she had available.

She and I had become friends when she came to me asking what I could do about a bad policy that impacted kids in the foster program. When Hansel Minyard was city solicitor in the mid-1980s, he had written a rule that prohibited all city employees from adopting or fostering a child in the city's system. It made no sense to her, or to me. The rule hinged on a section of the city charter that says no city employee can contract with the city. Clearly, while an adoption does require a contract, the provision refers to commerce. So I had written a new opinion that contravened the old, misguided one, stating, "The intent of the prohibitions is to preclude unethical conduct intended to benefit the employee, or actions where employees solicit or look for personal profit or gain."

Back in 1973, when I was at Temple Legal Aid, I'd filed a lawsuit against the city commissioners and the State of Pennsylvania, demanding bilingual voting ballots. The Voting Rights Act required that such ballots be provided whenever there is a 5 percent non-English-speaking population. With an election approaching, I had sued to have Spanish-language ballots in all the voting booths. Judge Joseph Lord, chief judge of the Eastern District Court, decided in our favor but it was too close to Election Day to replace the ballots, so we pasted a Spanish-language version on the side of every voting booth. Now, in 2002, as city solicitor, I asked the procurement commissioner to take the further step of publishing all the ballots in Spanish-speaking newspapers, to ensure that we were in compliance with the act. In 2004, Romy would reinforce the requirement with the court.

In October 2003, my time was winding down. I had committed to Mayor Street that I would stay through his first administration, and the election was approaching. Then everything blew up. On October 7, 2003, during a routine security sweep, the police found listening devices in the mayor's office that had been planted by the FBI. We had a month until the election.

As city solicitor, I represented the mayor, and so I began to work through the process. The FBI had made a couple of mistakes. It looked, for one, as though someone from the bureau had leaked the word to the Mayor's Office that the bugs were there, and, for another, whoever planted the bugs put them in the wrong place. Street never held his meetings in the office, so if anything underhanded was going on, the feds weren't going to hear it there.

The FBI came out with a statement acknowledging that, yes, they were FBI bugs, and, yes, it had placed them in the mayor's office, but it had not been targeting the mayor. Still, this episode could have been disastrous for Street, who was locked in another tough race against the Republican challenger Sam Katz. Street and Katz had run against each other in 1999, and Street had won by a narrow margin. It had looked as though this would be another close one. We didn't know how it would play out or a hundred other things. Would both newspapers endorse Katz as they had last time? Katz was running on lowering taxes, and he had a new anticorruption message that struck at the many scandals that swirled around Street while not embroiling him directly. This office bugging could have been a death knell for Street if not for some savvy campaigning. While I was working on preventing the mayor and his cabinet from being indicted, his campaign came up with a simple but effective plan. Blame the Republicans. Blame all Republicans. The Street campaign came out swinging against an attack by George W. Bush, claiming he was going after black mayors and East Coast cities. The bugging was all anyone wanted to talk about, and Sam Katz and his campaign were drowned out in all the clamor.

It worked. Street won by the widest margin he ever would in his career, at any level. African Americans came out to vote in support, and a lot of white Democrats who were thinking about voting for the pro-business, lower-taxes, anticorruption candidate—the one portrayed as the good business guy in the papers—were won back to Street's side.

I served until January 29, 2004, when the new administration began. As I looked back on the 14-year span from late 1990 to early 2004, I felt that I'd made good on the pact I'd made with God. I had taken my duties in public service very seriously, and I'd made a difference. I had been a prime mover in the effort to get a broken Philadelphia court system back to functional. I had worked to make public housing more livable across the country, resolving lawsuits, writing opinions, and helping to usher in a new era in which public and private enterprise worked together. And in Philadelphia, I had helped to uphold voters' and immigrants' rights, I had made changes in Family Court to allow it to function like a real justice system that considers the needs of the citizens it serves, I had helped the city's municipal utilities out of bankruptcy, and I had removed countless needless obstacles.

I was 57 years old, and I was ready to return to the private sector. Blank Rome welcomed me back. I began to serve on corporate boards, including Exelon's. I joined that board the day I resigned as city solicitor.

I would work at Blank Rome until 2007, when I moved over to Cozen O'Connor. I was there till 2011, when I went to Dilworth Paxson, where I stayed till the end of 2018 and resigned at the ripe old age of 71.

There was, however, one last detour to make, before coming to the end of my working career. In 2014, I decided to run for mayor.

10

RUN FOR MAYOR, PUERTO RICO
ELECTRIC POWER AUTHORITY,
REFLECTIONS

PHILADELPHIA IN 2014 HAD CHANGED a lot from the Philadelphia of my law school years. I had watched the transition from the Rizzo administration to the first black mayor, and the second, and the third. Ethnic voting blocs, unions, business interests, they all had a hand in determining who sat in the big office in City Hall.

Bill Green followed Rizzo as mayor, beating out my friend Charlie Bowser, but not by as much as he had expected. Green was a Kennedy-style liberal, and neither the unions nor the black population supported him. The police union particularly disliked him. Green saw the handwriting on the wall. He was also getting a handsome settlement from the local CBS affiliate after they broadcast a story that said the federal Environmental Protection Agency was about to indict him for polluting. Green was not going to be re-elected, and all he had to do was decide which path to take to the comfortable life that awaited him: bow out gracefully or suffer a humiliating defeat after a bruising campaign. He chose not to run. His managing director, Wilson Goode, who had read that same handwriting on that same wall, had been quietly campaigning during Green's term, visiting almost every police precinct under the pretense of reviewing the city budget. Goode had the support of the police and other unions—Henry Nicholas of the 1199C hospital workers' union was distributing "Wilson" buttons by New Year's Day—as well as the black community, and with that behind him, he became Philadelphia's first black mayor.

During Goode's administration the state took over the city's budget, the mayor initiated the disastrous MOVE bombing, and the city suffered a general sense of chaos and entropy. But still Goode served two terms, receiving 95 percent of the black vote when Rizzo ran as the Republican candidate in the 1987 election. After Goode and what seemed like an interminable slide toward disaster, Ed Rendell served for two terms and the city began to look as though it was turning around. In part this turnaround was simply a matter of Rendell's personality, a change in the public's perception, but those things are important in a leader, and the city's fledgling optimism made a real and tangible difference. We did some good in the courts and in housing during his administration, and because of his relationship to Bill Clinton and personal similarities to him, Rendell became known as the president's mayor. In Street's two terms that followed, I feel that things continued to get better. Michael Nutter's administration was, in my judgment, a mixed bag of self-canceling developments in real estate and gentrification and struggles with the Commonwealth.

The business landscape has changed as well since 1969. Many of the businesses that were anchored in Philadelphia when I arrived have been sold off. Rohm and Haas was a Philadelphia company, but it was sold to Dow Chemical, based in Michigan. First Pennsylvania Bank became CoreStates, then First Union, then Wachovia, and is now Wells Fargo, headquartered in California. PNB was bought by a Pittsburgh bank and is now part of PNC. SmithKline was sold and is now owned by a London-based company. All of these sales basing Philadelphia employers outside of the city have meant a big loss of business community leadership, too. What's left now is the Roberts family, who own Comcast, and a city full of great hospitals, including Children's Hospital of Philadelphia, Pennsylvania Hospital, Temple University Hospital, and the Hospital of the University of Pennsylvania, as well as nearby Lankenau Hospital on City Line Avenue and Cooper University Hospital in New Jersey.

The Greater Philadelphia First Corporation no longer operates today, but back in the 1970s and 1980s it was a political force. Most of those original 26 big Philadelphia businesses are gone. The wage tax acts as a suppressor to opening a business here, and Philadelphia is saddled with the reputation—not an entirely unfair one—of being unfriendly to business. The domino effect of the loss of business is felt everywhere, including in law firms, and many of Philadelphia's top firms—Morgan Lewis, Pepper Hamilton, Reed Smith, and Blank Rome—seek more business outside of the city and have set up offices in New York, Washington, D.C., and elsewhere.

I found myself taking stock of the city that had long ago become my home, and of my own life. I was serving on company boards and was a partner at Dilworth Paxson. Things were pretty good for me. But what had I accomplished? What was left to do? Had I fulfilled my deal with God to spend most of my time serving the poor and the vulnerable?

I had helped shape a court system that had grown wild and untended since 1776, adding judges, staff, and courtrooms without ever reorganizing. It had been running out of places to hold court and had never restructured to accommodate the needs of a non-18th-century city and the people who came to it seeking justice. I had had a determining role in the reform process.

I had helped to find a solution to a national crisis in public housing, bringing municipal affairs and private business together to make mixed-use housing a more desirable place to live. And I'd brought many of these solutions to the city itself, paving the way for a new era in improved living conditions for the poor and disenfranchised.

I had helped Peter Liacouras change Temple University from a commuter school to a premier research institution. Philadelphia's favorite safety school has become a prestigious place to go.

I had created a lot of nonprofit community development corporations and had brought the National Association of the Hispanic Elderly to Philadelphia. To this day, the best community development corporations in Philadelphia—the Hispanic Association of Contractors and Enterprises, Congreso, APM, Esperanza, Norris Square—are Latino organizations. At the federal level, I brought resources to the city beyond helping the Philadelphia Housing Authority, including funneling federal funding through the local Empowerment Zones.

Whenever I had filled a role never before occupied by a Latino, I was happy to be first, but I never wanted to be last. I wanted to build a staircase wherever I had climbed the ladder, so others could easily follow. I waited to leave the bench until another like me came along, and I was glad that Nitza Quiñones Alejandro, a gay Latina, was appointed judge before my time ended. She has continued to blaze a trail, too, and is now the first gay Latina to serve on the federal court.

I saw many Temple Law School and CLEO program students I had recruited go on to great things. Eduardo Rodriguez became the first Latino judge in Connecticut. Nazario Jimenez, a CLEO recruit, was the first municipal court judge from North Philadelphia. I brought Ricardo Montano to Temple, and he went on to become a political leader and city councilman in Suffolk County. Mari Carmen Aponte was a bilingual schoolteacher in Camden when I recruited her to Temple Law. I knew she was special, and I asked her to repay the opportunity to study law by giving five years to the community. When I went to D.C. as a White House Fellow, I left her in charge of the Committee on Service to the Spanish-Speaking Community, and out of that, in essence, she created the Hispanic Bar Association of Pennsylvania. She would become the first Puerto Rican woman chosen to be a White House Fellow and the first to serve as ambassador to El Salvador, which she did under President Barack Obama, and the first to serve as assistant secretary of state for Western Hemisphere affairs in the State Department. And Gil Medina, conservative Republican or not, has also done quite well.

That said, they didn't all have to make history. I was gratified to have the chance to help a kid get a law school education who would not otherwise have been able to afford it. What was important was providing access to a career, a key to unlock possibility. I'll never forget Mike Leon, the last student I helped to get into the CLEO program. Peter Liacouras had asked me to call Mike to see whether he wanted the last remaining seat we had available. Mike picked up the phone in a noisy house full of kids. I had made calls like this before, to crowded houses full of brothers and sisters and cousins, where promising students could often languish, never getting the chance to reach beyond that place, get off that street, that block, out of that neighborhood. I could barely hear him in all the shouting and commotion, and he could barely hear me. I almost had to shout the offer to him. But I remember when he finally understood what I was calling about, because he started to cry. He went on to graduate from Villanova University. I hope whatever he has chosen to do since then, he has enjoyed success and has helped others along the way.

I felt I had helped make progress in certain areas, but nowhere was anything finished. And there were problems I had not yet addressed, and I felt I had a responsibility to do so. The city's schools, for instance, were a mess. The city's budget per student was the lowest in the state, and the state's support had shrunk considerably. Governor Tom Ridge had decided in 1998 that the state should take over the management of the School District of Philadelphia. Such a move was unheard of, and no one in the city felt that a hostile Republican state administration was the answer to our problems. It took a few years of legal wrangling led by the school district board chair Pedro Ramos and Mayor John Street, but in 2001 the School Reform Commission took over the board, giving the state the right to appoint most of the members.

By that time, Ridge had left the Governor's Residence to join the Bush administration, and now Governor Mark Schweiker would over-see the negotiations on the particulars of the takeover. He worked with Street and Ramos, and while state control of Philadelphia's schools was not a good arrangement, throughout Street's and Rendell's administrations the School Reform Commission received increases in resources. All that ended when Tom Corbett became governor. Under Corbett, funding was choked off and all the schools suffered, with the exception of a few charter schools whose existence many people, including me, saw as a way to divert funding from the public schools as a whole and eventually to supplant the public school system in Philadelphia. The Corbett years were lean years for students. The schools were purposely underfunded, only to receive an occasional budgetary reprieve. It was like watching someone starve a child and then punish the child for not thriving.

Yet, even before this budget disaster that plagued the school system during the Corbett years, the school system had been failing students in fundamental ways. A school is a huge part of a child's life. Beyond the education children will take with them when they leave school is their well-being, which is profoundly affected by the environment their schools provide. In many Philadelphia public schools, that environment had for a long time been terrible.

But I had seen another way. Through Judge Eduardo Robreno I had become acquainted with Gloria Bonilla-Santiago and the school she ran in Camden, called LEAP Academy. Robreno, the senior judge in the U.S. District Court and the Operation Peter Pan kid from Cuba whom I had mentored after his graduation from law school, had called me to provide LEAP with some help and guidance. I told him I didn't want to get involved with Camden politics, but that I'd go take a look. That's when I met Gloria, the LEAP Academy CEO, in the school building at 5th and Cooper Streets. She walked me around and gave me her spiel about how every single kid who graduates from LEAP goes to college.

Then she took me to another building, which she wanted to buy. She told me she was running into all kinds of roadblocks and was looking for some guidance. Beneficial Bank had taken over the building when the owners went into default. I thought I could help her. The chairman at my law firm, Joe Jacovini, knew the president of Beneficial.

Joe and I took Gloria to the bank, only to hear that the bank already had the building under contract. It was not in good shape, and there would be a lot of work to get it up to code, especially for a school, including removing asbestos. But Gloria wanted it, and he changed his mind when she told him that her school could buy it within 30 days. So they agreed and worked out the financing, with some help from the Economic Development Administration (EDA) of New Jersey. At the same time, LEAP had a loan with the Reinvestment Fund, a Philadelphia trust company that had proven very hard to deal with, but I knew Robert Feldman, the company president from our time at HUD, and he helped us get a bond from the New Jersey EDA.

In all that time working on behalf of LEAP, I had been exposed to more of its mission, its methods, and the students and families it served. I had seen that it provided a great education to mostly minority kids, who looked just like the kids in North Philadelphia whom the city and the state had all but given up on. And more than the education, or perhaps it would be more accurate to say bolstering the education that LEAP offered, the school provided wraparound services to its kids and involved the parents and the community. The school signed contracts with the students and with their families. It employed chefs to prepare breakfast and lunch for the children. It provided a safe and up-to-date gymnasium that was open to the kids throughout the day. What LEAP was doing really worked, and I saw no reason why it could not be replicated on a larger scale across the river.

So there I was one Sunday afternoon in the fall of 2014, watching the Eagles play on TV, thinking about my life and my legacy. My mother, my stepfather, and my sister Cookie had moved in earlier in the year. It had all happened one Mother's Day. The three of them would come up for an overnight visit every Mother's Day, and Sara and I would put them in the TV room. My mother made it known that it wasn't her favorite place to stay—it wasn't even a bedroom—so Sara and I had converted it into an in-law suite. It was very nice, the biggest room in the house, compliant with the Americans with Disabilities Act, and more expensive than the original house had been. My mother loved it.

She and Pop and Cookie had been living in Puerto Rico in a nice place I had bought them, but things were changing. The last of Cookie's children, and my mother's favorite, had married and moved to Florida, leaving just the three of them in the house. Cookie was having more and more difficulty taking care of both parents, who were now in their 90s, especially because my mother was showing signs of dementia. On that Mother's Day in 2014 I had come to her, in her special room with the air conditioning set very low just as she liked it, and I asked her whether she was comfortable.

She said she was. And she told me she wasn't leaving.

And she wouldn't. Cookie rushed back to Puerto Rico, packed everything, and sent a lot of it to our house through the mail. And now our house was full of people, and full of love. Sara was a wonderful daughter to my parents, and a true sister to Cookie.

Things were good for me, inside and outside my home. Since leaving the city solicitor's office, I had been serving on the board of Exelon, a Fortune 100 company, thanks to my friend Walt D'Alessio. I had served for 12 years, and I could serve until I was 75, in 2022. I was one of the first mainland Puerto Ricans to serve on the board of a Fortune 500 company, hoping to keep the door open for others. I was making money and feeling secure. But the question that had always nagged at me returned: Was I still holding up my end of the bargain I'd made with God? Was I fulfilling my promise to help the poor?

I sometimes wish I'd just turned up the television to drown out the incessant doubts, but I didn't. Life was good, but I guess I have never grown too comfortable with things going smoothly. So why not ruin it? I could stay in my comfortable chair, in my study, watching the game and taking it easy, or I could do what I had always done and one last time yank the wheel hard to the right. I decided to run for mayor. I knew I had a way to address the problems with the school system. I had other ideas, too, but education was at the top of the list.

I started putting out feelers and unofficially threw my hat in the ring. Former city councilman Angel Ortiz, the first Latino to serve in that position, gave me a lot of encouragement. I'd been friends with Angel, another child of the New York City tenements, since I recruited Lydia Hernandez Velez to be a lawyer at Community Legal Services in 1976. Lydia recommended Angel, and I brought him in for an interview, not knowing they were married. Angel got the job. After serving there, Angel had been appointed to City Council by Mayor Goode in 1984 to fill John

Anderson's seat after he died. Angel's politics were very liberal, always, and he was a character. He'd served till 2002, when the papers found out that he'd been driving for 25 years with an expired driver's license. His was the first voice that encouraged me to run.

There was no candidate yet who seemed to hold much appeal to Latinos or to the key voting bloc in the Northwest. If I could secure those voters, I could reach out to other groups, perhaps some of the smaller unions in the city, such as PFT, AFSCME, 1199C, and 32BJ, and put together a loose coalition that would give the other candidates a real challenge. Perhaps the smaller unions would help me pull in some of the bigger unions. The key for Díaz 2016 seemed to be to get leadership in Northwest Philadelphia to come out for me. The Northwest was a largely black, politically active voting bloc that could be enticed to come out for the vote. I had three important contacts there: Cherelle Parker, who's now on City Council, outgoing city councilwoman Marian Tasco, and state representative Dwight Evans. I met with them to seek their endorsement, knowing that state senator Anthony Williams, a black candidate, was not doing well in the area. Williams had a problematic position on charter schools and was perceived not to be supportive of the public schools. Three of the last four mayors had been black—Goode, Street, and Nutter—and it seemed as though Williams needed more than just his ethnicity to win the black vote. With my strong civil rights record, I thought I had a chance.

The bad news was that I had to give up my seat on the board at Exelon if I was going to run for mayor. Serving on the board of a prestigious corporation had been a dream come true for me. It paid well and it was exciting and, I'll say it again, it paid well. Reaching such a position was an accomplishment few other Latinos had made, and in the hope of opening the door for others after me, I joined in the effort to form the Latino Corporate Directors Association. But I had to step down from board to run, so I did.

At my official announcement in the second week in January, in a room filled with supporters and Latino leadership, I felt good. I felt hopeful. Ken Trujillo, the Mexican American lawyer whom I'd replaced as city solicitor, was running. He had a full staff and substantial resources, but he was polling very poorly. Lynne Abraham, a judge and long-time district attorney for the city, had better numbers, but I thought I was better qualified. Williams, as mentioned earlier and with all of his issues, was running too. Back in 1998 he had slid into his father's state senate seat when, hours before the deadline to file, his father had abruptly retired. Then a state representative, Williams ran unopposed. He'd run for governor in 2010 and lost in the primary. In a weak field, he was looking like the early front-runner, but there were many developments still to come. At the time John "Johnny Doc" Dougherty, a wannabe Philadelphia kingmaker and leader of the powerful IBEWU-98, was trying to get City Council president Darrell Clarke to run. But Clarke was playing coy.

The mayor's race was one of the craziest things I have ever been a part of. Conditions changed constantly, and I had to continually recalibrate my expectations. Anything goes, and allies can be those who haven't found a more favorable horse to bet on. The main stage of big-time Philadelphia politics is more of an ecosystem, or perhaps a food chain, where alliances are struck and dissolved with dizzying speed, and favors can be either remembered or forgotten. But all I could do was announce myself and lay out the issues I'd be campaigning on.

My platform had five areas of emphasis:

- **Education.** Education is a civil right and every child is entitled to it. Since the founding of our nation, public education has lifted every generation until now, but Philadelphia's dropout rates are shameful and many students graduate without any preparation for either a job or higher education.
  - Abolish the School Reform Commission. Return the schools to the mayor and the parents who can be more responsible for their children than the governor. Schools should have greater autonomy, local control with decentralization.
  - Provide wraparound services to kids and families. Partner with local and cultural institutions and community groups.
- **Taxes.** Eliminate the city wage tax and reform the real estate tax system. The wage tax is too great a burden for the working class. Impose a real estate tax on the business community structured to put a commensurate burden on it and lower the real estate tax for homeowners. The current equal real estate tax structure is unfair to homeowners.
  - Establish a progressive tax system to bring business and employment opportunities from the suburbs into Philadelphia.
  - Use community college to train the unemployed for these new jobs. Make every citizen computer literate.

- **Police/community relations.** End the illegal practice of stop and frisk employed in minority sectors of the city. Establish a major community-policing program and establish a Police Athletic League in every precinct. A police force with good ties to the community will be a greater deterrent to crime than anything else and will end the fear of police in the black and Latino community.
- **Housing.** Any housing program or development that uses government funding must dedicate 20 percent to affordable housing.
- **The environment.** Philadelphia is the dirtiest city in Pennsylvania, partly because of oil and petroleum refinement. Phase out refineries and create clean jobs and renewable energy programs.

I had a very small staff. Denise Rawles was my political adviser; she had come to me from Angel Ortiz. She was on point to negotiate with the Northwest and the Latino community, and she found tough going on both fronts. Elliot Curson was an ad executive, the one who back in 1972 came up with the slogan "Philadelphia isn't as bad as Philadelphians say it is." They couldn't agree on whether we needed to have more boots on the ground to campaign for me or more advertising and publicity. My campaign didn't have much money, so what little I had needed to be used judiciously. Rawles wanted more staff, Curson more advertising, and they never could come to any kind of agreement. It wasn't long before Curson left.

Three days after I announced, Trujillo dropped out, claiming family issues. His staff would wind up on the staff of another candidate, City Councilman Jim Kenney, when he announced a month later, in February. I remember the day well, because it was the day I announced two grants from Exelon. On my behalf, as a parting gesture, Exelon made a $450,000 grant to the Temple Law School, endowing a chair, and a $50,000 grant to the Salvation Army. It was about 90 days before the election. Kenney had come up through the ranks as a protégé of Vince Fumo's and until recently had been conservative and, to my mind, a bit of a hothead. Of late he'd been remaking his image, getting a law passed that ended arrests for possession of a small amount of marijuana, and coming out against Chick-fil-A's opening a franchise in the city because of its record of discrimination against the LGBT community. What made Kenney most formidable, though, was that he had John Dougherty's backing. Johnny Doc had money and influence, and he almost instantaneously transformed the mayoral race into a struggle between Kenney and Williams. Dougherty circumvented contribution limits by forming a political action committee, to which, as the Supreme Court ruled in the *Citizens United* decision, unlimited funds could be given to be spent on a campaign. The unions could support Kenney with as much money as they wanted without being officially affiliated with him.

In the days and weeks that followed, everyone made calculations and seemed to be counting me out. That included my political adviser, who didn't have quite the same fire to run my campaign after Kenney appeared.

I had hoped for help from Councilwoman Maria Quiñones-Sanchez, but she owed Williams for contributions he'd made to her campaign and to the campaigns of her friends. The Latino community didn't like this move, since they were by-and-large opposed to Williams. The bloc of support I was hoping for was starting to dissolve at the edges. But my chances evaporated in early April at a meeting with the Northwest coalition when it said it was going with Kenney. Cherelle Parker had been trying to push my candidacy, but there was a lot of money flying around. It made my head spin. Carlos Matos and Representative Angel Cruz and his group asked me to contribute to other campaigns, including giving $102,000 to help an opponent of Quiñones-Sanchez's in the City Council race. My campaign didn't have that kind of money, but Johnny Doc did, and when he stepped up to pay it, the Latino officials and ward leaders revoked their endorsement of me. Dougherty had the money to offer support to all three of my main sources in the Northwest. He was going to help Dwight Evans's run for Congress, help Parker win her seat, and support Derek Green, who had been Marian Tasco's assistant. With Dougherty's money, they all went with Kenney. And that was that.

All's fair in love, war, and the Philadelphia Democratic mayoral primary. But I was shocked as I watched how things went down. I didn't like Kenney as a politician or as a person. For years I thought he was run by his temper, and I did not think he had done anything to support Latinos or blacks during his time on City Council. Late in the game he made a turn toward progressive politics, but it appeared to me to be about positioning and not about principle. There seem to be two Jim Kenneys: the guy who of late came out in support of the LGBT community and more lenient drug-possession laws, and the guy who once said in a City Council meeting that he thought a thief should have his hand cut off.[1] But he got enough people to believe in his chances of winning, and the money he had behind him did not hurt.

Politics is such an odd thing. It is as much about superstition as it is about polling data. Voters, voting blocs, patrons, the pundits, and the papers: even if they begin from an idealistic position, considering what they really want in a candidate and what issues they want their mayor to address, it's only a matter of time before everyone begins trying to predict how the election might work out and saying who they think can win. Principles give way to rooting for a team—much like watching a football game on television. Belief in a candidate's position is only one part. Voters have to believe that the candidate has the necessary support to win. They have to believe that there are enough believers. If voters don't believe you will win, they will seek out a candidate who they believe will. Only those who have enough people who believe they can win, can win. Changes happen quickly when it's all based on impressions and the ability to imagine someone being victorious. A campaign can vanish in a moment.

So it was that in the end my chances were unaffected by the promise of my platform. I didn't have the name recognition and I didn't have the money. My campaign lost its believers, as the saying goes, slowly at first and then all at once. When I saw people who had encouraged me to run move on to other candidates, I felt betrayed. But it was just business. My mentor and close friend Charlie Bowser saw how the machine worked and moved on. Latino leaders went with Kenney, too, but the Latino vote did not so neatly follow their lead. Kenney had the money and the patrons and he was building a coalition based on the backing of his South Philly neighbor Johnny Doc and the Northwest voters, delivered by Evans.

Later, when Kenney won the general election in November 2015, Evans announced he was running to take U.S. Representative Chaka Fattah's seat. Fattah, neck deep in a racketeering and influence-peddling scandal, was more vulnerable than he'd ever been. Fattah would lose the Democratic primary to Evans, and then Fattah would be convicted of felony. Two days later he'd resign his seat in the Congress. He's now serving 10 years in federal prison. Evans would win the general election and the special election to fill Fattah's vacant seat on the same day, and

---

1. See Ryan Briggs, "Kenney 'Embarrassed' by Stop-and-frisk, Crime Fighting Stances in 1997," philly.com, February 19, 2015, http://www.philly.com/philly/news/politics/mayor/Kenney_embarrassed_by_cop-and-frisk_.html.

he is now serving in the U.S. Congress, thanks to the support he received from Philadelphia for his help in getting Kenney elected.

But back to my campaign: my shot at being mayor was essentially dead before the Democratic primary, but I wouldn't drop out of the race, and I certainly wouldn't campaign with or for Kenney. Not just yet. I stayed in to keep attention on education and the other issues I thought were important. I had a plan to reform the tax structure to benefit both businesses and the poor, and I had an environmental plan to clean up the city. Philadelphia needed to bring back businesses, and it remains the poorest big city in the United States. So I went to almost every single forum during the campaign to keep my ideas in the public eye. I went to 72 in all, more than any other candidate, and I missed one. But when I missed the one, on immigration, I received bad press for it despite my long record of support for immigrants as city solicitor and throughout my career.

Kenney won the Democratic primary in a landslide, if a landslide can be achieved in a primary where fewer than a third of the voters come out. That was by design. The fewer the voters, the more you can influence the results, and a sustained effort was made to keep people home. In a low-turnout election, I was gratified to win at least the Latino vote. Kenney received more than 55 percent of the vote. Williams, his closest rival, barely registered a quarter. The Northwest voting bloc accounted for just over half of the votes cast, and it delivered a victory for Kenney. After the primary, the Philadelphia Democratic Party invited all the candidates to a Unity Breakfast to show an undivided Democratic front for the upcoming general election in the fall. I didn't want to go, but Lynne Abraham prevailed on me to do so. There were a lot of speeches and handshaking, and all the Democratic candidates got up to speak. I wasn't enthusiastic about joining the parade of the vanquished, but I stood at the podium and promised as a Roosevelt Democrat that I would never vote for the Republican.

Kenney won 85 percent in the general election, in which only 4,000 more voters came out in November than had for the Democratic primary in the spring. I do wish there were a better system in Philadelphia, one that is optimistic rather than one that cynically cultivates apathy in order to better take advantage of a depressed turnout.

It takes a long time to make a man, but even grown-ups still have lessons to learn. I just wish they weren't so expensive. I was dispirited after the election. I didn't understand why, after all the times I'd stood up for Latinos and African Americans and poor people, that they wouldn't stand up for me. I can be more philosophical about it now. I can see that that's just how it goes. You win or you lose, and you have to remember that what matters is doing what's right. I did what I did throughout my career to hold up the deal I'd made with God. I didn't always get the credit, but that wasn't why I did what I did. And in the long run, I feel that I've been blessed by doing what felt like the right thing, even if I had doubts about how it would affect me.

I didn't want to marry Vilma, but I did because it seemed like the right thing to do. I married young and our marriage was difficult, but it gave me three beautiful children and now grandchildren.

I wanted to finish my business education and pursue an MBA, to be an accountant and have a life without so many surprises. I would have been calmer, but I would never have become a lawyer or a judge, and I never would have been a White House Fellow.

I wanted to stay in New York, but Philadelphia has become my home, the place to which I always return.

As a kid I wanted to ride around in a convertible, to play the field and be a big deal in Harlem, but I would have had to sacrifice my faith, and the life of an activist had far greater rewards and satisfactions.

I have followed my heart. My plans have continually had to give way to each new opportunity to do the right thing. And whenever I've had to weigh what I think should happen against what God presents me with, it's always been a clear choice. It has not made me the richest man in Philadelphia. And I would be lying if I said I don't miss the money I sacrificed by, say, giving up my seat on the Exelon board. But so be it.

After the election, I went back to work at Dilworth Parson. In July 2016 I got a call from Russell Reynolds, the search firm, asking whether I was interested in a seat on the board of the Puerto Rico Electric Power Authority (PREPA), the electric company in Puerto Rico. My experience with Exelon made me a good candidate to oversee a utility company. The board wanted me to come to Puerto Rico right away for interviews, so I went, and then I didn't hear anything for months. It was the end of Alejandro Padilla's first term, and he had decided not to run for re-election. His party would lose in November to Ricardo Rosselló, son of Pedro Rosselló, who had served two terms as governor of Puerto Rico in the 1990s.

After the election, but before Rosselló's January swearing in, Padilla appointed me to the board and the Puerto Rican Senate confirmed me. I went to my first board meeting in December, where I was appointed vice chairman and was one of four independent appointees, along with Erroll Davis, an African American who had served on General Motors' Board of Directors and would chair the Audit Committee; Placido Martinez, a Cuban who had run an electric company in Australia and would chair the Infrastructure Committee, which oversaw equipment and power generation; and Rafael Díaz, a young Colombian from General Electric who joined the board late and demanded to be made chair of the Compensation Committee, which did not, at the time, exist, nor did it need to. Davis was calm and competent, and Martinez was meticulous. Rafael was young and brash and wanted to work on restructuring, an area where he'd found success at General Electric.

We had begun, and in January 2017, the new governor took office. I called the press and talked about the issues we faced—lax governance, a bloated workforce with duplicative functions, obsolete equipment, and crumbling infrastructure, all which amount to power that still runs on diesel and costs the consumers four times what it costs in the mainland United States—and they asked to have a meeting with the four new independent board members. As the one most familiar with Puerto Rican customs and the press, I organized the meeting. The press asked whether we'd met with the new governor yet. We hadn't. They said we would once the article ran, and they were right. When we met with the governor to discuss our mission, he pointed out that as a political figure he couldn't just institute changes with no thought to how they would be received by the mainland government, business interests, and the people.

Some of the measures we recommended he passed; others he didn't. Martinez and I opposed the method of awarding contracts without requests for proposal and pushed back against what seemed like sweetheart deals for friends of the new governor's administration. The previous governor's administration had spent $43 million on consultants, which to my mind seemed wasteful. We heard no response from the governor. The executive director wanted his friend to be the deputy director, even though he appeared corrupt and was alleged to have bribed a few officials to win the executive director's wife a seat on the court. Martinez and I voted against that appointment, which did not endear us to the new executive director, while Davis and Díaz voted for it. In June, at the executive director's request, the governor got rid of Martinez and me, despite our experience in running utilities. We were replaced with the expensive consulting firm on a $17 million retainer we'd voted against hiring. The firm was three years old and supposedly better qualified because of its familiarity with the language and the culture, but it didn't hurt that it was also run by friends of officials in the party in charge.

Martinez and I both had experience working with utility companies. I can only assume we had been appointed for our expertise. We saw the problems, the danger that awaited, but those who oversaw the work of Puerto Rico's power company were concerned with other matters. In 2017 Hurricane Maria wiped out power to the island for months. Not only was this destruction predictable; it had been predicted by everyone who knew anything about utilities.

Running up against people, time and again, with the authority to make real and important changes—changes that can profoundly help the vulnerable—who think first in terms of what will least inconvenience or annoy their unaffected friends and who become preoccupied with the politics of reward and returned favors can be disillusioning. The Puerto Rican power grid was flimsy and decrepit, just waiting for a hurricane to put it out of its misery. There were things we could have done, things that had long needed to be done. I had strong relationships at Exelon, the largest and best-run utility company in the United States, and they were ready to help, but their help was not wanted. The board was busy figuring out which consultants would win the contracts.

The issues with the power company are just one piece of the almost insoluble problem that is Puerto Rico and its finances, but they are illustrative. They exist within the context of the ongoing debt crisis that has long threatened to sink Puerto Rico. The financial crisis is almost built into the arrangement, helped along the way by inexplicable laws that make it impossible for the territory to find its way out of the mess. Even so, the reactions of the federal government and of the Puerto Rican government were disappointing. The executive director of PREPA signed a $300 million contract with a two-man energy company from Montana and was fired; his 72-year-old replacement wasn't Puerto Rican, spoke little Spanish, was paid a huge $450,000 salary, and lasted four months; his replacement lasted only a day and resigned when the governor demanded that he lower his $750,000 salary; and a week later José Ortiz was hired at a $250,000 salary. My friends at Exelon begged to be allowed to finish the job. They brought trucks, equipment, and people, and six months after the storm, they began work on a disaster that destroyed so much and caused so much suffering and death. I stepped up to help when asked, and I did all I could, but it's hard to help the Commonwealth of Puerto Rico.

WHEN CHRISTOPHER COLUMBUS SAILED OFF in search of India, the globe's geography and the prevailing winds brought him instead to the Caribbean. When he happened upon Puerto Rico, the smallest island of the Greater Antilles archipelago, he called it San Juan and claimed it, like everything else, for Spain. The island's Taíno inhabitants welcomed him, not knowing that he brought disease, war, and tyranny. Columbus and his three ships were about to unleash colonialism like a pestilence on the New World. And for good measure, they also brought pestilence.

Puerto Rico was for four centuries a Spanish territory. After Spain surrendered to end the Spanish-American War in 1898, it ceded Puerto Rico to the United States, along with the Philippines, and recognized the independence of Cuba. And while in time the other two territories became sovereign nations, Puerto Rico simply went from Spanish colonialism to American colonialism, where it remains under U.S. rule.

Once called "two wings of the same bird," Puerto Rico and Cuba have seen their histories fly in different directions. Cuba took the road of self-determination and became independent, but Puerto Rico did not. Social movements in support of Puerto Rican independence have come and gone, but whenever it has come time to choose, Puerto Ricans have always decided to remain a U.S. territory. We live in limbo, neither independent nor a full state. We are called a free associated state, but what we really are is a possession, a territory.

The old mentality of colonial subservience is hard to outgrow. It has informed our history and has come with us to the mainland as though we packed it in our suitcases. We have taken crumbs for a century in the hope that sooner or later they would add up to a meal, but they never have.

The colonized mindset has been Columbus's most lasting legacy, and the current debt crisis that threatens to cripple the island can be seen as a result of it. Puerto Rico has no power, no recourse, and no money. With no ability to fix what's wrong, it can only stand by and watch as things just get worse. Add up all that the Jones Act has cost Puerto Rico and the number might be roughly equivalent to the present deficit.

President Woodrow Wilson signed into law the Smith Act in 1917, which offers Puerto Ricans a curtailed U.S. citizenship, but citizenship nonetheless. We were granted some voting rights in a national election as long as we had taken residence in one of the then 48 states, but we

cannot vote while residing in Puerto Rico. We have no federal representation. And for 100 years we have been sitting in the middle of the
seesaw, unable to move toward full autonomy at one end or full participation at the other for fear of upsetting a balance that does not serve
us anyway.

Big issues of international finance, geopolitics, and history have affected my family and me in very personal and tangible ways farther
back than I can trace my roots. The hardships under which my grandmother raised her children were due in part to the stock market crash
in 1929, when many farmers on the island went bankrupt, banks closed,
and unemployment spiked. Many of those small farms and banks were
consolidated as larger businesses moved in, and by the end of the decade
nearly half of the Puerto Rican workforce was employed in the agricultural sector, with almost 30 percent of them, like my grandfather,
working in the sugar industry.

The agricultural market stagnated in the 1940s, and manufacturing
became the key to profitability in Puerto Rico. Investors saw cheap opportunities in programs like Operation Bootstrap, which was launched
in 1948 to bring manufacturing to the island through tax incentives,
new buildings and infrastructure, a cheap labor force, and tax exemp-
tions for as long as 30 years. As transformative as the 1940s were for the
island's economy, Puerto Rico's inhabitants were not much better off.

Some developments brought positive outcomes, especially in the
military, which offered new possibilities to Puerto Ricans after they returned home at the end of World War II. Veterans were able to qualify
for Federal Housing Administration loans and to go to college on the
G.I. Bill and even start businesses. Thanks to the postwar boom, for-
tunes called on the mainland, too. Many islanders turned to the promise
of abundant work in factories and on farms. America was the land of
opportunity, travel was cheap, and cheap labor was desirable. And thus
began the Great Migration that brought my mother to the mainland.

Over the years, most of the big corporations lured to the island have
left, and the jobs have dried up. Those who stayed on the island grew
more and more dependent on money coming back from the mainland.
But there was little production on the island, and a shrinking tax base.

Money had been drying up for decades, so when the Puerto Rican
government needed to finance its operations, it borrowed on its own
publicly traded and tax-free municipal bonds. Wall Street bought the
bonds, assuming the same guarantees offered by most municipal and

state governments, and bankers were happy to refinance them. Call it what you want, sweeping troubles under the rug, kicking the can down the road, or whistling by the graveyard, this was an engagement in financial magical thinking and everyone was willing to fantasize. Puerto Rico has acquired debt at an alarming rate, but (thanks in large part to Senator Strom Thurmond, who introduced an amendment excluding Puerto Rico and the District of Columbia from a bankruptcy bill that was being debated in the Senate in 1984) it can neither declare bankruptcy nor restructure that debt. We never seem to reap any benefits, only consequences.

Refinancing looked too good to be true because, of course, it was. The practice of heedless refinancing was a poor substitute for fiscal responsibility, and those in charge of budgeting were derelict and overly optimistic in their duties. At a time when you would never see a rate of more than 4 percent, in 2014, Puerto Rico was refinancing at 6 percent interest tax free, and many investors made record returns. And since the Puerto Rican government is one of the few remaining employers on the island, it was borrowing on the pensions of its own municipal employees—its teachers, clerks, and police officers.

And that is how you create a financial disaster.

The debt stands at about $132 billion as of this writing. And because the Bankruptcy Act doesn't apply in Puerto Rico (thank you again, Strom Thurmond), the obligation to all those bondholders remains. In 2015, when it became clear that the Puerto Rican government couldn't pay the interest on the bonds, the federal government passed the Puerto Rico Oversight, Management, and Economic Stability Act, known as PROMESA, creating a federal committee to oversee the budget of Puerto Rico. It's a nice name, but there is no promise that it can keep.

If Puerto Rico were a state, it would have five representatives and two senators in Congress to take up for it. If it were independent, it could negotiate a way out of this impossible situation. But because of its colonized status, Puerto Rico is at the mercy of an unconcerned federal government that does little but cluck its tongue and institute half measures more punishing than helpful.

It's untenable, but where the Cubans turned to revolt in the face of injustice and oppression, Puerto Ricans employ a different tactic: they leave. Wherever they are, they go to the other place.

The colonized mindset means you really have no home. Everywhere is a foreign land. The first migrants to come the mainland in the 1940s and the 1950s did not come to participate in democracy as a U.S. citizen, or to buy into the American dream. They came for no more high-minded reason than to earn some money to send back home and at some point to go back themselves. Cheap travel made it easy to go back and forth, and until the 1980s, as many as one million people in a year did so.

Puerto Rico and New York City stood as alternatives to each other, and neither place was home. There was always an out. Each place took on the aspect of a refuge when viewed from the other. Each was a place to flee to when things became difficult. When the money ran out in Puerto Rico, there was money to be made in New York. When New York became too oppressive or too alienating, there was Puerto Rico, waiting just a cheap plane ticket away, offering comfort, familiarity, rest, and a dream.

Mexicans, Cubans, and other noncitizens who come to the United States do not have the option of leaving and returning. They have to go through an immigration process, and when they come they have to stay for fear of never being able to get back. Their mindset is different. They can send money home, but there is no easy come, easy go for an immigrant.

The political parties in Puerto Rico have engaged in a game of push and pull—either independence or statehood—that has kept the island neither/nor, floundering, and now teetering on ruin. In the history of the United States, four U.S. senators have been of Cuban descent, two of Mexican descent. There has yet to be a Puerto Rican U.S. senator.

I recently went to Camden with Sara to take in a concert by El Gran Combo, a Puerto Rican band that has been around for almost 60 years. Some of the performers have moved on and been replaced, but the songs are timeless, beautiful, and very catchy, and the group that evening was dynamic. People were dancing in the aisles and in their seats. Sara enjoyed herself, and she wanted me to dance with her. But I couldn't bring myself to dance.

Here we all were, listening to a group of musicians sing songs about the island, how beautiful it is, and how the food tastes and the sun feels—singing as if it's gone and there's nothing anyone can do. We're all here in New Jersey singing about a home that we don't live in, not because we can't or because it is no more, but because we don't want to. We have a nostalgia for a thing that isn't even gone, but it is being crushed. I looked around at the crowd, smiling, dancing to songs about the water, singing along to songs about coffee. We visit the island, of course, but we do so to stare at our past while living in the present, feeling homesick while standing in our homes. Puerto Rico is a living place, but it's as if we look at it behind glass. It is a homeland that is not my home. Something about it feels as close as the blood in my veins, but at the same time it is as distant as an island paradise in a children's book or in a song about coffee. It's not a home or a homeland, but it's not gone either. And while it sinks, we dance. Because we accept that that's just the way it is. What can you do?

We are a people who feel grateful just for being allowed to be here. But our invitation to the party means only that we gain entrance. We don't really participate; we just watch from the doorway and think how much worse it would be out in the street. We don't consider ourselves worthy of constitutional rights, and we don't know how to demand them. We fear losing what little we have, because it was granted to us. We didn't earn it. We didn't take it. Ironically, if we did demand those constitutional rights, we'd get a lot more.

But for the foreseeable future, we are a people who are neither here nor there. That's the unofficial motto of the Puerto Rican: *No soy de aquí ni de allá,* which translates in English to "I am accepted neither here nor there." But I hope that's not always going to be true. We need more fighters for the world we want. I was lucky to have grown up among African Americans during the fight for civil rights. Doing so helped shape me into the person I became. But Puerto Ricans have to find an identity of their own. It's hard when you have no place that you're really from. In New York, I was just a Puerto Rican, and in Puerto Rico I was *americanito,* a Nuyorican. Many of us have just tried to pass. If we're light-skinned, maybe we can pass as white; if dark-skinned, as black; and in between, maybe as Italian. We do it to ourselves, which is why it's so hard for us to break through. Whom do we have to look up to as a real success? Supreme Court justice Sonia Sotomayor is a shining light. But after her, whom?

I do not know what the future holds for Puerto Rico. I didn't solve any of the problems I addressed, but I hope that I made things better by being here. In a life full of unexpected changes, I always tried to do what seems like the best thing. I spoke truth to power and I stood up for those who needed it. And if the places I went required a ladder, I trust that behind me I left a staircase for others more easily to follow.

Puerto Ricans remain the poorest Latino community in the United States, and if Puerto Rico were a state, it would be the poorest state in the Union. The long reach of colonialism affects us in some ways more than it does any other Latino group. If anything, we have grown poorer and less powerful and less determined to improve our situation.

I am now retired. I have done what I could for justice and equality. I may not always have gotten the credit, but I accept what blame I deserve. I can only look to the next generation of activists, firebrands, and just regular folks who stubbornly live their lives and refuse to take less than what they deserve. They have a great opportunity and a huge responsibility to solve a problem that has been puzzled over for 400 years.

I was lucky to have convictions that motivated me. I have always believed in defending and upholding human rights, all over the world, whether they be the rights of my friends and neighbors or the rights of Refuseniks in the Soviet Union or of Indians along the banks of the Amazon. I served my fellow human as best I could, and all I can hope is that I helped create a slightly kinder, more accepting world for all people to live in. All the rest is just chatter.

EPILOGUE

EVERY NIGHT IN THOSE YEARS when she and Pop and Cookie lived with us, before she turned in, my mother would cut up orange slices and leave them in a cup for me. I would come home from work or after a long day campaigning, and even if everyone had gone to bed, the little cup of orange slices would be waiting for me on the kitchen table.

Cookie told me that one winter night in a bad snowstorm my mother was distraught to find that there were no oranges left in the house. It was late, and outside was a blizzard, but my mother wanted to go to the store to get some more. No, Cookie wasn't going to drive in these conditions at this hour just to get a few oranges. Surely our mother's oldest could go one night without his orange in a cup. My mother wouldn't hear of it and she started bundling up to go out into the snowy night, 90 years old, not knowing where she was going or how to drive the car.

I count myself lucky to have been born to a mother as fiercely concerned with my welfare, who would ask me to go to church with her as a birthday present, who would chase me home with a baseball bat, who never shied away from a frightening journey for my sake, whether it entailed boarding a gigantic ship and leaving behind everything she knew to make a life for me, or driving through a blizzard to make me my cup of orange slices. As a child, I had to walk a very narrow path for her, but as an adult, I could do no wrong in her eyes.

The house for those last two and a half years of her life was a happy place, full of love. She said they were some of the happiest years of her life. But Mom's health was declining. Her heart, which had borne so much and carried so many within it, was giving out. She was still strong and could still get around, and she still swept the back patio every day, especially in the fall. She loved to sweep, but she was forgetting things and got mixed up more and more. Sweeping was almost a compulsion for her. We found out after she passed, when we had some trouble with the ducts, that she had treated the vents in the floor like little dustpans, convenient places to sweep the piles of dirt she'd collected in the room. As much as she loved her air conditioning, she didn't understand how it worked.

Maria Cancel Rodriguez, mother of three, wife to Miserain Rodriguez and survived by him and those three children, eight grandchildren—all of whom had married—and 15 great grandchildren, finally went home on the evening of October 14, 2016. She died peacefully in her sleep in a suitably chilly room, surrounded by people who loved her, and I take great comfort in the belief that she died without any worries about those she was leaving behind.

It takes a long time to make a man, but I could become who I am only because of Maria. It was her love, ruthless, unyielding, and bottomless that shaped me and formed the foundation for my character. My story is the story it is largely thanks to her, and I dedicate this book to her memory and her fierce spirit.

I thank my wife, Sara, for her unending support and for her love and care of my parents. She taught me a great deal in these past few years about what kindness is and what patience is. It was Sara who insisted that we build the room for Mom and Pop, and it was she who furnished it and made it a welcoming place my mother never wanted to leave. Every day of my life beginning when I was probably 15 years old, I would sing the old song "Once Upon a Time," about hoping to find my true love. When I finally met Sara, 30 years after growing up in the same building she did, I never felt the need to sing it again.

There are many others to thank for helping and guiding me, for giving me their mentorship and their kindness. Growing up in New York City in the 1950s as I did, things could have turned out very differently for me, but by luck or the grace of God—which may just be two different names for the same thing—I thrived under the watchful eye of selfless men.

Leroy Otis found me when I was 10 years old, having just moved to the high-rise apartment building. He had played ball in the Negro Leagues and coached a group of us for years with a combination of hustle, resourcefulness, and strategic acuity. He saved my life and helped me get over my asthma.

Leroy had set up baseball as a bulwark against a life of gangs and crime, keeping us too busy in three different leagues to find trouble. The ministry of David Wilkerson and the spiritual guidance of my future mother-in-law Delia Ortiz helped fortify that bulwark with faith.

Thomas Stapleton, chair of the accounting department at St. John's University recommended me for the Council on Legal Education Opportunity program, and Peter Liacouras cast the line and kept on casting until I bit, and then wouldn't stop reeling till he'd landed me at Temple Law School. Carl Singley partnered with me at law school and taught me how to study—which meant that I would survive. He and I formed the Black Law Student Association, which was my first definite foray into activism and organizing. Marvin Wachman negotiated with us in the spirit of fairness and treated us both as students and peers. He also placed me on the board of Temple Hospital.

Judge Clifford Scott Green encouraged me to reapply to the White House Fellowship program—and did not care that I was doing it only to file a lawsuit—which changed my small-time career and broadened my small-time perspective to a worldview perspective.

Vice President Walter F. Mondale and his staff taught me about big-time politics and policy, and most important, showed me that you never have to compromise your decency or your humanity no matter the stakes.

After my years in Washington, D.C., I was blessed with mentors in Philadelphia who showed me the ropes in the professional world.

Howard Gittis was never anything but supportive. He was more like a father confessor than a boss. Throughout my time at law, Howard gave me his time, counsel, and support, negotiating my election to the bench and every law firm job I had until he passed away in 2010. After he died, I was ready to give up the law, but Joseph Jacovini at Dilworth Paxson stepped in and worked with me for eight more years.

Without the guidance of Howard and David Girard-diCarlo, my career in the private sector would not have been a success. More than anyone else, David taught me how to be a lawyer in a private firm and how to be a rainmaker.

Longest in my life, though, and the man who helped me find a seat on a corporate board—in some ways the job of my dreams—is Walt D'Alessio. He seemed to be on every board, corporate or civic, of any importance. He never steered me wrong, and he and Howard helped me to achieve my financial independence.

Bob Garcia taught me about politics, and the value of his advice and support is immeasurable. Henry Cisneros may be the smartest person I ever worked with, and I remain very proud of what we achieved together during those exciting years in the Clinton administration. We changed things for the better. Between Bob and Henry, I learned a valuable lesson about a life in politics. They offered me two sides of the same coin. Bob showed me throughout his career never to treat anyone like an enemy and to serve everyone equally. Even after heated campaigns, Bob dealt with everyone who came to him the same way, even those who had said terrible things about him. He never lost sight of the fact that it is more important to be a public servant than a public figure. While Bob showed me how to treat people, Henry set me straight on what I should expect from them. Henry used to say that in politics you have no permanent enemies and no permanent friends. That saying should be engraved on a piece of granite and displayed on the Mall in Washington, D.C.

Hank Lacayo provided me with important political and union support and friendship. His sister Carmela and Bob's sister Aimee Cortes were invaluable for their spiritual support. Carmela prayed for me for 40 years, perhaps second only to my mother, and Aimee taught me never to hate anyone, even those who hate you.

No matter what happened to me, or what I inflicted on myself—derailing my own career, being criticized, sued, or ostracized—I always had someone there to pick me up. I was continually and repeatedly set back on the path forward, no matter how many twists and turns it took.

One last thank-you goes to perhaps the quietest presence in my life. Miserain Rodriguez married my mother when I was three years old and has been a calm and loving presence in my life for more than 65 years. Pop never spanked me when I was a child and rarely said an unkind word to me. A religious man who grew up a farm boy in San Antonio, Aguadilla, he told great stories of his farming days and about working on the Air Force Base. He loves to pray and drink *café con leche* after every meal. He attributes his long life to both habits. And somehow along the way, quietly, almost secretly, Pop showed me how tough the truly cheerful are. He is always ready with a smile and a joke. For 67 years my mother and he stayed together, through good times and hard times. He lives with me still, with no signs of slowing up.

From the bottom of my heart I thank him for showing me that being a man begins with humility and kindness.

At my 60th birthday party. From left to right: *To my left are Leticia Manich, my sister-in-law; Nelson, my son; and Sara, my wife.* To my right are Mom; Pop; Vilmarie, my daughter; Cookie, my sister; and Bob Garcia.

INDEX

Page numbers followed by the letter f refer to figures.

After graduating from St. John's University in 1969 and from Temple University Law School in 1972, **Nelson A. Díaz** became the first Puerto Rican lawyer to pass the Pennsylvania bar examination and the first Latino judge, administrative judge, and partner in a top-100 law firm in the state. Appointed by President Jimmy Carter to a White House Fellowship and by President Bill Clinton as general counsel to the U.S. Department of Housing and Urban Development, he has served as a public defender, as Philadelphia city solicitor, and as a member of several corporate boards—including Exelon Corporation, a Fortune 100 company—during his legendary career. His fight for civil and human rights and his promotion of neighborhood economic development and judicial and housing reform have paved the way for others.

Díaz lives in Philadelphia with his wife, Sara Manzano-Díaz.